The Limits of
Educational Reform

Educational Policy, Planning, and Theory
Series Editor: Don Adams, University of Pittsburgh

The Limits of Educational Reform

MARTIN CARNOY
HENRY M. LEVIN

*Stanford University
and Center for Economic Studies*

DAVID McKAY COMPANY, INC.

NEW YORK

Developmental Editor: Edward Artinian
Editorial and Design Supervisor: Nicole Benevento
Design: Angela Foote
Production and Manufacturing Supervisor: Donald W. Strauss
Composition: Maryland Linotype Company
Printing and Binding: Haddon Craftsmen

Library of Congress Cataloging in Publication Data
Main entry under title:

The Limits of educational reform.

(Educational policy, planning, and theory)
Includes bibliographical references.
1. Education—United States—Addresses, essays, lectures. 2. Educational sociology—United States—Addresses, essays, lectures. I. Carnoy, Martin. II. Levin, Henry M.
LA209.2.L49   370'.973   76-5509
ISBN 0-679-30302-2

To Pax and Pilar

Acknowledgments

Chapter 2 represents a considerably expanded version of "Educational Reform and Social Change," *Journal of Applied Behavioral Science* 10, no. 3 (August 1974): 304–20. The chapter was originally presented as a paper for the conference on "The Public Interest in Education: Toward a Policy for the United States" sponsored by the Center for the Study of Democratic Institutions, Santa Barbara, California, March 19 and 20, 1973.

Chapter 5 was published in Martin Carnoy, *Education as Cultural Imperialism* (New York: David McKay, 1974).

Chapter 6 was published in James H. Block, ed., *Schools, Society, and Mastery Learning* (New York: Holt, Rinehart, & Winston, 1974), pp. 75–88.

Chapter 7 was published in John Pincus, ed., *School Finance in Transition* (Cambridge, Mass.: Ballinger, 1974), pp. 177–98.

Chapter 9 draws heavily upon "School Is Bad; Work Is Worse," *School Review* 82, no. 1 (November 1974): 49–68. The chapter was originally prepared as a paper for a special issue of the *School Review* (November 1974) devoted to a review of James Coleman et al., *Youth: Transition to Adulthood*. The research reported was performed pursuant to a grant from the National Institute of Education, Department of Health, Education, and Welfare, under the aegis of the project "Educational Requirements for Industrial Democracy." The opinions expressed do not necessarily reflect the position or policy of the National Institute of Education, however, and no official endorsement by the National Institute of Education should be inferred.

Chapter 10, part 1, was published in the *Harvard Educational Review* 44, no. 1 (February 1974): 178–87, as a book review of *The World Educational Crisis* by Philip Coombs. Part 2 was published in *Convergence* 7, no. 3 (1974): 53–59.

Chapter 11 was published in Martin Carnoy, ed., *Schooling in a Corporate Society* (New York: David McKay, 1972).

Contributors

William H. Behn is a member of the Center for Economic Studies.

Martin Carnoy is a member of the Center for Economic Studies and an associate professor of education and economics at Stanford University.

Michael A. Carter is a member of the Center for Economic Studies.

Joyce C. Crain is a member of the Center for Economic Studies.

Henry M. Levin is a member of the Center for Economic Studies and a professor of education and economics at Stanford University.

Contents

1

Martin Carnoy and
Henry M. Levin

Introduction

Perhaps the noblest function that has been commonly assigned to the American schools is that of alleviating poverty. Over a century ago, the leading advocate of the common school movement, Horace Mann, preached that "Education . . . prevents being poor." The provision of a minimum amount of schooling for everyone was expected to create skill levels that would enable the entire population to participate in the labor force at a high enough level of productivity to avoid poverty. Of course, the economy was expected to be able to employ all those who wanted to work, so that the condition of poverty would be due only to low productivity or a lack of preparation for work in the expanding industrial sector of the latter nineteenth century.

Apparently the faith in the schools as the social and economic leveler, or what Greer has called "the great school legend," was pervasive.[1] For the system of education expanded historically so that by the middle of the twentieth century a substantial majority of Americans were completing secondary school, and virtually all entrants to the labor force had an education that included at least some high school. A sizable number of persons were undertaking college and university training as well. Educational participation was so great that in 1960 the entire population between the ages of 6 and 13—29 million youngsters—was attending school, and about 86 percent of the 11.2 million youngsters between the ages of 14 and 17 were enrolled.[2] At the same time, some 3 million students were attending college. As estimated 44 million persons, or one-quarter of the total population, were in school.[3]

Accordingly, it was with some surprise that the nation rediscovered in the 1960s the remarkable extent to which poverty persisted despite these schooling accomplishments. In 1962 an estimated 38 million Americans, or 21 percent of the population, were living in poverty.[4] Poverty was especially heavily concentrated among blacks, Chicanos, Native Americans, and other minorities, although it showed a substantial incidence among whites as well. Poverty within the midst of plenty became the concern of the social reformers of the 1960s, culminating in the War on Poverty. And, if such a war was actually declared during this period, then education and training were its artillery.

Like the social philosophers of a century before, contemporary social reformers saw education as a powerful device for achieving social change (in this case, the elimination of poverty). They viewed not only the low incomes of the poor as emanating from inadequate education, but they also saw discrimination in employment and housing as the result of lack of education in other segments of society. If only poor blacks, Chicanos, whites, Puerto Ricans, and Native Americans could be given more schooling and training for jobs, they would receive higher-paying jobs that would remove them from poverty; if only textbooks could be altered to make them multicultural, minorities would be accepted by white students on their own term; and if only employers, landlords, and fellow workers would be properly educated, they would cease to discriminate against minority workers. The reformers viewed this lack of education as something that would be provided by the public schools and government training programs only if the schools and programs were characterized by reforms designed to achieve these ends.

Attempts to reform education and training in the decade of the 1960s were pervasive. For the very young there was Head Start with its emphasis on improving the skills of preschool youngsters from low-income families in order to prepare them for entry into primary school. At the primary and secondary levels the Elementary and Secondary Education Act of 1965 provided between one and two billion dollars a year to school districts for instituting and financing compensatory education programs for poor children. These funds were used to retain teachers, reduce class size, hire more remedial specialists, acquire new materials and instructional technology, and modify curricula in order to improve the rate of learning of children from low-income backgrounds. For school dropouts and potential dropouts there were training and education programs such as Job Corps and the Neighborhood Youth Corps, and a variety of programs was expected to increase the participation of the disadvantaged in higher education. And for adults there were manpower training programs, especialy those provided under the Manpower Development and Training Act of 1962.

In addition, a concerted effort was made by the courts, government agencies, and some citizens groups to achieve racial integration in the urban schools of America. Special teacher-training programs such as those sponsored by the National Teacher Corps were designed to train new teachers in rural and urban settings characterized by "difficult" conditions and chronic teacher shortages. Multicultural education became a new catchword as state and local school systems began to scrutinize their textbooks in order to eliminate stereotypes and racial bias from the official curriculum, and in-service training courses and institutes arose to change the values and pedagogy of teachers in these areas. Finally, the teacher-training programs of colleges and universities altered their offerings to include preparation for teaching in urban and rural environments. Courses on the "disadvantaged child" and teaching English as a second language proliferated among such institutions.

By almost all observable standards, these programs failed to achieve their ostensible objectives. Test scores of disadvantaged children did not appear to improve despite the massive efforts in this direction.[5] Inner-city and rural schools retained their unenviable characteristics despite massive increases in expenditures and personnel. Racial segregation grew worse over the period as middle-class families migrated from the cities to the suburbs, increasingly isolating the minorities of the cities. And other training programs also seemed to have little or no impact on educational fortunes or on poverty reduction.[6]

This volume questions the premise that educational reform can resolve social dilemmas that arise out of the basic nature of the economic, political, and social system itself. The fact that the United States had the highest per capita income and the most highly schooled labor force in the world in 1960 while such a high proportion of its citizens remained impoverished must certainly raise serious questions about the educational solution to poverty. And where the establishment and expansion of a universal system of compulsory education had not solved the problem, it was expected that the institution of a substantial number of educational reforms would. Why did education fail, and can it succeed in eliminating poverty and achieving other "desirable" social changes? In our view the schools of a society serve to reproduce the economic, social, and political relations, and the only way that schools can change those relations is through their unforeseen consequences rather than through planned and deliberate change. In this sense we argue that a society based on largely unequal positions of power, income, and social status among adults will not be able to alter those relations through the schools. To the contrary, the schools will tend to reproduce the inequalities in order to contribute to the legitimation of adult society.

A useful way of looking at this dilemma is to consider the functioning of a capitalist society. Even the staunchest defenders of capitalism recognize that "a capitalist system involving payment in accordance with product can be, and in practice is, characterized by considerable inequality of income and wealth."[7] Under the conditions of monopoly capitalism, where the markets for goods and services are dominated by relatively few economic entities—the universal state in advanced capitalist societies like the United States—the inequalities tend to increase over time.[8]

But the schools do not deal with the overall economic and political structures that create this inevitable result. Rather, they attempt to graft on to these inequitable structures an institution that will alter the distribution of cognitive knowledge and values and attitudes in order to make these more equitable; they expect that more equal human attributes will create more equal social, political, and economic outcomes. As we emphasize, the nature of the economic system has a great deal more influence on the distribution of income and occupational status than does the system of schooling. In fact, the empirical evidence suggests that such bastions of monopoly capitalism as Mexico and Brazil show evidence of *increasing* inequalities between the poor and the rich in spite of rapid economic growth and unprecedented expansion of the schools.[9]

The educational reforms of the War on Poverty were based primarily on the tenet that certain groups were below the poverty line mainly because they lacked the skills to be productive in a system that rewarded merit. They tended to have less schooling than nonpoverty groups; and disadvantages in their homes, discrimination, and inferior schools were thought to provide a lower-quality education to them than to their more advantaged counterparts. The basic educational reforms were predicated on overcoming these shortcomings through correcting the biases in the school system and compensating minority students for the inadequacies of their sociocultural background.

While most observers agree that this strategy failed, they differ on the reasons for the failure. Many reformers feel it failed because the effort was neither large enough nor sustained enough. Others, like Jensen and Hernstein, argue that the basic premise of capability is wrong and that blacks specifically lack the intellectual capacity to obtain parity with whites in spite of compensatory education programs.[10] Jencks argues on the basis of his statistical results that there is little connection between differential educational attainments and differences in income— and that educational reform cannot bring about equality because the basic premise of causality between schooling and income is incorrect.[11]

Yet, none of these critics addresses the fundamental issue: even if the assumptions of capability and causality were correct, would it be possible significantly to equalize income distribution, employment opportunities, and social positions without changing the basic structure and functioning of the economy? Consider the following normal characteristics of our economic system which contribute to inequality:

1. The government is unwilling or unable to create full employment, so several million Americans must be unemployed at any one time despite their educational attainments. In periods of crisis this number may exceed 8 million, as it did in 1975.

2. Employers are able to obtain similarly educated females and nonwhites at lower wages than they pay to males and whites regardless of the educational level at which employees are hired.

3. The majority of minimum-wage or low-paying jobs in the occupational pyramid at the bottom of the occupational hierarchy are not altered according to the educational characteristics of the employee. Rather, they are defined by the nature of the production enterprise and the technical characteristics of the organization as well as the facilities and equipment that are used.

4. About one-third of national income is derived from the ownership of physical capital rather than from work, and ownership of this source of income is very heavily concentrated among the wealthy. For example, a recent estimate shows that the wealthiest 1 percent of the population owned 61 percent of corporate stock, and the wealthiest 5 percent owned 83 percent.[12]

In all these cases the equalization of educational results would have little or no impact on the distribution of income or the existence of poverty because the sources of inequality emanate from the economic system itself rather than from inequalities in educational attainments. Accordingly, educational reforms to equalize educational attainments among all segments of the population would not change these basic realities of the economy. And there is no assurance that the reform would succeed in the first place, as we assert in the chapters that follow.

Indeed, we argue that the source of most economic inequality has little to do with the schools per se except as they reflect the inequalities of the larger society. We also reject the view that the inequalities are due primarily to genetic inequalities in intellectual capability. To accept the genetic assertion that those who do badly in the economic system do so because of a lack of intelligence (Hernstein 1973) requires that the income associated with a job and the cognitive intelligence required to perform it are closely linked. That is, higher productivity requires greater intelligence under the apparently complex and technological conditions of advanced capitalism. Yet systematic studies of the relationship between economic success and IQ or other cognitive measures show that IQ scores are relatively poor predictors of income.[13]

It is true that as an individual obtains more schooling he is likely to increase the probability of getting a better job and higher income and avoiding unemployment. But this act will not serve to equalize income; for as some people improve their positions, those of other workers worsen.[14] Indeed, as average educational attainments increase, many older workers with less schooling find themselves out of jobs or forced to accept lower-paying jobs. As long as there are inadequate numbers of jobs to employ all those who wish to work at nonpoverty wages, no improvement in educational attainments of the population as a whole or the bottom segment of the population will eliminate poverty. Of course, such changes in educational accomplishments may redistribute poverty.

The overriding theme is that the principal cause of failure to reform the social and economic system through educational institutions stems not from the incompetence of the reformers, but from the inability to alter a schooling system that is largely functional to the existing polity: the system reproduces the inequalities created by its system of production. As we discuss in several essays in this book, a significant improvement in income distribution, a full-employment policy, and even a gradual elimination of racism and sexism will require a movement away from the capitalist system of production toward one of greater participation and equality in work organizations themselves as well as the social ownership of capital. The capitalist structure of production—particularly the monopoly capitalist form which dominates the U.S. economy today—is characterized inherently by hierarchies of alienated workers with vast differences in rewards from the lowest to the highest paid.

Reformers cannot expect monopoly capitalism to do anything it does not perceive as increasing its profits and accumulation of capital. The needs of the poor and the oppressed can be met under monopoly capitalism only if such policies make these powerful economic entities better off. Any change that helps the poor at the *expense* of profits will be resisted and will fail. And the historical domination of the capitalist over the labor force has been dependent upon the very factors which create inequality, that is, the social division of labor and fragmentation of jobs as well as a vast unemployed or underemployed labor force.[15] The former is integral to the control of the enterprise and domination of the production process by the capitalist class, and the latter is functional for providing a self-disciplined work force that will work at relatively low wages for capitalist firms for fear of being among the unemployed. Eliminating poverty and reducing economic inequality can be achieved only by dismantling monopoly capitalism.

We argue, therefore, that the failure of the educational reforms of the 1960s to create beneficial social changes was due to the "reformist" nature of the reforms which accept tacitly the structural sources of inequality. As Andre Gorz has emphasized:

> A reformist reform is one which subordinates its objectives to the criteria of rationality and practicability of a given system and policy. Reformism rejects those objectives and demands—however deep the need for them—which are incompatible with the preservation of the system.
>
> On the other hand, a not necessarily reformist reform is one which is conceived not in terms of what is possible within the framework of a given system and administration, but in view of what should be made possible in terms of human needs and demands.
>
> In other words, a struggle for non-reformist reforms—for a anti-capitalist reforms—is one which does not base its

validity and its right to exist on capitalist needs, criteria, and rationales. A non-reformist reform is determined not in terms of what can be, but what should be. And finally, it bases the possibility of attaining its objectives on the implementation of fundamental political and economic changes. These changes can be sudden, just as they can be gradual. But in any case they assume that the workers will take over power or assert a force (that is to say, a non-institutionalized force) strong enough to establish, maintain, and expand those tendencies within the system which serve to weaken capitalism and shake its joints. They assume structural reform.[16]

Our argument that the elimination of poverty, unemployment, racism, and sexism can be met only by changing the structure of work—from an extremely hierarchical and competitive one that maximizes the needs of the capitalist class to a more nearly equal and cooperative one that satisfies the needs of workers—also has important implications for school reform. First, and obviously, the argument rejects the premise that social reforms can be achieved by providing poor people with more and better schooling. While such an endeavor might be worthwhile on its own merits, more schooling will not affect the hierarchical form of production or the profit-maximizing, antilabor behavior and organization created by capitalist management. These elements are part and parcel of capitalist production and are necessary to its survival, and they are the sources of the problem. Differential schooling attainments are only a symptom.

But, second and more important, our analysis implies that the schools are an *integral part* of the capitalist system. Rather than being independent of the production hierarchy, they serve that hierarchy as school administrators, students, teachers, and parents derive their values and norms about work, success, competition, and status largely from the values and norms of corporate capitalist ideology. Thus schools attempt to meet the needs of monopoly capitalist organizations (both unwittingly and through "career education") by developing lower-class children to be better workers and middle-class ones to be better managers in the corporate economy and by reproducing the social relations of production in the schools to inculcate children with values and norms supportive of capitalist work organization.[17]

The educational reforms of the 1960s did not accept this postulate. Rather, they were based upon the assumption that the schools could produce results that were independent of the economic system or that the capitalist system could be made equitable by using schools as the mechanism of equalization and of poverty elimination. In this set of essays we critique a number of these types of reforms and attempt to show how, in each case, it is crucial to understand the role of the reform in the overall context of the economic and social system. Our pervasive theme is that educational reform is limited in its ability to produce social change by the inherent structures of corporate capitalism and because the school system is geared to fulfilling the needs of corporate capitalism rather than changing it.

In chapter 2, Henry Levin summarizes our views on educational reform. "Educational Reform: Its Meaning?" describes a model for understanding the role of formal schooling in a society and the sources of contradictions in that role which *may* lead to educational change and, more remotely, to social change. Levin analyzes the function of schooling by what he calls the "correspondence principle": "In brief, this principle suggests that the activities and outcomes of the educational sector corresponds to those of the society generally. That is, all educational systems represent an attempt to serve their respective societies such that the social, economic, and political relationships of the educational sector will mirror closely those of the society of which they are a part." Thus, we argue that if a society emphasizes competition and hierarchical relations in production, then the schools will reflect these attributes in their activities. In contrast, if a society emphasizes cooperative social and economic relationships, we would expect the schools to reflect these cooperative goals.

Using this principle, Levin looks at the various elements of the schooling sector and shows how they interact. He concludes that educational outcomes are produced in line with desired social, economic, and political outcomes through educational resources, the schools' budget, and the educational processes taking place in the schools themselves. Even so, he argues that change may still occur. Such change, however, is not attributable to deliberate educational policy. Rather, it is created by the *contradictions* that emerge within the educational sector as well as in the economic and social structures of the larger society. One such contradiction is reflected in the relatively recent phenomenon of the creation of more persons with higher educational attainments than the economic system can absorb. The legitimacy of schooling as both a selection device for jobs and as an agent of social mobility requires a constant expansion of enrollments at successive levels in order to absorb the social demand for increases in educational attainments. But occupational upgrading has not expanded as rapidly, so that educational requirements for jobs have been rising. As the increasing occupational and economic aspirations of more recently educated workers are stymied, such workers are increasingly difficult to integrate into the traditional wage-labor system. This contradiction is evidenced by increasing problems of worker turnover, absenteeism, sabotage, wildcat strikes and slowdowns, drugs, and alcoholism. Accordingly, the capitalist system may have to change the nature of production in order to avoid costly disruptions.

Levin suggests the kinds of reform that might occur in the economic structure in order to attempt to absorb the contradiction. He posits that if the capitalist structure of production were to be altered in the direction of greater worker control and participation or other forms of worker democracy, the schools would tend to put greater emphasis on cooperation in learning, on mastery of particular skills by *all* students, on the ability to handle new situations and learning opportunities, and on other worker traits that would assume increased importance in the work process. He stresses, however, that the commitment to social change will occur prior to the educational changes.

The dynamic processes of correspondence and contradiction are central to understanding the nature and limits of educational reforms. In "Contradiction and Correspondence: Analysis of the Relation of Schooling to Work," Michael Carter focuses on the substance of this process which we believe provides the boundaries of stability as well as the impetus for change. Carter develops a philosophical analysis of the concepts and attempts to apply them to the relations between education and change. The first part of his essay sets out the overall framework within which we believe correspondence and contradiction operate, and then he outlines the more specific relations with respect to education and work. The value of Carter's essay lies in its explication of the workings of correspondence and contradiction in the educational context and its implications for educational reform.

Levin's "A Taxonomy of Educational Reforms for Changes in the Nature of Work" applies the concept of correspondence to an analysis of educational reforms that might arise from changes in the organization of work. Both work reforms and educational reforms are classified into micro- or macro-changes of either a technical or political nature. Specific work and educational reforms are then described and placed into one of the four categories.

One focus of this typology is to emphasize the limitations of micro-technical changes for social change whether implemented in the educational or the economic sector. While the majority of reforms are in this category, such modifications do little more than enable the system to produce essentially the same results somewhat more efficiently. In general they fail to alter the social relationships of schooling or the type of work and work structures for which children are prepared. For political changes to occur in schools, changes in the governance and control of the workplace would have to precede them. Chapters 2 through 4, therefore, sketch our position on the relationship of schools to work and to the organization of production. They emphasize that the direction of reform must proceed from changes in the nature of work to supportive changes in schooling, rather than the other way around.

While Levin and Carter provide a basic framework of analysis for understanding the limits of educational reform, they do not attempt to provide historical evidence that supports this view. Martin Carnoy's "Educational Reform and Social Control in the United States, 1830–1970" sets out a brief historical context in which the links between the needs of a developing capitalist system and the responses of the schools in terms of educational changes and reforms are emphasized. Carnoy argues that micro-

and macro-political changes occurred in the organization of work, and in both cases the alterations increased the capitalists' control and manipulation of workers. The two major periods on which Carnoy focuses are the development and consolidation of the factory system in competition and then monopoly capitalism phases and the later application of principles of "scientific management" by capitalists which created an increased fragmentation of work tasks with a concomitant increase in the social division of labor and alienation of the work force.

Both of these profound changes in the capitalist system of production had implications for the nature of work and the characteristics of workers, and each is tied to major school reforms. The first development was related to the initiation and growth of a corporate system of schools whose main function was to prepare workers for the realities of the factory system with its impersonal and bureaucratic relations. The second change was characterized by the systematic differentiation of pupils for future work roles through the development of testing and tracking devices. These educational reforms represented an attempt by the schools to rationalize the preparation of students for the emerging structure of work in a more scientific and systematic manner that would correspond to the extreme differentiation of work roles demanded by "scientific management."

Although Carnoy devotes little attention to present-day reforms in this chapter, it provides a bridge between the previous theoretical discussions and the analyses of more specific recent attempts at educational reform. The next three chapters analyze three different common educational reforms that have been widely discussed or adopted for improving the educational and social fortunes of children from low-income backgrounds: equalizing financial support for schools through changes in the methods by which states fund their educational systems; equalizing the attainment of cognitive skills through curriculum reform in the direction of "mastery learning"; and compensatory education to provide remedial resources for such children in order to compensate for "deficiencies" in their home backgrounds. In each case the reform is shown as not likely to have the equalizing effects claimed for it.

One of the major educational reform efforts of the late 1960s and early 1970s has been the attempt to change the method of state financing of education from its present reliance on the local property tax to one that creates a more equitably distributed basis for raising educational funds. Under the existing system, the school districts with high property values are able to spend relatively large amounts on their students at relatively low tax rates, while poorer school districts must levy high rates merely to obtain minimal educational spending levels. This phenomenon has been challenged in the courts of many states and in the federal courts as violating the "equal protection clause" of the Fourteenth Amendment of the U.S. Constitution as well as the state constitutions. The final outcomes of many of these cases will not be known for some time because of appeals and reformulations of the original legal strategies when they have failed, but several states including New Jersey and California are under court-imposed mandates to revise their methods of financing schools.[18]

Levin's chapter in "Effects of Expenditure Increases on Educational Resource Allocation and Effectiveness" addresses itself to how increases in educational spending will affect the educational fortunes of children from low-income school districts. On the basis of a political model that describes the various interest groups, their goals, possible coalitions, and their relative power, Levin concludes that the principal beneficiaries of policies to equalize school spending will be the educational professionals in the school districts that receive the additional funds. While a more equal distribution of educational resources among school districts is a *necessary* condition for more equal educational outcomes, it is not a *sufficient* condition.

Levin posits that the school bureaucracy is involved in the struggle over how additional resources will be used, while poor children and their families have little input or power into that arena. In essence, teachers and administrators will be able to increase their own employment and salaries without concomitant improvements in the educational attainments of the students. Furthermore, the state apparatus has no ostensible interest in intervening on behalf of the poor since the state is dominated by other interests. Levin concludes that "without massive changes in the political structure of our society, the *Serrano* decision (the landmark California case) has all the earmarks of a bold and humanitarian gesture that will not produce the ultimate result that the court had in mind."

According to our analysis, the equalization of the financial base for supporting the schools will have little impact on unequal educational outcomes. Some would assert that financial equity must be accompanied by curriculum reform if it is to be successful at reducing educational and social inequalities. In "The Economic Implications of Mastery Learning," Levin analyzes the major curriculum reform devoted to equalizing educational results, mastery learning. This reform is based upon organizing the classroom so that all students achieve some predefined level of mastery in each important competency area. In contrast to the conventional approach to instruction which assumes a highly unequal distribution of educational attainments, the mastery-learning paradigm assumes that all students can achieve functional competence in all important domains. The attainment of this objective is carried out through the unequal distribution of resources in favor of those who are slowest to reach mastery as well as differentiating the type of instruction according to the aptitudes of the learner.

Levin argues that mastery learning may improve the internal efficiency of resource use in the schools, but it is not likely to have much effect on social mobility or the distribution of economic success, the external results of schooling. The social justice inherent in the mastery-learning concept is not reflected in a corresponding set of social institutions. Thus, Levin concludes that the mastery-learning strategy will not be adopted in any systematic way; or, if adopted, the outcomes for which mastery learning will be implemented will not be important ones with regard to the social selection process. That is, he contends that if mastery learning is successful in being adopted and in equalizing certain educational outcomes, the outcomes themselves will lack importance in the social process by which individuals are selected to fill roles within the occupational and income hierarchy.

Both the school finance and mastery-learning reforms are

analyzed conceptually for their effects on equalizing educational and social results. Empirical support for these propositions is found in the chapter by Carnoy, "Is Compensatory Education Possible?" During the 1960s and early 1970s, the most important policy for improving the educational attainments of students from low-income backgrounds was the application of additional educational resources in order to attempt to equalize their performances with those of their more advantaged counterparts. In his analysis of compensatory education, Carnoy introduces data to show that in the mainland United States and in Puerto Rico (which has a similar system), the addition of massive educational resources that appear to have the most hope for improving the test scores of poor and minority children would not come close to equalizing their performances relative to those of students from majority and wealthier backgrounds. Carnoy concludes that without structural changes in the school itself, the addition of resources alone can have little effect on the distribution of outcomes. But he believes that these structural changes will require prior changes in the society at large, as our overall thesis implies.

Accordingly, three current reforms that are being advocated, litigated, or adopted do not seem to or are not likely to have the equalizing effects claimed for them. In all these cases we have maintained that the social structure will dominate any attempts at reform within the schools. However, it can be argued that these are piecemeal reforms that do not address the overall role of schooling in society. The next two chapters address system-wide changes that have been proposed for the schools in order to improve their function in preparing the young for adulthood.

One of the more recent large-scale proposals has been to reduce the amount of compulsory formal schooling required of youth and to substitute for it activity in the workplace. This represents the dominant theme of the highly publicized report of the Panel on Youth of the President's Science Advisory Committee, *Youth: Transition to Adulthood*.[19] "School Is Bad; Work Is Worse," represents a response by Behn, Carnoy, Carter, Crain, and Levin to the recommendations and arguments contained in that report. The report argues that the prolonged schooling of youth is injurious to their development. It is maintained that schooling prepares students only for individual and cognitive development rather than for social development. In contrast, the workplace is considered the appropriate environment for fulfilling the "idealistic creative, and constructive impulse of youth."[20]

In this chapter we assert that the school is an excellent preparer for the world of work. Schools inculcate those attitudes and values that function to integrate persons into corporate, capitalist production. As the chapter suggests, most of the activities and organizational aspects of the school environment correspond closely with those of the work environment; from the alienation of workers and students from the work process, to the hierarchical differentiation of students and workers in both settings, to the external reward structures of grades and wages that are used to manipulate behavior in the direction desired by those who control both enterprises.

Nevertheless, the present organization of work is so unfulfilling for most people that with higher educational attainments they have an increasing difficulty in adapting to its conditions. Up to a generation ago, the need for income, food, clothing, and other basics was reason enough for conforming to job demands; but today's youth have grown up in an age of relative affluence where financial survival is no longer a powerful motivation. Increasingly, young people are refusing to accept the psychologically debilitating and developmentally limiting nature of traditional jobs which evolved for reasons of capitalist control and profit maximizing rather than for reasons of human need. We argue that an earlier integration of youth into the work force will not change this pattern, since it is the organization of work that is at the heart of the dilemma rather than a prolongation of schooling.

The problem is that the schools are a reflection of the actual work setting, and a transition from the former context to the latter will not alter the repugnant characteristics of the workplace. In this case the educational reform implied by shifting students from schools to jobs at an earlier stage may accelerate the disenchantment with work rather than alleviate it. Without a movement toward a work situation that satisfies human needs for the many instead of the accumulation of profits and capital for the few, the reduction of schooling and its replacement with work experiences will have little effect on the basic unwillingness of many youth to embrace either schools or work.

Ironically, while the role of schooling for alleviating poverty and improving the distribution of income is being questioned increasingly in the United States, it is still argued as the principal basis for the expansion of education in developing societies. Indeed, the most important educational reform in those countries is that of expanding the schooling system to encompass a larger proportion of the population, and the major debate seems only to revolve around the mixture of formal vs. nonformal educational opportunities. In Carnoy's "International Education Reform: The Ideology of Efficiency," this phenomenon is reviewed through a discussion of a book by one of the leading international educational reformers, Philip Coombs, as well as a report for UNESCO on this subject. Along with other "developmentalists," Coombs had maintained in the 1960s that one of the keys to increasing economic growth rates and alleviating inequality was to expand and modernize school systems to prepare a skilled labor force which would be part of an overall efficiency drive in the society.

Carnoy argues that although Coombs is probably correct in assuming that expanding the skilled and socialized labor force through schooling will increase profits, thus increasing incentives for investment, the strategy does not address the goals of social transformation which Coombs attributes to the schools, nor does it focus on the situation of the masses. Coombs does not ignore the relationship between social structure and the educational system it fosters. He blames the rigid structures of traditional societies for the educational inefficiencies and inequities in those countries, and he suggests that under more modern societies the schools will become more efficient and equitable. Carnoy agrees that the inequities of traditional societies tend to be translated into similar patterns of schooling; but he points out that the movement to a modern, capitalist society based upon production hierarchies and capitalist elites will continue to produce massive social injustices as evidenced by the history of such transitions.

In the second portion of this chapter, Carnoy reviews the

orthodoxy of the 1970s as reflected in the UNESCO report *Learning to Be*. While the reformers of the present decade show more sophistication in arguing for a direct intervention in the distribution of income rather than relying on educational expansion, they fail to confront the nature of the capitalist order in molding the results they believe are so distasteful. First, they believe that science and technology can solve social problems, avoiding the issues of the class structure of production and its implications for the distribution of work, income, and learning. They also ignore completely the question of control of technological development and adoption and the historical records that reflects on whose behalf technologies were utilized.

Second, Carnoy argues that the reformers had a particular view of societal change in mind in recommending their reforms, one based upon pluralism. This view suggests that society is an association of many different groups, each sharing more or less equally in the fruits of development, technological change, and economic growth. Under this assumption, change can occur smoothly, and everyone can participate in its rewards. If the society is composed of inherently conflicting groups, however, the proposed reforms are more likely to favor the most powerful interest at the expense of the others. It is clear that the latter context is the actual one which characterizes most developing societies, and the lack of recognition of this reality simply serves to legitimate the view that educational reforms are always created in behalf of social betterment for a pluralistic society rather than in behalf of the interests of a relatively small ruling class.

In the final chapter we ask what kinds of reforms in the schools and other institutions might lead to social change in corporate capitalist societies such as the United States. In general we suggest that strategies which exploit emerging contradictions will have a greater likelihood of success than those which attempt to make the existing system more efficient. The ultimate goal, we argue, is to dismantle the vast system of monopoly capitalism and to replace it with a highly democratized form of socialism where work institutions and political ones would be governed by a high degree of day-to-day involvement of workers and constituents.

Following Gorz, we suggest that we should take every opportunity to exploit the contradictions of the capitalist system by encroaching on the traditional prerogatives that support its operation.

With respect to schools, this means that the schools should be viewed as a workplace in which increasing control of all "workers" (both educators and students) is desirable. The goal is to raise teacher and student consciousness about the nature of the system they serve by obtaining *joint* control as a single class over the learning process. Perhaps this is the weakest part of our thesis, for once having argued that schools are not a powerful agent for social change, it is inconsistent to assert that they are an important part of the strategy for altering the society that sponsors them. But our claims for such a strategy are modest in that we believe that every workplace represents a potential application of this encroachment strategy, and the schools should certainly not be ignored in its adoption.

Notes

1. Colin Greer, *The Great School Legend* (New York: Basic Books, 1972).

2. U.S. Department of Health, Education, and Welfare, "Selected Statistical Notes on American Education," HEW Publication No. (OE) 74–11703 (Washington, D.C.: May 1974), p. 27.

3. Ibid.

4. Robert Plotnick, "Progress and Poverty in Recent Years," in *Poverty Report, A Decade Review* (Madison: Institute for Research on Poverty of the University of Wisconsin, 1975), chap. 3, pp. 3–4a.

5. V. Cicirelli et al., "The Impact of Head Start: An Evaluation of the Effects of Head Start on Children's Cognitive and Affective Development" (Report presented to the Office of Economic Opportunity, Contract B89–4536, Westinghouse Learning Corporation/Ohio University, June 1969); Michael J. Wargo et al., "ESEA Title I: A Reanalysis and Synthesis of Evaluation Data from Fiscal Year 1965 Through 1970" (Palo Alto, Calif.: American Institute for Research, March 1972); Henry M. Levin, "A Decade of Policy Developments in Improving Education Training for Low-Income Populations" (Re-

port prepared for the Conference on a Decade of Federal Anti-Poverty Policy: Achievements, Failures and Lessons of the Institute for Research on Poverty, University of Wisconsin and the Johnson Foundation, 6–7 February 1975).

6. Levin, "Decade of Policy Developments."

7. Milton Friedman, *Capitalism and Freedom* (Chicago: University of Chicago Press, 1962), p. 168.

8. Paul Baran and Paul Sweezy, *Monopoly Capital* (New York: Monthly Review Press, 1966); Richard C. Edwards, Michael Reich, and Thomas E. Weisskopf, eds., *The Capitalist System* (Englewood Cliffs, N.J.: Prentice-Hall, 1972).

9. David Barkin, "Education and the Distribution of Income" (Lehman College, CUNY, April 1972), mimeographed; Albert Fishlow, "Brazilian Size Distribution of Income," *American Economic Review* 62, no. 2 (1972): 391–402; Martin Carnoy, "A Distribuição da renda e Desenvolvimento economico no Brasil: umcomentario," *Revista de Administração de Empresas* (Sao Paulo) 14, no. 4 (July–August 1974): 86–93.

10. A. R. Jensen, "How Much Can We Boost IQ and Scholastic Achievement?" *Harvard Educational Review* 39 (1969): 1–123; Richard Hernstein, *IQ in the Meritocracy* (Boston: Atlantic Monthly Press, 1973).

11. Christopher Jencks et al., *Inequality* (New York: Basic Books, 1972).

12. Frank Ackerman et al., "The Extent of Income Inequality in the United States," in Edwards, Reich, and Weisskopf, *Capitalist System*, p. 209.

13. Samuel Bowles and Herbert Gintis, "IQ in the U.S. Class Structure," *Social Policy*, November/December 1972–January/February 1973, pp. 1–32; Samuel Bowles and Valerie Nelson, "The 'Inheritance of IQ' and the Intergeneration Reproduction of Economic Inequality," *Review of Economics and Statistics* 66 (February 1974): 39–51.

14. Lester C. Thurow, "Education and Economic Equality," *Public Interest*, no. 28 (Summer 1972): 66–81.

15. Stephen A. Marglin, "What Do Bosses Do?" *Review of Radical Political Economics* 6, no. 2 (Summer 1974): 60–112; Harry Braverman, *Labor and Monopoly Capital* (New York: Monthly Review Press, 1974); Katherine Stone, "The Origins of Job Structures in the Steel Industry," *Review of Radical Political Economics* 6, no. 2 (Summer 1974): 113–73.

16. Andre Gorz, *Strategy for Labor* (Boston: Beacon Press, 1968), p. 78.

17. Samuel Bowles, "Unequal Education and the Reproduction

of the Social Division of Labor," in *Schooling in a Corporate Society*, ed. Martin Carnoy (2nd ed.; New York: David McKay, 1975).

18. John Pincus, ed., *School Finance in Transition* (Cambridge, Mass.: Ballinger, 1974).

19. James S. Coleman et al., *Youth: Transition to Adulthood* (Chicago: University of Chicago Press, 1974).

20. Ibid., p. 137.

2

Henry M. Levin

Educational Reform: Its Meaning?

As philosophers have noted, the manner in which a question is formulated has a profound shape on the answer that is forthcoming. In this sense, the "right" answer to the wrong question becomes the wrong answer to the initial problem. Thus, one must devote at least as much energy to raising the right questions as to providing answers to them. In this paper I argue that the prevalent viewpoint reflected by such questions as "What is the public interest in education?" is a misleading one since it implies that education is shaped in a deterministic fashion by academics, wise citizens, and politicians, rather than by a larger set of controlling forces.

In contrast, I attempt to demonstrate that the educational system corresponds to the social, economic, and political institutions of our society and that the only way we can obtain significant changes in educational functions and relations is to forge changes in the overall social, economic, and political relationships that characterize the polity. As a major corollary of this view I maintain that no educational reforms will succeed if they violate the major tenets of our social, economic, and political system; and in any stable (nonrevolutionary) society the educational system will always be applied toward serving the role of cultural transmission and preserving the status quo despite the emergence of academic debates and utopian visions on the issue.

Schools and Society: Which Serves Which?

On these subjects there are two principal views of the world. One approach assumes that the schools exist as an agent of social reform and that the limits of their ability to change society are conditioned only by the limits of our imagination and the difficulties of obtaining consensus. Beyond these boundaries it is the duty of educators and citizens to use schools as the major lever to create a fair and productive society. Although these assumptions are never stated this explicitly, they clearly appear to be the values that undergird the literature and debate on educational reform.[1]

In contrast, I am assuming that schools exist as an agent of the larger social, economic, and political context which fosters them. Accordingly, they correspond to the institutions of the larger society and serve the functions assigned to them for reproducing the social, economic, and political relationships reflected by the prevailing institutions and ideologies.[2] According to this approach, the schools serve society, and meaningful educational reform is not possible. The former view suggests that the schools dominate society; the latter one suggests that society dominates the schools.

Which view is more nearly correct? The attractiveness of the educational reform position is considerable. Psychologically the schools loom large in importance for all educated persons because of their substantial domination of our values. That is, the schools have been such a salient factor in our lives that we tend to assume that they are a principal, independent force for determining the shape of society. Little wonder that students who opposed the Vietnam war tried to destroy their universities rather than the munitions plants. The frustration caused by a nonresponsive government was visited upon the father-image of the schools. In this sense so-called liberals and radicals expect educational change to be a liberating force for attaining the good society. Whether this is brought about by burning buildings or reforming curriculum is less important than the common ideology that by creating pressure for educational change, we are creating pressure for social change.

In addition to the psychological underpinnings that support the educational reform position, there is the argument of logic. If we change the functions of schooling, we change the functions of socialization. Altered socialized patterns lead to changes in social institutions. While such a causal chain seems reasonable, it assumes that the functions of schooling can be modified without concern for the demands on schools created by the dominant political, economic, and social institutions. That is, the assumption is that meaningful educational reform is viable even when it conflicts with the larger set of social demands. This argument lacks empirical support.

Finally, a romantic image of schools persists that is promulgated by the early works of such philosophers as Horace Mann and Henry Barnard, and it underlies tacitly much of the recent educational reform literature as well. Even in these days when criticism of schools no longer makes the press because of its repetitive quality, the basic goodness of the "potential" of school reform is largely unquestioned.

While Silberman views the "crisis in the classroom" as no more than a lack of good ideas and commitment, so does his revisionist adversary, Colin Greer.[3] After attempting to demonstrate that schools have served historically to reproduce the class structure, Greer concludes that if only schools would address themselves to their lofty rhetoric of equality, they would succeed. Underlying both points of view is the romantic notion that the schools can remake society.

Our psychological dependency on schools, the apparent logic of school reform, and the romantic tradition of school reform are heavy adversaries of the notion that one cannot use the schools to alter important social, political, and economic institutions. Accordingly, the remainder of this paper is devoted to a demonstration of the assertion that while schools will adapt to changes in the polity, the traditional view that school reform can effect changes in the sponsoring society is improbable.

The Correspondence Principle

The most important tenet underlying our approach is the correspondence principle. In brief, this principle suggests that the activities and outcomes of the educational sector correspond to those of the society generally. That is, all educational systems serve their respective societies such that the social, economic, and political relationships of the educational sector will mirror closely those of the society of which they are a part.

Since the schools and educational policy are commonly discussed without reference to their outcomes on society, it is easy to ignore the correspondence principle. For example, much of the educational planning literature concentrates only on such aspects of education as the proportion of the national budget allocated to the schools or the proportion of youngsters at each age level who are enrolled. This type of analysis implies that it is these foci that are the concern of society, rather than the link between schooling and social outcomes per se.

One way of seeing more clearly the nature of the relation between schools and the larger social, economic, and political framework is to consider the process by which youngsters attain competencies with regard to their adult lives. In this respect, Inkeles has proposed a model that provides a conceptual role for the schools and other social institutions.[4] According to Inkeles, every society creates specific demands for competency upon its adults, and it is the purpose of all institutions of socialization to fulfill these demands by socializing the population to attain these competencies. Obviously, the specific demands change from society to society, so that a hunting and gathering society requires very different competencies than does a modern industrial nation. The latter situation requires that adults possess

> certain levels of skill in the manipulation of language and other symbol systems, such as arithmetic and time; the

ability to comprehend and complete forms; information as to when and where to go for what; skills in interpersonal relations which permit negotiation, insure protection of one's interests, and provide maintenance of stable and satisfying relations with intimates, peers, and authorities; motives to achieve, to master, to perservere; defenses to control and channel acceptably the impulses to aggression, to sexual expression, to extreme dependency; a cognitive style which permits thinking in concrete terms while still permitting reasonable handling of abstractions and general concepts; a mind which does not insist on excessively premature closure, is tolerant of diversity, and has some components of flexibility; a conative style which facilitates reasonably regular, steady, and persistent effort, relieved by rest and relaxation but not requiring long periods of total withdrawal or depressive psychic slump; and a style of expressing affect which encourages stable and enduring relationships without excessive narcissistic dependence or explosive aggression in the face of petty frustration.[5]

Even this list of competencies represents only a partial enumeration of the traits that a postindustrial society normally expects of its adult population; and the process of socialization requires that somehow during the period from infancy to adulthood these and other attributes are inculcated. Among the agencies of socialization charged with these tasks are the family, community, church, schools, and perhaps other organizations; but surely the school represents the principal means of socialization for many if not most of the tasks that require social, political, and economic relations beyond the family. In this context, the role of the schools is clearly to carry out a responsibility delegated to it by the needs of the larger society; and this is essentially what is meant by the assertion that in every stable social setting the activities of the schools will correspond to and serve the social, economic, and political relations of that society.[6]

Indeed, this correspondence should be evident across societies in that differences in their social relationships should be reflected in their schools.[7] Specifically, if a society supports large inequalities among its population in political, economic, and social position and status, then the schools will reflect closely that situation. That is, the large inequalities of the society will be visited upon the schools in terms of very unequal educational outcomes among the population in terms of schooling attainments and qualitative differences in education. Moreover, we would expect to find that the financing, governance, and operations of schools would serve to reinforce these inequalities, rather than finding that such inequalities were the result of "institutional mindlessness."[8] In short, we would expect the schools to serve an important role in selecting and allocating students to their ultimate positions of inequality on the social, economic, and political hierarchies of status.[9]

Stated more strongly, we would expect to find direct evidence of the correspondence in both the outcomes and the process of schooling. That is, the nature of the society is visited upon the schools in their entirety. If a society emphasizes competition and hierarchical relationships in production, then the schools too will reflect these attributes in their activities.[10] If the work force requires workers who labor for extrinsic rewards such as wages and salaries and who must accept alienation from and boredom with their work circumstances, then the schools will prepare workers for such an eventuality by socializing them to, and legitimating, these conditions. It takes little imagination to see the correspondence between grades for school performance and wages for work performance; to see the alienation and boredom of the assembly line; to see the competition among students for grades parallel the competition among workers for advancement; and to see the teacher in the classroom impose his arbitrary values on his underlings, just as does the boss on the job (neither legitimacy of authority resulting from a democratic election).

In contrast, if a society were to emphasize cooperative social and economic relationships, we would expect the schools to reflect cooperative goals as well. That is, the schools would be likely to focus on cooperative solutions to learning and human development, and there would be a tendency to disdain strict hierarchical relations.

One confusion that arises in assimilating the correspondence principle is the fact that in most countries the schools are given a romantic aura that conflicts with the observed characteristics of their societies. The schools represent the great hope for social change. Thus, schooling and its expansion are often said to be the major elements for improving "equality of opportunity" in societies that have large inherent inequalities. Unfortunately, we are often too quick to accept the "publicly declared intent" of our schooling institutions rather than examining their processes and outcomes. We will assume that the "true intent" can be better observed from the actual activities and results of the schooling sector than it can from the rhetorical claims associated with it.

Thus, if schools are financed in such a way that they invest far more in children of the rich than in the children of the poor, this is a better indicator of intent than the liturgy of equal opportunity.[11] If tracking and curriculum serve to sort and select children in such a way that the children of blue-collar occupations or unemployment and the children of the elite will be socialized for positions consonant with their class or origin, then we need not torture our senses by suggesting that these are not consistent with intent. In a mature and long-standing institution, the actual operations and outcomes can be considered to be the *best* reflection of the true intent of that institution.[12]

In summary, the correspondence principle underpins the view that the schools are socially functional. Along with other agencies of socialization such as the family, the church, and the community, the schools prepare children for adult roles in society; and most of the organization and activities of the educational sector can be related to the society which sponsors that sector.

The Educational Sector

In order to pursue a more systematic analysis of the correspondence principle, it is useful to show its application to the various activities of the educational sector. Of utmost importance in this analysis is the question of how controlling interests in the society are visited upon and reinforced within the educational setting. Accordingly, this section reviews briefly the various activities that comprise the educational sector. It devotes special attention to their relationships with one another and with the sponsoring society.[13]

Figure 2.1 shows a flow diagram of the educational sector. The activities of the sector are described by a set of six boxes connected by a series of arrows describing a closed loop and a seventh box representing external influences on the system. The arrows represent flows of decision outcomes, resources, and socialization outcomes from one stage to another. Throughout this description we will be referring to the formal educational sector or schooling sector as if the two were identical. While we are omitting a discussion of other educational influences, I do not believe that their inclusion would modify the pattern of interpretation.

Polity   The polity refers to an organized society with a specific ideology and form of government. Thus, the polity has various properties that will create demands on its educational sector. These properties include such characteristics as the nature of the economic and political system; social, religious, and cultural factors; the level of industrial development; and relationships with other societies. Emanating from the polity are a set of demands or socialization objectives for transmitting the culture and reproducing and maintaining the economic, political, and social order. These demands take the form of laws that define and affect the schools; governing relationships that will inevitably weigh the demands of some constituencies more heavily than others; and a resource or budget that will be allocated to educational activities.

In addition, the polity will affect educational activities by creating values and expectations on the part of citizens with regard to their roles in society and the educational requirements for fulfilling those roles. To this degree, the educational values and expectations for any individual will themselves emanate from the role that he perceives for himself (or that his parents perceive and transmit to him). It appears that a large portion of the differential socialization effects of the schools and families are related to the roles assigned by the polity to different classes

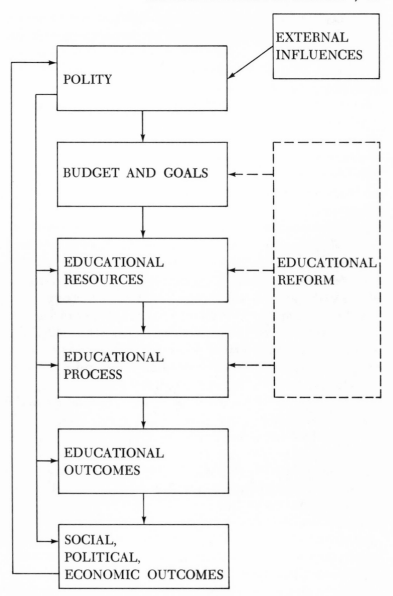

Figure 2.1

The Educational Sector

of individuals. For example, Melvin Kohn has found the values of children are consistently related to the social class of the father.

> The higher their class position, the more highly they value self-direction and the less highly they value conformity to externally imposed standards.[14]

Other researchers have drawn similar conclusions regarding family position in the class structure and the values transmitted to children by the mother that will affect learning, attitudes, and attainments.[15] That is, the reality that individuals experience in their daily lives leads to educational and social expectations on their part as well as their perceptions of the "rules for success." Persons occupying different vantage points in highly stratified societies will emerge with different values and expectations. These studies suggest that the children of working-class families will be more capable of taking orders, and those of ruling-class families will be more adept at giving orders. These attributes will not be treated neutrally by schools that undertake to select children by testing and curriculum assignment in order to fill out the class structure for the next generation.[16]

In addition, the government and private enterprises create specific demands for workers with certain characteristics to fulfill the hierarchical relations of production. While such demands are, in part, generated through the formal governing arrangements for schools, their pervasive influence is transmitted through hiring standards and mobility patterns that signal to students and workers what their "proficiencies and values" should be if they wish to succeed. In many respects these signals and the class-derived values of citizens may be far more important in determining educational outcomes than the direct governance of the educational sector.

Thus, in explaining educational outcomes we should be cognizant not only of the formal government policies, but also of the values and attitudes and expectations inculcated by the polity with regard to themselves and others. The subtle interaction among the governmental outcomes of the polity, the direct demands of government and private agencies, and the effect of the polity on the formation of individual and class values will determine the operations and results of the educational sector. Accordingly, figure 2.1 shows that the influences of the polity extend not only to the determination of budget and goals; they also determine the selection of educational resources, educational processes, and educational outcomes; and they determine how educational outcomes will be translated into social, political, and economic outcomes.

Budget and Goals One of the most direct ways in which the polity dominates the operation of the educational sector is its determination of goals and budgets. The goals reflect the institutionalized demands of a formal and informal nature that the society visits upon its schools, and the budgets represent the resources allocated to fill those demands. Goals may be reflected in laws such as those that mandate compulsory attendance and require the provision of schooling by the appropriate government agencies. Moreover, the laws that set out licensing requirements for educational personnel reflect educational goals because such requirements determine the types of formal socialization experiences and self-selection that will be mirrored in the attitudes and values of teachers, administrators, and other educational professionals.

In most cases the goals will not be transmitted directly; but they will be veiled in the laws, operating procedures, licensing requirements, curriculum and personnel requirements mandated upon the educational system. That is, it is difficult to find any list of objectives that is communicated to the schools by the polity other than the ambiguous and rhetorical ones which seem to have little operational value. Examples of such rhetorical objectives that characterize societies with vastly different forms of government and values are "equality of opportunity" and "training for literacy." In fact, these objectives are often discharged through the mere expansion of schooling enrollments and through the assumption that any person completing a particular level of schooling (e.g., the fifth year) is literate. The actual goals of the polity are mirrored in their policies on personnel selection, school organization, compulsory attendance, and budgetary allocation.

The budget represents the monetary value of resources that the polity wishes to allocate to the schooling process. Obviously, the budget has little educational value until it is transformed into the purchase of resources that can be used to operate the educational organizations. Such resources include teachers, administrators, other personnel, buildings, facilities, books, other instructional materials, and so on. In most cases the allocations of the budget are determined by forces far removed from the schools where the money is spent. That is, budgets are not lump-sum amounts that are allocated to schools to be alloted to educational resources according to the professional views of educators or the priorities of local communities. Rather, the budgetary categories and their allocations often follow from the specification of resources and their organization that are dictated for the educational system.

For example, in many situations the schooling process is specified in remarkable detail with regard to the number of teachers, nature of facilities, and other inputs, and the budget represents only a description of the total value of these resources.[17] In contrast, it is sometimes suggested that the polity allocates a budget indicating the amount it is willing to pay to achieve its goals and that managers of educational organizations allocate their budget according to the relative costs and effectiveness of different inputs.[18] While this latter version of budgetary determination appears logical under a technocratic approach to managing the educational sector, it does not appear to reflect the reality of the actual relationship between the polity and educational operations.

Educational Resources   As noted, budgets are only useful for educational purposes when they are transformed into educational resources. Accordingly, at this stage the process of resource selection is made. The salaries of teachers and other personnel are set and the system of remuneration is developed. Decisions are made about the types of facilities and materials that will be used in the educational process. In large measure the impact of the budget on educational outcomes will be contingent upon the types of resources that are brought into the schooling process. As stated, most of these decisions are made by the polity, so that in many respects the determination of the budget and the resource inputs that it will purchase are made concurrently.

The choice of personnel is one area of resource selection that deserves special scrutiny. To a large extent, educational personnel seem to be hired less for their skills than for their values. The licensing and selection requirements in most settings focus little attention on intellectual proficiencies or measures of success in attaining educational objectives. Rather, high-level administrators are chosen according to their "philosophies" of education, and they are expected to hire other administrators and educators according to such values. In addition, the control of certification of educational personnel and the establishment of "educational requirements" for such certificates means that the polity can assure itself that teachers will be socialized in a manner consistent with the interests of the state. In fact, the training programs themselves act as self-selection devices in filtering out those individuals who do not subscribe to the values and content that seem to underlie teacher-training programs and licensing requirements. In the United States, for example, the paths to teaching in elementary and secondary schools tend to be systematically inhabited by intellectually less-able groups.[19]

Schooling Process The educational resources that are obtained with budgets are organized in particular ways in order to produce certain educational outcomes. For example, schools are arranged in hierarchical fashion with respect to administrators, teachers, and students. Curriculum requirements are set with regard to how personnel and students will interact in any particular setting. Various types of competitive activities are sanctioned, both academically and athletically. A particular amount of time is normally spent in each activity and grade level, and so on. In addition, success according to the norms of the school is sanctioned with strong social approval and such extrinsic rewards as high grades and high class rankings. Poor performance, according to such norms, is punished with detention, other coercive sanctions, and low grades.

Children are tested and on the basis of such results are allocated to the various curricula and to their educational experiences. Counselors attempt to shunt students toward particular schooling paths and careers toward which their academic grades, test scores, and "interests" are consistent; and students who represent "problems" to the school organization are stigmatized with visits to school psychologists, low grades, dismissal from school, or other such devices which punish a failure to accept school norms. Educational settings are usually dominated by the educators themselves in that few choices are made by the students; rather, most of the decisions that will affect the school experiences of each child are made by teachers, administrators, and governing agencies in the form of inflexible personnel configurations, curriculum, lesson plans, and so on. Indeed, most of these decisions are made as they will apply to any child, long before he arrives on the educational scene, and they reflect the values of the polity rather than the persons who are involved in the process. Little or no effort is made to adapt the educational strategy to the specific needs of the child as evidenced by his characteristics, so-called individualized instruction.

Educational Outcomes   Contrary to those who suggest that the above processes are mindless, we maintain that they are functional in producing outcomes that the polity desires. That is, the educational resources selected are organized in particular ways to obtain educational outcomes consistent with the roles expected of adults in society. What are some of these outcomes? Because the popular appeal of the schools is based upon their contribution to increasing literacy and knowledge, we often tend to think of schools as producing only such cognitive outcomes. That is, productive schools are commonly thought of as those which produce students with high proficiencies on standardized tests of reading, mathematics, and general knowledge.

As noted, the demands of modern industrial societies on their citizens are far more complex than just the requirements suggested by the cognitive goals. All kinds of values and personality attributes are also required for effectively functioning social units that individuals comprise. For example, appropriate political behavior and values require that the schools and other agencies of socialization inculcate the "proper" formation of political attitudes. The same is true for the moral development of each citizen. Additionally, the fact that so much of our lives is devoted to work means that these attitudes and relationships must be formed to fulfill appropriate demands. Accordingly, much of the energy and organization of the schools is devoted to the transmission of attitudes, values, and institutions. In this context the hierarchical relations of the school, boredom, the alienation from one's activities, the emphasis on conformity in some settings and intense competition in others is functionally related to the demands of the hierarchical work organizations that characterize modern societies.[20] It is much more difficult for the family, church, or other more traditional institutions to obtain these outcomes than it is for the school to do so.

Social, Political, and Economic Outcomes   The end product of the schooling process is the effect that the schooling outcomes have on reproducing the social, political, and economic results desired by society. In this respect, schooling has an important role in preparing people to assume their ultimate responsibilities as adults. The economic system must depend on an adequate supply of persons who are properly trained and inculcated with the attributes that sustain both the nature of production and consumption. Adults must be politically acculturated in order to contribute to an effectively functioning political system based upon a widely accepted set of political values and structures. The acceptance of social and cultural traditions is necessary in order to transmit values and social organization from one generation to the next. Schooling must necessarily play an important part in fulfilling these outcomes.

Usually, the results of the schooling process are stated in more positive terms than these. Thus, it is widely asserted that the schools contribute to economic and political development and increase the amount of social mobility within the polity.[21] Schooling is considered to be a nationally unifying force because of the common set of values which are promoted among all the populations it touches. Moreover, schooling is supposed to provide a more interesting and diverse cultural milieu by increasing the level of artistic activity, aesthetic appreciation, and literacy. Whether or not schooling does these things has been much less explored than the popularity of the claims suggests.

Finally, whatever the effects of schools, the impact is one that affects the nature of the polity in a dynamic setting. These effects are both determined by and influence the structure and behavior of the polity. Thus the polity determines the relative value of different amounts of education by race and sex through market discrimination against nonwhites and females.[22] That is, even with given levels of educational attainments, the polity will value differentially the occupational, income, and status values of those attainments.[23] Moreover, the impact of the educational sector is visited directly upon the society by serving to reinforce its dimensions over time. These reciprocal relationships are reflected in the arrows in figure 2.1 that feedback the social, economic, and political outcomes to the polity as well as the arrow from the polity that influences the translation of educational outcomes into social, economic, and political outcomes. Thus the correspondence of the values and goals of the larger society with those of the educational sector are complete, and they operate in a continuous and reinforcing flow.[24]

Education and Social Change

The assertion that the educational sector serves to reinforce the existing social order should not be construed to mean that change does not take place. To the contrary, a dynamic process of social change is constantly evident, but it is not attributable to deliberate educational policy. The purpose of this section is to comment briefly on the origins of change and their relationship to education. In carrying out this charge I attempt to compare the concepts of change implicit in this approach with those implied by the champions of change through educational reform.

There are three ways in which the polity can change with

regard to its structure, organization, and values. First, natural disasters such as earthquakes, floods, droughts, and volcanic eruptions can have an enormous impact on the shape of all social, economic, and political institutions. Second, societies that are highly dependent on external influences can be affected deeply by externally induced factors. For example, imported technology and values, immigration or emigration, wars, and substantial changes in export and import prices for key commodities represent possible disturbances from external sources that can have powerful consequences for changing the existing social, economic, and political order. Finally, a society can change because of internal contradictions that arise within it. Since the first two sets of forces are largely self-explanatory with regard to their change-inducing properties, it is best to dwell at greater length on change-through-contradiction.

Although the social, economic, and political forces that dominate society attempt to reproduce their relations from generation to generation, contradictions emerge through unforeseen consequences. In order to sustain the existing social, political, and economic order it is necessary to eliminate those contradictions by adapting to them while attempting to preserve the traditional order. For example, changes in technology that are created for one purpose may have unanticipated consequences which affect profoundly the society and force it to comply with a new set of conditions.

As an illustration of this type of contradiction one might consider the advent of simple and inexpensive methods of birth control. Although such devices were developed for purposes of capitalizing on a market demand for mechanisms to plan families with greater precision, and a possible desire on the part of the government to reduce the population growth of the lower classes, the actual effects of modern birth-control technology have been much more profound. The availability of birth-control devices has apparently had a profound effect on attitudes toward family planning and family size, sexual behavior, and population growth.

In turn, these factors are affecting the nature and formation of families, the growth of economic markets, and the pattern of political behavior as the age composition of the population changes; population size stabilizes, and sexual activity outside marriage becomes more widely acceptable. All these changes represent contradictions to the existing social, political, and economic order; and they were largely ignored by the developers of the new technology. Accordingly, legal, economic, political, educational, and other institutions must adapt to the consequences created by the widespread use and acceptance of birth-control devices.

A Marxian approach would suggest that a capitalist society must continually react to such emerging contradictions in order to be able to continue to reproduce the social division of labor.[25] That is, the concept of change through contradiction is a version of the dialectic by which every thesis is countered by an antithesis, and change is the *modicum* of the synthesis. While many Marxians would apply this concept only to capitalist societies, I would argue that the state socialist societies (such as those of the Eastern bloc) are characterized by similar contradictions that force change.

In this sense, changes in the educational sector will be permitted to take place only when the educational sector is contradicted by relationships in the larger society. Under such circumstances the schools will change in such a way as to eliminate the contradiction. Thus, if a society goes through a revolutionary change that alters the traditional economic, political, and social relationships, the traditional schooling would tend to be contradictory to such changes. Accordingly, we would predict that planned changes in the educational sector would parallel the transition in the society at large in order to remain functional; and we have living evidence of this change through correspondence and contradiction in the cases of Cuba, Tanzania, and China.[26]

Such contradictions can also emerge *within* the educational sector. Assume that for some unforeseen reason the schools produce citizens whose attributes do not correspond to those which are functional in the polity. For example, the legitimacy of schooling as a selection device and an agent of social mobility requires a constant expansion of enrollments at successive levels in order to absorb the social demand for increases in educational opportunity and access. But job opportunities for educated persons have not expanded commensurately with increases in educational attainments, so that educational requirements for jobs have been rising.[27] Thus the expectations of higher-level jobs have not been met; and the overall social system has contradicted itself. In response, many persons with higher educational attainments have begun to reject the normal world of work in order to exist marginally on welfare payments and food stamps under communal or semicommunal arrangements. In many cases they have chosen to pursue arts and crafts and other countercultural endeavors as well as to partake of drugs and undertake new religious experiences.

All these reactions to the contradiction between expectations and the lack of consonant opportunities also manifest themselves in other ways. For example, developing life styles offer new alternatives to others who might have otherwise accepted traditional work roles for lack of other opportunities. They also tend to induce younger persons to forgo additional schooling and to join some of the new experiments in living. It is clear that in order to preserve the relationship between schools and the organization of work, some radical changes will have to take place. The concluding section describes one such possibility. What is important to note is that schools can serve as an agent of change only when their activities and outcomes contradict the larger social order.

In contrast, the educational reformer believes tacitly (if not explicitly) that changes can take place in education without reference to the polity and that the results of such educational change will be social change. This view is symbolized by the dotted box to the right of the flow diagram in figure 2.1. The three dotted arrows suggest that educational reforms are directed at altering the budgetary support and goals of the educational sector, the types of educational resources used, and the organization of these resources in the educational process. Presumably the reforms would create different educational outputs as well as altering social, economic, and political outcomes, and the result of this influence would be a change in the polity. To the degree that such reforms do not correspond to the social, economic, and political order, our previous analysis would suggest that they must fail.

Indeed, I believe that a review of major school reform movements that violated the precepts of the polity would show that they either failed to be adopted or failed to show the expected results. One need only compare the criticisms of the major reformers at the turn of the century with recent critiques. For example, John Dewey's trenchant indictment of school practices written in his 1899 essay on "Schools and Society" is strikingly similar to that of Charles Silberman in his 1970 work, *Crisis in the Classroom*.[28] Yet, the two works were separated by seven decades of school reform spearheaded by Dewey's own progeny, the "progressive education movement."[29]

More recent times have seen several attempts to change substantially the ways in which the schools function, but in each of these cases the reforms were not consistent with the values and premises of our larger social system. Thus, attempts to individualize instruction were established on the basis that the needs of each child should be diagnosed individually and that an individualized program of learning should be prescribed and implemented for him. Such a process obviously violated the need for socializing group values, conformity and class-related interchangeability among individuals in the hierarchical organizations that characterize both industry and government in our society.

Attempts to provide "compensatory education" for youngsters from low-income backgrounds in order to improve their relative opportunities in the competition for status with children from more advantaged backgrounds have also failed.[30] Again, the correspondence principle suggests that the schools are not going to succeed in reducing the competitive edge that the advantaged have over the disadvantaged in the race for income and status. The failure of the 1954 *Brown* decision of the Supreme Court to prevent the almost complete segregation of the schools by race is yet another example of the failure of school reform; and there is every indication that the attempts to equalize financial support of the schools will also fail in a society which regards as a privilege the ability to provide a greater educational background for the children of the rich than those of the poor.[31]

In short, the underlying viewpoint in this work is that the educational sector and all its activities are dominated by the sponsoring society. As long as there are no contradictions between that society and its schools, any serious attempt at "school reform" will fail since the schools will follow their master, and not vice versa. Moreover, it will not be possible to use the schools as a platform for social reform since their operations will always be overshadowed by the operations of the host society. Schools are to be viewed as functional in obeying the rules of the game set out by the larger society, and analysis of the educational sector must take this tenet into account. In effect, only when there is a demand for educational reform by the polity will education reform succeed. The historical record bears out the view that the "turning points" in the functions of the schools coincided with major movements that changed the social order.[32]

Contradiction and Educational Reform

In order to apply the concepts that have been presented, it is helpful to use them to predict changes in education. Consistent with our approach is the requirement that we stipulate the contradiction that is emerging and the probable response of our society for preserving itself. Following this we can deduce the probable impact on the educational sector that will be engendered by the response. In this particular instance we attempt to demonstrate that certain educational reforms that would not be adopted on their own merits might be acceptable as reforms that correspond to modifications in the larger social order.

As noted, recent years have seen extensive contradictions arise between work and schooling with the swift upgrading in educational attainments. Each of these contradictions has led to a rising dissatisfaction with the conditions of work that await educated persons. What are some of these inconsistencies? First, with the enormous increase in the number of young persons with college credentials, it appears that traditional job opportunities for college graduates have not expanded as rapidly as the number of graduates. The result is that individuals with college training are being employed increasingly in jobs which formerly required only high school credentials. Thus, one of the normally expected linkages between more education and higher productivity is being violated as more and more highly educated persons assume relatively low-productivity and low-status occupations.

Second, the fact that rising educational attainments lead to increasing job expectations and that many of these expectations cannot be met has led to rising dissatisfaction with work itself. That is, most college enrollees have the expectation that their additional educational accomplishments will be reflected in occupations with higher prestige, earnings, and greater entrepreneurial options or at least greater control over activities on the job. As it becomes obvious that their expectations exceed the actual availabilities of such opportunities and jobs, dissatisfaction with work is the fruit of dashed expectations.

Third, the constant tendency for technological change to reduce the number of functions of workers as specialization increases means that workers increasingly feel redundant in a production process that demands only very limited aspects of the human potential. At virtually all levels of employment from professional positions such as physicians, lawyers, and professors to production workers, the tendency toward greater specialization of function is evident. The fact that more schooling of the labor force has created an increased exposure to a wider variety of cognitive experiences while job requirements have become more highly specialized has certainly contributed to worker dissatisfaction.

The symptoms of these sources of contradiction between education and jobs are increasingly reflected by a number of indicators. For example, it is widely viewed that the quality of workmanship has been deteriorating in recent years and that quality control is one of the most serious problems faced by industry. Moreover, industry and government are plagued by rising incidences of job impairment due to alcoholism and drug usage, employee absenteeism and turnover appear to be rising, and production is increasingly disrupted by wildcat strikes and employee sabotage.[33] The specter of increasing sabotage is especially frightening to employers since relatively simple acts can do vast amounts of damage to sophisticated machinery, and the interdependence of particular manufacturing and service activities mean that a single act of sabotage can disrupt production even for those plants and equipment that are intact.

These consequences have become so serious that the problem has been recognized at the national level by a recent report of the U.S. Department of Health, Education, and Welfare, *Work in America*.[34] This controversial report has suggested that if the nature of work does not change in such a way as to increase the participation of workers in decision making and to reduce worker alienation, major disruptions of normal production activities and reduced productivity can be foreseen.

One response to these concerns is to change the organization of work so as to increase the degree of participation of workers in the production decisions that affect their welfare. Such an adaptation would preserve the underlying ownership of capital while reducing the threat of costly destruction and disruption. There are many different forms of these changes in work organization, but all would have the effect of attempting to reduce the alienation and dissatisfaction of workers and to increase productivity by changing the nature of workers' relationships to the firm and its decision-making mechanisms. Some approaches would allow workers to organize into teams that would rotate specific jobs and cooperate to meet production schedules. Others emphasize the use of workers' councils that would advise management on ways to improve working conditions. Still other approaches would enable workers to elect their bosses. This broad family of alternatives can be thought of as attempts to increase the degree of "industrial democracy."[35] Recent experiments in the United States and abroad with industrial democracy suggest that this phenomenon will become increasingly important as a strategy for improving worker satisfaction and output.

Given major changes in the organization of work, important changes in the function of schools are implied. In this respect, industrial democracy will require that workers possess those characteristics that enable them to participate more fully in decisions regarding the production process. A glimpse of these processes suggests that workers will need abilities and interpersonal traits that are not required at present or developed by existing educational institutions. For example, industrial democracy will lead generally to somewhat less specialization in production tasks, and individual initiative will be encouraged through cooperative or team production and decision making. The reward of work will become substantially more internally oriented than it is under the present system.

Corresponding changes in the nature of schooling are likely to emerge. A much greater emphasis would be focused on cooperation in learning, on mastery of particular skills, on the ability to handle new situations and learning opportunities, and on the other worker traits that assume increased importance in the work process. It would not be surprising to see the acceptance in the schools of such reforms as the mastery-learning approach of Bloom for assuring that all workers have mastered the minimum competencies required for their participation,[36] the open classroom advocated by Charles Silberman for inculcating students with the ability to take responsibility for particular school and production decisions,[37] and the tutorial community where students assist other students to learn new proficiencies.[38] Even the deschooling solution proposed by Illich would be likely to be partially accepted as it became more useful for students to acquire some of the necessary competencies for worker democracy through on-the-job training programs rather than through formal schooling.[39]

Paradoxically, if the scenario I have sketched takes place, the advocates of school reform will celebrate the victory of having changed society through educational "progress." Indeed, the coincidence of work reforms with educational reforms will reinforce their view of the world. But such a conclusion will derive from a misinterpretation of the data in conjunction with their educational reform ideology. The commitment to social change will have preceded the educational changes.[40]

A Brief Conclusion

In my view, the debate on the role of schools in our society is valuable in forcing us to consider the nature of our reality. Such a discussion should enable us to understand better how the present society works as well as assisting us in describing a better society. Perhaps the proliferation of utopian visions has value in itself in speeding up the rate of contradictions encountered by the polity. I, too, would like to believe that the creation of a just and better society can be achieved through educational changes and that educational reform requires only the best of intentions and imagination of educated men.[41] Unfortunately, I don't have any assurance that this is so.

I am left with the story of the two businessmen from New York who see each other sunning at Miami Beach during their busy seasons. The first explains that his business was destroyed by a fire and that he is using part of the $50,000 in insurance money to take a vacation. The second man is surprised by the coincidence, for as he explains, he is vacationing under similar circumstances. It seems that his business was destroyed by a flood and he received $100,000 in insurance money. The first man looks at the second man and says: "Tell me, how do you start a flood?"

How do you start a contradiction?[42]

Notes

1. See, for example, Charles Silberman, *Crisis in the Classroom* (New York: Random House, 1970).

2. A supporting view is Samuel Bowles, "Unequal Education and the Reproduction of the Social Division in Labor," in *Schooling in a Corporate Society*, ed. Martin Carnoy (New York: David McKay, 1972).

3. Compare Silberman, *Crisis in the Classroom*, with Colin Greer, *The Great School Legend* (New York: Basic Books, 1972).

4. Alex Inkeles, "The Socialization of Competence," *Harvard Educational Review* 36, no. 3 (Summer 1966): 265–83.

5. Ibid., p. 281.

6. See particularly the notes of Louis Althusser, *Lenin and Philosophy and Other Essays* (New York: Monthly Review Press), pp. 127–86, on these relations.

7. For a comparative view of schools in the United States and the Soviet Union, see Urie Bronfenbrenner, *Two Worlds of Childhood* (New York: Russell Sage Foundation, 1970).

8. Silberman states unequivocally: "What makes change possible,

moreover, is that what is mostly wrong with the public schools is due not to venality or indifference or stupidity, but to mindlessness." Silberman, *Crisis in the Classroom*, p. 10.

9. See Herbert Gintis, "Towards a Political Economy of Education," *Harvard Educational Review* 42, no. 1 (February 1972): 70–96.

10. See Robert Dreeben, *On What Is Learned in School* (Reading, Mass.: Addison-Wesley, 1968), for an analysis of some of these attributes. For similar implications see Philip W. Jackson, *Life in Classrooms* (New York: Holt, Rinehart & Winston, 1968). For Empirical data see Herbert Gintis, "Education, Technology and the Characteristics of Worker Productivity," *American Economic Review* 61, no. 2 (May 1971): 266–79.

11. A description is given in John E. Coons et al., *Private Wealth and Public Education* (Cambridge, Mass.: Harvard University Press, 1970).

12. Bowles, "Unequal Education," illustrates numerous aspects of this process.

13. A parallel description is presented in Henry M. Levin, "A Conceptual Framework for Accountability in Education," *School Review* 82, no. 3 (May 1974): 363–91. Somewhat more detail is provided with regard to describing the political dimensions of the process.

14. Melvin L. Kohn, *Class and Conformity* (Homewood, Ill.: Dorsey Press, 1969), p. 171.

15. E. G. Olim, R. D. Hess, and V. C. Shipman, "The Role of Mother's Language Style in Mediating Their Pre-School Children's Cognitive Development," *School Review* 75 (Winter 1967).

16. Althusser, *Lenin and Philosophy*.

17. There is a remarkable parallel between the conditions that await workers and those that await pupils. In both cases the tacit assumption that underlies "production" is that they are interchangeable and that the fine detail of their circumstances can be set without specific knowledge of their attributes other than their class origins.

18. See the criticisms of this view in Levin, "A Conceptual Framework."

19. The evidence on this point is rather consistent. For example, in 1951–53, of almost half a million men who took the Selective Service Qualification Test (verbal and nonverbal), 62 percent equaled or exceeded the critical score for draft deferment. But, only about one-quarter of the educational majors met the standard, a performance that was far inferior to that of any other group. See Educational Testing Service, *Statistical Studies of Selective Service Testing* (Princeton, N.J.: ETS, 1955). Moreover, Wolfle's classic study of human resources found that education majors scored consistently among the lowest groups on standardized tests of intelligence regardless of which degree

level one was comparing. Dale Wolfle, *America's Resources of Specialized Talent* (New York: Harper & Row, 1964), pp. 286–96 and chap. 8. More recently it was found that college freshmen who intended to become elementary or secondary teachers performed below the average for all college students in all five areas that were tested, and they showed fewer high school courses in mathematics, sciences, and foreign languages than did other college students. See E. Haven, *The Freshman Norm Sample for the General Examinations of the College-Level Program* (Princeton, N.J.: ETS, 1967). Even among students in public teacher colleges it appears that the students with higher performance levels on both verbal and nonverbal tests are less likely to choose teaching as an occupation than those with lower performance levels. See James Coleman et al., *Equality of Educational Opportunity* (Washington, D.C.: Government Printing Office, 1966), chap. 4.

20. For a more extensive discussion of the correspondence between educational outcomes and the social relations of production see chapter 3; Gintis, "Worker Productivity" and "Towards a Political Economy"; Bowles, "Unequal Education"; and Althusser, *Lenin and Philosophy*. A general view of socialization for competence is found in Inkeles, "Socialization of Competence." The Inkeles view does not deal with the requirements for differential socialization in hierarchal societies. Rather, it addresses itself to a general set of competencies that all citizens are "expected" to possess. In contrast, the literature that links schooling to the social relations of production tends to focus on differential socialization for differential competencies of a hierarchal nature.

21. See the review of some of these claims in Greer, *The Great School Legend*.

22. See Lester Thurow, *Poverty and Discrimination* (Washington, D.C.: Brookings Institution, 1969), for an example of the discrimination literature.

23. See B. Duncan and O. D. Duncan, "Minorities and the Process of Stratification," *American Sociological Review* 33 (1969): 356–64. Also see Randall Weiss, "The Effects of Education on the Earnings of Blacks and Whites," *Review of Economics and Statistics* 52 (May 1970): 150–59.

24. Since the translation of educational results into social, economic, and political results is itself influenced by governmental policy, market factors such as discrimination, and other characteristics of the polity, even changes in educational outputs, will not necessarily be converted into expected social, economic, and political changes. That is, not only does the polity control the educational process, but it also controls the reward or value structure for converting educational results into social results.

25. For a discussion, see Mao Tse-tung, "On Contradiction," in *Selected Works of Mao Tse-tung* (Peking: Foreign Languages Press, 1967), pp. 311–47.

26. For some documentation on the Cuban experience, see Samuel Bowles, "Cuban Education and the Revolutionary Ideology," in *Schooling in a Corporate Society*, ed. Martin Carnoy (New York: David McKay, 1972), pp. 272–303; Richard Fagen, *The Transformation of Political Culture in Cuba* (Stanford, Calif.: Stanford University Press, 1969).

27. The phenomenon and its consequences are discussed in Ivar Berg, *Education and Jobs: The Great Training Robbery* (New York: Praeger, 1970), and Murray Milner, *The Illusion of Equality* (San Francisco: Jossey-Bass, 1972).

28. Compare John Dewey, *The School and Society* (Chicago, 1899), with Silberman, *Crisis in the Classroom*.

29. The most noted history of the Progressive Education movement is found in Lawrence Cremin, *The Transformation of the School* (New York: Vintage, 1964). See also the visions outlined in John Dewey, *Democracy and Education* (New York, 1916).

30. See the evidence of this in Henry M. Levin, "Effects of Expenditure Increases on Educational Resource Allocation and Effectiveness," in *School Finance in Transition*, ed. John Pincus (Cambridge, Mass.: Ballinger, 1974), pp. 177–98; and chapter 9 of this volume. This does not mean that there were not a few individual successes. Rather, the assertion is that such policies will not succeed in a systematic sense. That is, the real question is whether compensatory educational policies have shown success on the average rather than in isolated instances.

31. See Levin, ibid., for a political model that would predict this result. This view is also supported by the 1973 decision of the U.S. Supreme Court to overturn the decision of the federal district court in *Rodriguez* v. *San Antonio*. The lower court had ruled that the present system of financing education in Texas—and by implication in all other states except Hawaii—violated the Equal Protection Clause of the Fourteenth Amendment because it provided greater educational support to children in wealthier school districts than in poorer ones. Even if similar decisions are upheld in individual states, the educational outcomes among children drawn from different class origins are not likely to change.

32. See Michael Katz, *The Irony of Early School Reform* (Boston: Beacon Press, 1968); David B. Tyack, *Turning Points in American Educational History* (Waltham, Mass.: Blaisdell, 1967); and Raymond Callahan, *Education and the Cult of Efficiency* (Chicago: University of Chicago Press, 1962).

33. See Health, Education, and Welfare, *Work in America* (Cambridge, Mass.: MIT Press, 1973), especially chaps. 2 and 3.

34. Ibid.

35. See ibid., chap. 4; Carole Pateman, *Participation and Democratic Theory* (New York: Cambridge University Press, 1970); and Gerry Hunnius et al., *Workers' Control: A Reader on Labor and Social Change* (New York: Vintage, 1973).

36. James H. Block, ed., *Mastery Learning: Theory and Practice* (New York: Holt, Rinehart & Winston, 1971), contains several essays and a description of the literature on the mastery learning paradigm developed by Benjamin Bloom.

37. Silberman, *Crisis in the Classroom*, sect. 3.

38. This was advocated by John Dewey, and it is reflected in a number of educational projects. In particular, the New York City-based National Commission on Resources for Youth headed by Judge Mary C. Kohler has been promoting and implementing the "kids tutoring kids" approach on a national basis.

39. Ivan Illich, *Deschooling Society* (New York: Harper & Row, 1971).

40. It is important to recognize that the speed of adaptation will depend on the availability of implementable ideas. In this sense the educational reformers will tend to increase the rate of change in the educational sector in response to contradiction if they can provide models for change that can be readily diffused.

41. Also I agree with the values that seem to underlie many of the reforms suggested by Dewey and others. The distinct point of disagreement centers around differences in assumptions regarding the conditions under which educational and social change proceed.

42. See the view of Mao Tse-tung, "On Contradiction," on the subject.

3

Michael A. Carter

Contradiction and Correspondence: Analysis of the Relation of Schooling to Work

All social scientific research must begin with a view of the world, or rather, a way of viewing the world. A basic organizing concept that informs our study of social institutions and social change is the centrality of the work experience. That is, we view the institutions and structural relations of the labor process as the center of gravity of the entire social structure. Ultimately, it is the institutions and structures of work that pull the other institutions of society into line with their motion. Given this viewpoint, any understanding of the other institutions in society must comprehend them in two ways: in themselves, and also in their relationship to the institutions and structures of the workplace. This is especially true if we wish to understand how and why these institutions *change*, or what possibilities of changing them exist.

In particular, the dynamics of reform and change in the schooling process cannot be understood without understanding the relationship of schooling to work. This paper analyses this relationship utilizing the concepts of *correspondence* and *contra-*

diction. This brief introduction discusses our methods of analysis, introducing our concepts and explaining their interrelationships. The remainder of the paper applies these concepts to develop a relatively concrete specification of the interrelationship of schooling and work processes. From this analysis the following conclusions emerge.

Contradictions within the existing structures of work processes are responsible for the current widespread worker discontent and problems of "labor discipline." Through their correspondence to workplace structures and relations, existing schooling processes prepare workers for their future work roles and thus diffuse much potential discontent, or at least prevent it from coalescing into unified class-conscious opposition to the capitalist organization of production. At the same time, the schooling system has overexpanded and increasingly produces more people with relatively high educational attainments who are socialized to expect more nonroutine, high-status jobs than existing job structures can accommodate. This overexpansion is particularly difficult to halt because it results not merely from the dynamics of the schooling process itself, but also from the role that schooling has played in mediating potential conflicts in work processes. For example, the expansion of schooling is taken as evidence of the ever-improving equality of educational opportunity and, prospectively, equality of economic opportunity. The implication is that individuals need only seize the opportunity to acquire more education to extricate themselves from undesirable work circumstances. This correspondence of schooling portends increased demands by a more highly educated work force for greater participation in decision making in production and decreasing legitimacy in workers' eyes of existing structures of hierarchical control.

Contradiction and Correspondence: A Definitional and Methodological Discussion

The central organizing precept of our analysis is that the production process together with the structural forms and social relations under which it is carried out ultimately determine the other social institutions and practices in society. This statement is prior to our analysis; it is a method of viewing the "facts," of defining the "facts." Therefore it is not directly testable against "objective fact"; i.e., it is not refutable by contrary empirical facts because there are no facts independent of the statement itself.[1]

Our views on the centrality of the working experience and its associated institutions stem from the observation that a major portion of adult life is spent on the job and that the income earned there quantitatively limits the opportunities for nonjob activities and thus ultimately (though not directly) determines these as well. Thus our view is empirically reasonable, if not empirically refutable. And it is compelling as well because of the important questions this perspective opens to inquiry.

The structural forms under which production is carried on are not, however, immutable. For example, within the United States a transformation has taken place during the last two hundred years from production characterized by small independent farmers, artisans, and shopkeepers employing only family labor to production characterized by large corporations and government bureaucracies employing thousands of wage laborers, each performing specialized functions and organized in pyramidal hierarchies.[2]

Contradiction and Change in the Organization of Production
In our view the sources of change in the organization of production inhere in contradictions internal to the organization of production. These contradictions may initially be latent or mediated temporarily by other institutions of society, but eventually they develop to a point where production can continue only if the structural forms under which it is carried out are changed radically. For a time, output and profits may be increased by dividing work into smaller tasks capable of more rapid repetition, meanwhile relying on wage incentives to motivate workers. But once most of the workers who are regularly employed have attained a certain standard of consumption outside the job, their major consumption desire may become an increase of interest or leisure on the job. Once this point is reached, wage incentives cease to prevail as a method of extract-

ing labor from these workers. This example illustrates how latent contradictions may become manifest and operate as barriers only after material conditions in the economy have developed sufficiently to "uncover" them. Indeed, the very element in the production structure that ultimately is the barrier to increased productivity—the relation of the worker to his work as a mere means to "individual" consumption—initially was a factor in spurring worker industriousness.

But contradictions in the structure of production do not switch from a latent to a manifest state overnight; they develop gradually and in varying degrees among different groups of workers at different structural positions within the productive process. This pattern of slow and uneven development increases the possibility of using institutions outside the work process, namely schools, to mediate or suspend temporarily contradictions that are essentially rooted in the work process. For instance, boring, stultifying routines and authoritarian pedagogical methods in schools can condition workers to accept from the outset that work must necessarily be boring; as adults, therefore, the workers are not so likely to demand that their work be self-actualizing. On the other hand, both schooling and a multitude of media influences can socialize workers to heightened expectations and needs for material consumption. Thus the schools in two distinct ways act to mediate the aforementioned contradiction in the work process. These mediating factors operate to postpone the time when workers become relatively satiated with commodities and begin to treat the job itself as a commodity.

Correspondence Between Schooling and Work, and the Mediation of Contraditions in the Workplace When we speak of "correspondence" between the schooling process and the work process, we are referring to the mechanisms and structures through which schools mediate contradictions in the work process and thereby contribute to the reproduction of existing structures and social relations on the job. Indeed, in our view the institutions of schooling as they exist today arose in response to the need to mediate the contradictions in workplace structures.[3] Moreover, the present form and content of these institutions are still largely determined by this objective need. For instance, the emphasis on individual achievement in school rather than on group learning is necessary to reconcile the ideology of equal opportunity with the reality of enormous and systematic inequalities in incomes by representing the resultant individual achievement differences as the source of the income inequalities.

While correspondence to existing production structures is the raison d'être of schools and therefore the primary organizing principle we use to understand many aspects of their practice that would otherwise seem irrational or random, schools frequently and increasingly produce outcomes that are dysfunctional to the production of existing relations of production. Thus correspondence not only arises out of contradiction but also develops new contradictions. For instance, the emphasis on achievement in school leads ultimately to an undermining of the ability to cooperate with others, an ability that is critical in many production situations. Or again, the emphasis on educational credentials as signs of superior ability leads to a massive diversion of effort into the attainment of those credentials, rather than into developing the knowledge and abilities they supposedly represent. This behavior subsequently generalizes when the student enters the work force into a cultivation of appearances rather than a development of productivity.

Emergence of New Contradictions and Exacerbation of Latent Contradictions in the Production Process The correspondence of schooling processes to workplace requirements, which mediates contradictions and helps reproduce existing structures and social relations on the job, eventually breaks down for two major reasons. First, and most basic, the existing hierarchical structures of production and their associated property relationships are *inherently self-contradictory*; they therefore require sets of attitudes, values, and behaviors that are inconsistent. Thus, attitudes of individual competitiveness and a desire for individual advancement, which hierarchical structures use to elicit the voluntary cooperation of subordinates with the goals and directives of superiors, inherently work against the cooperation and teamwork necessary for the efficient execution of these directives.[4] When schools grade on curves, they necessarily sow egotism along with competitiveness, necessarily contradict workplace requirements even as they correspond to these requirements. (Of course, through organized sports and other extracurricular activities, schools attempt to develop "teamwork" and allegiance to a productive unit larger than oneself and thus harness competitive egotism to the pursuit of corporate goals. But these activities are secondary to the main pursuits in schools, so the contradiction remains).

A second reason for noncorrespondence between particular aspects of the schooling process to existing hierarchical structures is that schools are not directly controlled by private enterprise. Once established as formally separate institutions staffed by individuals paid out of public funds rather than private profits, they acquire a logic of development of their own. This proceeds in part independent of, and even in opposition to, the needs of private enterprise. For instance, hierarchical production structures require schools to produce relatively great numbers of people who will docilely accept subordinate positions and relatively few people with the "credentials" and attitudes appropriate to high-status, high-paying jobs. Yet the schooling system, propelled by parental demands for increased educational attainments for their children and trapped by its own public image as a provider of equal opportunity, has a tendency to overexpand and produce relatively too many college-educated students. When this glut of college students cannot find high-paying, high-responsibility jobs, they must settle for jobs lower in the hierarchy. But they will be more bored and frustrated in these jobs than if they had never attended college. Thus, on an empirical level, particular aspects of the schooling process do not correspond to the needs of hierarchical production structures and even contradict those needs. Schools are failing—most noticeably by the expansion of schooling as evidenced by rising educational attainments—to mediate contradictions.

Analysis of Change Utilizing the Concepts of Contradiction and Correspondence   The concept of correspondence, however, remains useful at an abstract level as a powerful key to understanding the logic of the system as a whole. It enables us to understand how the present system of hierarchical relations, both at the level of school and work, reproduces itself as a system independently of any self-conscious direction by individuals or groups of individuals. A particularly important insight embodied in the correspondence principle is the idea that an institution (e.g., the school) is not in essence a thing in itself; its essence lies elsewhere, i.e., in its relations to the institutions and processes of work. The specification and understanding of these relations is therefore the key to understanding the schooling process. Even though ultimately we are interested in *change* and how to bring it about, we must know *what* we are trying to change. The correspondence principle directs our attention beyond the empirical institutions and practices of the schooling process to their fundamental reality, their relation to the work process and its associated structures.

Considered by itself, the correspondence principle is an inadequate interpretation of the system of schooling and work relations. It gives us many insights into the unity of that system and into the mechanisms that facilitate *reproduction* of the system, but masks the contradictions and tensions within the system. And it is precisely these contradictions and tensions that augur change! Hence the concept of correspondence must be augmented by a concept of contradiction. Correspondence directs our theoretical version toward *what is to be changed*: contradiction steers us toward where it *can be changed and is changing*.

Let us summarize the conceptual and methodological world view underlying our analysis. Basically, we view the process of production together with its characteristic set of institutions and structural relations as the center of gravity for the entire set of social structures and processes. The forms and structures of work and schooling act and react upon one another, but the importance of the work process so much outweighs the importance of the schooling process that the motion of the former ultimately determines the motion of the latter. Put differently, the dynamics of work structures and relations can be largely understood in terms of their own movement, i.e., as a sequence of institutional responses to contradictions internal to the work process itself.

Nevertheless, a concretely rich understanding of the ways in which internally generated contradictions in the work process appear on the surface of society, of the ways in which these contradictions are resolved, and of the changes to which they lead, requires an analysis of the schooling system and its correspondence and contradictions to the work process. On the other hand, an understanding of the schooling system and its dynamics requires *from the outset* an understanding of its connections to the work process, although its dynamics cannot be understood solely in terms of these connections.

In addition to this concept of the centrality of work processes, the concepts of contradiction and correspondence also underlie our method. The concept of contradiction is the dynamic principle in our analysis. Any set of structures is said to be internally contradictory if it tends to produce by its own functioning conditions which hamper its own reproduction. Such a situation sets up pressures for, and may eventually force, qualitative changes in those aspects of the set of structures that are responsible for producing the contradictory conditions. Similarly, two relatively autonomous structures are said to be contradictory if either produces conditions that hamper the reproduction of the other. Contradictions of this type generate pressures for change in both structures. However, reproduction of existing structures can proceed despite the existence of contradictions of both types. The possibility of reproduction in a situation of external contradiction depends on the degree of autonomy of the sets of structures in question. In situations of internal contradiction the possibility of continued reproduction depends on the existence of structures, either internal or external, which mediate or temporarily suspend the contradiction.

This brings us to the concept of correspondence. Correspondence between two sets of structures is a major mechanism of mediating contradictions internal to the dominant set of structures. Indeed, the mediation of contradictions within the dominant set of structures is often what calls the subordinate set of structures into being, and in all cases it determines the basic form that these subordinate structures assume. Thus a concrete understanding of correspondence is necessary in order to understand the subordinate set of structures, and an understanding of the incipient contradictions in the dominant set of structures is necessary to understand correspondence. Precisely because the subordinate set of structures by assumption constitute a separate set of structures, however, they possess a relative autonomy from the dominant set of structures which permits them to develop in part according to an internal dynamic, to develop internal contradictions, and even to develop contradictions to the dominant structures.

The Interrelationship of Schooling and Work

In order to clarify the basic relationships among the concepts on which our methodology is based, the discussion thus far has been abstract. This section uses our methodology to derive a relatively concrete specification of the interrelationship of schooling and work processes. This specification is still primarily theoretical, but provides a framework within which empirical studies can be situated.

The Work Process and Basic Contractions   From the previous discussion it follows that our analysis must begin with the structures and institutions of the work process, and must identify the salient contradictions within these structures. The more basic contradictions in work structures derive ultimately from the fact that, at present, production takes place for the purpose of making profits, not for the satisfaction of the consumption needs of workers or for the purpose of workers' job satisfaction. Of course, the worker toils in order to satisfy his consumption needs, and the present organization of production depends crucially on these needs to motivate the worker. But what must be emphasized here is that the existence of these needs notwithstanding, no employer will hire a worker or continue to employ him unless he expects to profit from the worker's activities. Production is for the purpose of making profits in the sense that production takes place at all only upon the expectation of profit.[5] The needs of the workers are structurally subordinate to the profit requirements of capital.

Not only are the needs of workers subordinate to profit requirements, but they also are concretely opposed to those requirements
as a direct consequence of the organization of production on a
wage-labor basis. The worker is paid a given wage. This wage
payment is contingent upon the expectation that the worker will
work hard enough and long enough to produce goods and services
whose value exceeds the wage plus the cost of materials, depreciation, and so on. But since the worker does not own or have
any claim over what he produces, he has no direct interest in
increasing his output. Indeed, to the extent that increasing his
output necessitates expending increased energy, he has a direct
incentive to minimize such expenditures (contingent upon keeping his job) and "save" his energy for activities outside the job.
Therefore, from the outset, the wage-labor form of production
pits the interests of the worker against those of the employer.
This implies that once the employer has hired a worker and
agreed upon a wage, he must have some means to extract labor
from the worker. That is, no direct incentive arises out of the
wage form that would cause the worker actually to supply the
labor upon which the wage payment is predicated.[6]

*Approaches to the Extraction of Labor under Wage-Labor
Organization of Production, and the Role of Schooling* There
are two general approaches to the extraction of labor. One
method is to rely on tight personal supervision backed up
by threats of dismissal. The second method is to enlist the
worker's cooperation with the firm's goals by providing various
sorts of indirect incentives. We now examine each of these
methods in turn, and the interactions of schooling processes with
each method.

*Close Supervision and the Threat of Dismissal: The Secondary
Labor Market.* The method of close supervision coupled with a
dismissal sanction was the dominant approach used to extract
labor from workers until the last decades of the nineteenth
century. Even today it survives as the dominant method of control in the secondary labor market.[7] An examination of the
characteristics of jobs in the secondary labor market suggests
the conditions under which this approach to labor-force control

is practicable. First, there must be few skills specific to the particular job, and what skills there are must require a very short learning time. Otherwise it will be very costly to the firm to fire refractory employees and train new ones. The costs to the firm in such situations include not merely the direct training costs and lost output during the time the new employees are learning their job, but also the potential permanent loss of market share as the firm's competitors rush to fill the orders it can no longer supply. Therefore, the more important job-specific skills are to the firm's productivity, the more costly and risky is a pure "hard line" approach to labor-force discipline.

A second circumstance that renders this approach excessively costly and risky is a high degree of mechanization of production. Where production is highly mechanized, detection of poor performance and attribution of the poor performance to particular individuals may be difficult and involve time lags during which large losses in output (in the form of defective goods as well as below-quota production) would be incurred. Moreover, in situations where each worker is in contact with large amounts of capital equipment, and where various equipment is interconnected so that a breakdown at any point in the production process causes a bottleneck which can idle most of the plant for hours, the sabotage potential of each employee is very high. It is thus very risky to antagonize the work force through tight supervision and frequent firings when job-specific skills are important, where production is highly mechanized, or when an individual employee's actions and decisions can affect sizeable capital investments.

Correspondence of Schooling Processes to Relations of Production in the Primary Labor Market. Before describing the relatively sophisticated mechanisms that have evolved to control the work force and secure its voluntary cooperation with the goals and objectives of management, we should discuss how correspondence operates in the context of the secondary labor market, where direct supervision is still the dominant method of control. These are jobs that require little advanced education or job-specific training and jobs in which the worker uses little capital equipment so that job stability is an unimportant attribute of firm productivity. In short, these are jobs that virtually anyone can do. Wages on such jobs are low, both because of the large potential supply of laborers and because physical productivity is necessarily low given the absence on these jobs of either capital or responsibility for capital. Therefore, given the low wages and poor job security these jobs involve, few people would do them if they had any real alternatives. Yet such jobs continue to form a quantitatively significant proportion of all jobs—even in the technologically advanced U.S. economy.[8]

As long as our economic and social system can produce a sufficiently large number of people who must work to support themselves and their families, but who have no real alternative to employment in the secondary labor market, competition among these people will permit employers to pay low wages and rely on threats of dismissal to enforce discipline. But there is a problem for the system as a whole of producing and reproducing in sufficient quantities people who feel that they must accept such jobs and the working conditions they entail; that they have no hopes either as individuals or as a class of acting to improve their situation. This problem is complicated by the myths of mobility and equal opportunity.[9] These myths suggest that everyone has a stake in this society and that all benefit in the same way (if not in the same amount) by increased production.

To broad segments of the work population these myths appear plausible as they personally experience rises in material living standards. But for those confined to secondary labor markets, this experiential correlate to the myth has been absent. Their reality has been low wages, insecure working conditions, and harsh living circumstances.[10] The threat that this reality poses to the system is the threat of massive social unrest and violence resulting from frustration and envy, from a perception that "the system" is responsible for the reality, or from a combination of these. That is, the contradictions that hierarchical wage-labor system engender in the secondary labor market appear as incipient generalized violence. The concrete problems that such systems must solve is the mitigation of the frustration and envy of those who are trapped in such jobs while sustaining the ideology of open and mobile society.

The role that the schools play in solving this problem is to provide "objective" evidence in the form of standardized test scores, grades, and years of education completed that demonstrate that great ability (and presumably productivity) differences exist among individuals. The structural failure of the system to provide meaningful, remunerative work for a significant percentage of the population thus appears to the child through his/her schooling experience as a failure of ability or motivation.[11] The child's experience of failure in school corresponds to his/her subsequent "failure" at the workplace.

We are not suggesting that schools deliberately fail particular students. Rather, they do little to overcome the differences in cognitive background, self-image, and modes of self-presentation with which children from low-income families enter school.[12] Indeed, these initial disparities in cognitive styles and modes of self-presentation may well be so large that individual teachers or principals, no matter how well motivated, cannot overcome them. The point is that the schooling system with its "objective" tests distracts attention away from the objecive effects that real poverty exercises on children. When they emerge from twelve years of schooling with an eighth-grade reading level, no one, presumably, can blame the class structure of society or the hierarchical structure of production for their failure to find decent jobs. It is merely a question of their own failure to attain the ability standards necessary to function productively on complex, responsible jobs.[13]

While the schools succeed in producing large numbers of workers with the low level of cognitive achievement that restricts them to secondary employment, while some of these workers may to varying degrees become reconciled to the notion that they can expect no better jobs, and while some may even come to blame themselves and not "the system" for their failure, contradictions remain. Most evidently, the basic sources of frustration and rebelliousness—low wages and poor working conditions—are not changed by schools. Children who are destined for these jobs learn at an early age that the schools, whatever they might do for others, won't help *them* to get better jobs. Hence, the whole schooling process is at best frustrating, at worst a constant conflict with disciplinarian teachers and truant officers. The schooling experience of these children thus comes to mirror their later work experience; the conflicts and frustrations of the latter are reproduced in the former. Though the ultimate source of these conflicts—the hierarchical wage-labor structure of production—is obscured by the schools, they are powerless to mitigate the hostility, bitterness, and violence engendered by confinement within the secondary sector.

Hierarchy and Incentive Systems: The Primary Labor Market. We now turn to the primary labor market comprised of those jobs where the level of either job-specific skills or of responsibility for large amounts of capital is high and, consequently, regular reliance on a dismissal sanction to extract productive performance from labor is excessively risky and costly. In such situations a variety of structures have emerged *within the organization of the work process itself* which attempt to mediate the contradictory interests of labor and capital. The general effect of these structures is to increase the apparent material advantage to the *individual worker* of maintaining a steady high level of productive effort and cooperating with the goals of management. At the same time, these structures serve to distract the attention of workers from the overall distinctions between themselves as a class and capitalists as a class, by interposing structural distinctions among fractions of the working class itself. These institutional structures fall into two groups. One group is associated with jobs whose content can be more or less routinized; the other is associated with jobs where unique situations regularly arise requiring decisions and actions not specifiable in advance.

The content of jobs that can be routinized is specifiable in a set of rules and standard operating procedures. The major problem of management (apart from designing the standard operating procedures) is to secure conformity to them. By their very nature, these jobs afford the worker little intrinsic satisfaction. Hence the motivation to perform them must come from outside the job, from its "circumstances" rather than from the job itself. In this situation the dominant method of eliciting steady high levels of performance and output has been to arrange the various jobs in hierarchical structures. Jobs higher in the hierarchy not only have higher pay but also require less physical effort or less constant concentration, and they give the worker more autonomy over his actions while on the job. They may also involve more responsibility or slightly higher levels of skills, but these are not necessary conditions.[14]

The major point is that jobs higher in the hierarchy are more desirable on virtually every criterion. Access to these coveted jobs is determined generally on a seniority basis—not on the basis of productivity. Nevertheless, a regular high level of productivity must be maintained on jobs at the lowest level of the hierarchy if the employee is to attain seniority. Thus this scheme holds out to the worker the promise of relatively easy work at increased wages in the future, if only he/she works hard, follows the rules, and doesn't "rock the boat." Although management must pay higher wages to those few workers at the top of the hierarchy than it would if workers were allowed to compete for these jobs, it recoups its losses in terms of increased productive effort and reduced hostility on the part of the bulk of the workers who are located in the more alienating, more exploited jobs at the bottom of the hierarchy. Viewed from this perspective, these promotion patterns and relative wage structures constitute a sophisticated mechanism for extracting a regular high level of labor from the labor force, at the same time sustaining the appearances of equal opportunity and of individual self-determination.

Before we discuss the contradictions inherent in these institutional structures, let us describe briefly the institutions for extracting labor on nonroutinized jobs.[15] The critical feature of such jobs from the standpoint of management is that they require that the employee make decisions and take actions which can neither be specified in advance nor supervised directly. Whereas routinized jobs require adherence to the rules and hard work to meet standards, nonroutinized jobs require internalization of the rules and creative application of effort and expertise to the concrete problems of the firm in earning profits.

Because the decisions and actions of even a single worker in such a job can have potentially substantial direct and indirect effects on profits, individual ability and skill differences are more directly rewarded in terms of wages and promotion opportunities than they are on routinized jobs. Although wages rise regularly with seniority on these jobs, there is substantial competition between firms for employees who perform exceptionally well, and younger employees are regularly promoted past older employees whose productivity has peaked. Thus an individual's power, income, and status are fairly closely linked to the firm's profits. Nevertheless, the wage structure itself is relatively fixed and unresponsive to the potential supply of qualified employees. Since these jobs are critical for profits, it is much more important to get and hold someone "good" in the job than it is to pinch pennies on wages. Despite the individual competitiveness engendered by these arrangements, a camaraderie exists among employees in this sector. Even when a firm is in such serious financial difficulty that it must lay off some of these employees, it deals with them gently, giving them substantial severance pay, long notice, and so on. Moreover, during noncrisis periods, employees who have once performed well but whose productivity has sagged are often "carried" by the firm for a substantial length of time. These institutional arrangements combine to give individuals in this sector a strong sense of identification not only with the profitability goals of their employer, but also with the general values and methods of hierarchical organization of production.

While these institutions mediate to some extent the basic antagonisms between labor and capital within the primary labor market, they still contain latent contradictions and impose requirements on schools with respect to both skill and value transmission. The most salient contradiction remaining within the routinized segment of the primary labor market is that the job-ladder and wage-incentive structures provide the employee with only an indirect interest in maintaining a high level of productivity. Indeed, all that is necessary from the employee's point of view is to maintain the appearance of high productivity.

The very fact that the jobs are routinized leaves the employee's mind largely free to devise schemes to "cheat" the system and use time spent on the job for his own purposes. Although the concrete possibilities for enacting such schemes vary from job to job, and management systematically attempts to design plant and equipment layouts to minimize the possibilities for "cheating,"—pilferage, gold bricking, etc.—the contradiction remains. These schemes absorb the creative energies of the employee that cannot find outlets in the routinized activities of the job itself. It is important to note that this sort of cheating is normally associated with an individualistic, instrumentalist orientation toward the job. As such, it represents an acceptance of the hierarchical wage-labor system and a determination to maneuver within it for one's own benefit. Hence, such activities are not as threatening to this system as concerted class-conscious opposition would be. Nonetheless, in the context of competition among capitalists of different countries, the rise in production costs that ensues when such cheating becomes generalized and accepted behavior is a serious matter and directly threatens the markets and power of capitalists in that country.

In the primary nonroutinized sector the major contradictions are between competition and cooperation, between maintenance of friendly relations with fellow workers and making profits for one's employer.[16] That is, those who hold the nonroutinized jobs within a firm—the engineers, analysts, and management personnel—must cooperate with one another in exchanges of information and in executing and enforcing directives. Yet the individualist competitive reward structures in this sector encourage withholding of information and ideas until the individual thinks he/she can reap full benefit from them. Each of the separate branches and departments within the firm seeks to misrepresent its situation to obtain more resources, funds, and personnel for itself.

Moreover, those who hold these nonroutinized jobs must constantly take actions and make decisions on the basis of profitability criteria. Given the basic antipathy between the interests of capital and labor under the wage-labor relation, this means that employees in the creative sector must constantly exercise their creativity in ways that increase the amount of labor extracted from fellow employees. Thus employees in this sector must constantly take actions that isolate them from and antagonize other workers. The pressures generated by this situation, on top of the pressures to produce and beat out one's competitors, render even these high-paying, high-status jobs alienating. Despite the institutional structures of primary labor markets, therefore, contradictions remain within both the routinized and the nonroutinized segments, although the concrete forms in which the contradictions appear vary between the two segments.

Correspondence of Schooling Processes to Relations of Production in the Primary Labor Market. We now examine the correspondence of the schooling process to the organization and content of work within the primary labor market. More important, we focus on where and how correspondence breaks down and emergent contradictions shape the changing relationship between schools and work. As we have seen earlier the increasing inability of schools to diffuse the hostility and incipient violence that conditions in the secondary labor market generate, so we also see here their inability to mediate the conflicts arising out of the structures specific to primary labor markets.[17]

Through the end of high school the schooling process typically involves the performance of boring, highly structured, fragmented tasks assigned by the teacher—a figure who combines attributes both of "the boss" and "expert." In this sense the work content of schooling mirrors the work content of jobs. The student-teacher relationship resembles the relationship that primary routinized workers have to management and to engineering and scientific personnel. The teacher assigns tasks to the students, supervises their performance, determines their grades and promotability. However, the teacher's authority to extract "labor" from the students derives not merely from a hierarchical relation to them, but also from superior knowledge and expertise. Thus in technical, intellectual matters the teacher is always assumed to be infallible. It is very important to inculcate in students this belief in the teacher's superior knowledge and intellectual attainment so that the students come to accept the teacher's control of the work content of their schooling as being in their own best interests, despite contrary impulses.

The interrelationships among the students in the schooling process also replicate their relationships with one another on the job. There is a constant emphasis on the individual, on individual achievement or individual accountability; but the broad majority of students are promoted each year regardless of individual differences in performance. Only those students who seriously violate standards of conduct or attendance fail to graduate with their peers. Hence, while students are never taught to work cooperatively or to help one another, and while they are imbued with an individualistic perspective, most of them are not particularly competitive about their academic performance. Only among those students who are near the top of the grade distribution and are destined for college and jobs in the nonroutinized professional and scientific sector are competitive attitudes toward grades and studies inculcated.

The general skills taught at this level include not only literacy and computational skills, but also skills in following and executing instructions, and skill in managing one's time in accordance with a clock. While general analytical skills and skills in symbolic manipulation are developed to some extent during these years, little attention is paid to the creative application of these skills to realistic problems; and critical use of the skills is discouraged (i.e., in the task of problem identification). Textbooks, like teachers, are always assumed to have the correct answers. History, civics, and social science courses consist of uncritical presentations of U.S. history and institutions as the progressive realization of the actions of free individuals and democratic processes. Correspondingly, "science" is pictured as a universal good, its attainments the result of the progressive unfolding of human knowledge.

In sum, in primary and secondary schools the bulk of children receive practice coping with situations structurally similar to those encountered in the routinized sector of the primary labor market. Social relations with the teachers and peers, promotion patterns, content and structure of tasks all have qualitatively similar analogs on the job. Basic cognitive and analytical skills are imparted, but their use is confined to increasing ability to digest information, understand complex instructions, budget time, and the like. The critical intellectual faculties are neglected and their spontaneous use discouraged during this phase of schooling. Most important, schools attempt to impart a respect for expertise, particularly expertise learned in school and evidenced by degrees and technical language. The emphasis is always on the expert and on science as universal benefactors against whose cumulative wisdom and knowledge the contrary experience of the average layman cannot hope to stand.

Once the process of schooling at the lower levels has inculcated this respect for expertise, college and postgraduate programs train a select few to become the "experts": the technical, professional, and managerial workers who will hold the high paying, nonroutinized jobs. The students who reach this level have in general aready demonstrated by earning high grades not only that they have the analytic abilities necessary for nonroutinized jobs, but also that they are willing to sacrifice some popularity among their peer group in order to achieve. In college, although the academic competition and its associated pressure intensifies, a sense of membership in an elite group is cultivated. While the student faces constant pressure to do more, perform at a higher level, he/she also gets the feeling of having "arrived," and expects to assume a high-paying, high-status job as a matter of course. This feeling of being part of a leadership elite is communicated not only in addresses by the college president, but directly in the curriculum. For example, assignments now read, "How would you advise the chairman of General Motors . . .?"

In addition to reinforcing these self-images of membership in an elite group, culturally and intellectually superior to those with only a high school education, college also develops the cognitive abilities and work attitudes necessary for performance of nonroutinized jobs. Most obviously, task assignments are much less structured in college, and there is much less direct supervision on a daily basis of actual work done, although the volume of material to be covered increases and the indirect pressures to produce intensify. In addition to cultivating the self-discipline to work under such circumstances, college also hones the ability to reduce complex situations to sets of symbols and to manipulate those symbols to find "solutions" to problems. These latter abilities are intimately bound up with the legitimating ideology of technocracy. This process is most evident in the training of students to prepare mathematical representations of complex social, economic, and political processes in order to analyze a

problem and develop solutions. The fact that problem identification and hence the solutions posed are conditioned by the
mathematical techniques employed receives scant attention. For
example, mathematical techniques are best suited to analyze
equilibrium conditions or slight deviations therefrom as opposed
to situations of conflict and large social change.[18]

While the solution to many technical problems requires the
compactness of thought made possible by symbols, many problems that workers in the nonroutinized sector face are largely
social and involve conflicts of interest between labor and capital.
The reduction of these social problems to symbols, and their
subsequent solution on this level, obscures the fact that the
solutions taken reflect the interests of capital and injure the
interests of labor. By way of illustration, the design of technology
involves issues of work satisfaction and control over production
on which workers' interests diverge from those of capital. But
since the entire situation is enshrouded in mystifying symbols,
the class interests of capital (i.e., the resolution of the work
process into small standardized units and the minimization of
the time required to perform the sum of these units) assume in
the eyes of the industrial engineer the appearance of efficiency
and scientific progress.[19] Associated with the development of skill
in symbolic manipulation is a strengthening of the respect for
technical expertise and division of labor, and a reinforcement of
the belief in its objectivity and value neutrality. Thus, for
example, the scientist learns that his job is to develop atomic
power; its use is to be decided by the politicians.[20]

Finally, the ability to use critical intelligence to perfect the
operation of existing structures is developed. It is not enough for
the worker in the nonroutinized sector to follow "the rules" or
even to internalize them. He or she must be able to redesign the
rules so that they achieve their ends more surely and efficiently;
and for this critical abilities must be developed. Nevertheless,
these abilities must be exercised only within narrow confines
and not extended to a critical analysis of the functioning of the
system as a whole. In this regard the particular patterns and
methods of symbolic manipulation learned in each discipline,
and the respect for expertise and division of labor which is gen-

erally inculcated in college, serve to bound the domain over which the expert will let his critical faculties range. Thus college and postgraduate training exposes students to work situations that correspond to those encountered on nonroutinized jobs, develops the general cognitive skills and particular technical skills necessary to function effectively on these jobs, and heavily reinforces the ideologies of meritocracy and technocracy which legitimate the antiworker nature of the actions that students will have to take as employees.

Despite the correspondences just discussed between the particular stages of the schooling process and various labor-market segments, contradictions remain and create pressures for structural change in both schools and firms. Most evidently, primary routinized and secondary jobs continue greatly to outnumber primary creative jobs while increasing numbers of students are earning college and advanced degrees. This situation has led to a legitimation crises. It is increasingly difficult to sustain the myth that those in the high-paying, high-status jobs are there because of superior ability when many individuals hold college credentials. But this is not the most serious aspect of the crisis. More important, increasing numbers of students who have been socialized through college education to think of themselves as "experts" and to expect nonroutinized, high-paying jobs are being forced to accept subordinate, routinized jobs. This frustration of expectations is a potentially explosive situation which directly threatens the routinized structure of the bulk of jobs today.[21] The regular but relatively slow mobility patterns of the routinized sector will not satisfy these workers. They will not settle for work that is a mere means to a living. They have come to expect more control over the conditions of their work, to make decisions, and by making the right decisions, to rise rapidly.[22]

A similar contradiction is potentially inherent within the hierarchical structure of the routinized sector. That is, if the rate of growth of the economy permanently slows down from its post-World War II pace, the movement of employees up the seniority job ladders must necessarily slow down as well, leading to a situation of frustrated expectations. Moreover, the slower the growth rate of the economy as a whole, the greater will be the number of overeducated individuals crowded into the primary routinized sector (leading in turn to new primary sector workers with mere high school credentials being de facto thrust down into the pool of secondary labor through an inability to find jobs in the primary sector). The glut of overeducated workers will arise not merely because of the slower growth rate of high-level jobs, but also because of a prolongation of education due to a reduction of alternative wage-earning opportunities.[23]

This last factor is important to bear in mind when analyzing the impact of the present economic crisis on demands for more fulfilling, interesting work. Quite naturally, when output and employment suddenly dip, the first reaction of workers' whose jobs are threatened is defensive, i.e., the focus of their agitation shifts to job and wage guarantees. Issues of job content and work control slide into the background. Viewed from a long-run perspective, however, the crisis contributes to the oversupply of workers educated to expect high-wage, high-status jobs. Workers displaced from their jobs pursue more education to improve their job prospects conditioned on holding certain educational credentials. As a consequence, dissatisfaction with the conditions of work will reassert itself with renewed force as the state of the economy improves because adverse economic conditions encourage further expansion of schooling. In this way the present economic crisis is heightening the most salient contradiction between the educational process and the structure of workplace requirements. It is increasing the structural base on which worker demands for more control over their jobs is predicated, at the same time that it dampens the immediate demands for worker control.

General Contradictions Which Schools Cannot Mediate   Our analysis also points to other potential contradictions between schooling processes and workplace requirements which, though not as immediately related to issues of work content and structure, still augur increasing discontent both in schools and workplaces. Indeed, it may be more accurate to describe these as contradictions imminent within the present structure of work relations, which the schooling process cannot mediate but can only exacerbate. The most salient of these antagonisms can be grouped under three headings: materialism vs. morality, competition vs. cooperation, egotism vs. sociality.

In order to function smoothly, the production process requires that the workers be honest, cooperative, and place the welfare of a wider social unit ahead of their own; firms in primary labor markets cater to the individualist, materialist, competitive impulses of individuals in order to pit laborers against one another and enlist the individual cooperation of each with the goals of the firm. Schools attempt to mediate this contradiction through extolling morality, cooperation, and help-thy-neighbor. But the structural correspondence of schooling institutions to labor-market structures, the replication in the former of peer and authority relations in the latter, contradicts these principals in its very operation. Moreover, the greater the number of students with college aspirations and education relative to the number of high-paying jobs, the more fiercely the competitive struggle will rage within schools and the more obvious the gap between the ideology schools preach and the reality they signify will become. Thus as presently structured, schools can only reproduce at an earlier and more formative age the cynicism, materialism, and indifference to the social consequences of one's actions that present relations of production foster.

Summary Note on Methodology and Principal Contradictions That Portend Change in the Relations of Schooling to Work

The relations between schooling and work processes, and the dynamics of change within these processes, are complex. In order to interpret these complex relations we introduced the concepts of contradiction and correspondence.

A process or institution is self-contradictory when it tends to produce by its own functioning conditions that hamper its own reproduction. When such a situation occurs, pressures for change in the process or institution in question are generated. The present organization of production based on wage-labor is inherently self-contradictory in that the interests of management and labor are directly opposed. Management seeks to extract the maximum amount of labor for a given wage (in part, as a consequence of competitive pressures from other capitalist enterprises). The wage payment is contingent on the expectation that the workers will produce goods and services whose value exceeds the wage plus the cost of materials, depreciation, and so forth. But since the worker does not own or have any claim over what he produces, he has no direct interest in increasing his output and acts to limit the work he does at a given wage.

The frictions caused by the ensuing struggles over wages and work conditions are a continual threat to interrupt the production process, and in extreme cases, jeopardize its basic structure. We have described a variety of institutions that have arisen historically within the labor process itself that smooth over these frictions, segment workers into various groups, and enlist the voluntary cooperation of strategically important or difficult to replace workers with the goals and methods of management through various cooptative salary and promotion schemes. Despite these institutions, however, the basic contradiction remains, but manifests itself in less direct forms.

Correspondence is defined as a relation between two processes that mediate contradictions in the dominant process and thereby facilitate *reproduction* of the structures and institutions of that process. The need to play this mediating role is what ultimately determines the form of the institutions and structures in the subordinate process. Thus the schooling process mediates incipient contradictions in the labor process by replicating the relations to peers, authority figures, knowledge, and control over work content that students wil subsequently face in their work lives. More particularly, the relations within each of different tracks and levels of schooling correspond approximately to the relations within the different segments of the labor market. The early and continuing subjection to these relations makes them appear natural and inevitable, and thus helps to prepare individuals for (and reconcile them to) their position within them. This differential socialization to competence is most apparent in the contrasting schooling experience at any given grade level of the affluent as opposed to the poorest in our society. The relations within college, graduate school and their preparatory tracks attended by upper SES children correspond to relations within the primary creative segment of the labor market. The schooling experience of inner-city youth in grammar school and high school prepare them for the secondary labor market. The relations of high school, junior college, and nonelite four-year colleges experienced by middle SES students correspond by and large to the primary routinized segment.

As long as schools are functioning to facilitate reproduction of the existing social and structural relations of the labor process, the concept of correspondence predicts that little significant change will occur in schooling processes. Our analysis suggests, however, that the mechanisms of correspondence are breaking down. The most salient breakdown is the overexpansion of the schooling system at higher levels relative to the requirements of existing job structures for highly educated workers with a capacity and desire for responsible decision-making roles. At the same time, minority students and students from inner-city high schools, who increasingly recognize that the schools are not the key to mobility for them, become cynical and hostile. Our analysis thus locates the source of the much discussed "crisis in education" in the breakdown of its correspondence mechanisms—a breakdown that is rooted in (and reacts back on) a crisis of reproduction of existing relations in the workplace.

Nevertheless, the logic of cost minimization in a hierarchically organized and controlled production process dictates that as many jobs as possible be routinized and simplified so that more easily replaceable workers with less training can be hired at lower salaries. This trend implies a stagnant or even dwindling supply of high-paying, responsible jobs relative to demand except when the overall growth rate of the economy is high.[24]

In this context, the use of schooling credentials to ration access to these increasingly scarce high-paying, high-status jobs —i.e., to represent this assignment of jobs as the outcome of individual differences in ability and effort—has backfired. People have believed that, by studying hard, anyone with sufficient ability could get ahead; this has fueled a tremendous expansion of the schooling system. Now they are finding that in a hierarchically organized production process, not everyone who registers the appropriate achievement level gets ahead. This situation results in many workers with aspirations to primary creative jobs being forced to accept routinized jobs, thereby experiencing disillusionment and cynicism with the system of production. We hypothesize that the decreasing legitimacy of existing workplace hierarchies coupled with the frustration of expectations derivative from the oversupply of educated workers will result in increasing pressures over the next decade for more democratic, participatory forms of work organization.

If these pressures force large structural changes in the forms of work organization and in the social relations of the work process, then our correspondence concept predicts that forces will be generated to change the content and structure of schooling processes in corresponding ways. By studying the operation of existing mechanisms of correspondence, and by identifying the structural elements of industrial democracy[25] that specifically distinguish it from present organizations of production, we gain insight into the ways in which schooling processes must change in order to correspond to democratic work structures and to facilitate change in that direction.

Notes

1. Indeed, in our view all thought is founded on such organizing precepts and thus in principle untestable against empirical observation. Theories change not because they are refuted by the "facts" but because they prove inadequate to solve practical problems. Unfortunately, we cannot explore this epistomological position here. Thomas Kuhn, *The Structure of Scientific Revolutions* (2nd ed.; Chicago: University of Chicago Press, 1970), treats this problem at some length. He lays more emphasis on theoretical inadequacy (i.e., the accumulation of anomalies) than on practical inadequacy as a source of change in organizing precepts.

2. See Martin Carnoy, "Capitalist Change and the Changing Structure of Labor Markets" (Center for Economic Studies, Palo Alto, Calif. (August 1975: mimeo.), for a more detailed summary of these changes in the organization of production.

3. See Samuel Bowles and Herbert Gintis, *Schooling in Capitalist America* (New York: Basic Books, 1976), for a summary of these arguments.

4. See Herbert Gintis, "Towards a Radical Theory of the Firm," discussion paper No. 328 (Harvard Institute of Economic Research, Cambridge, Mass., October 1973), for a discussion of the use of job-ladder structures to enlist worker cooperation with management objectives.

5. Obviously we are speaking here only of the private sector. The inclusion of the government sector in the analysis, while desirable, poses a number of problems that will not be taken up here.

6. This observation is discussed in more detail in Gintis, "Towards a Radical Theory of the Firm."

7. Segmented labor markets are labor markets differentiated by the nature of wage and benefits structure, the degree of job stability, the existence of career ladders, etc. According to segmentation theories, most jobs in the economy can be grouped into one of three major segments—the primary independent, primary subordinate, and secondary labor market. Each segment requires a different set of worker traits and, as a result, draws upon different pools of workers. The distinguishing characteristics between segments are as follows:

The primary independent sector comprises jobs in which the work is nonroutinized, nonmenial, and involves decision making that affects workers in subordinate layers of the hierarchy. The nature of tasks in this sector precludes direct supervision by superiors; hence, the specific substance of productivity in this sector is the ability to do what one would have been told without being told. This requires acceptance and internalization of corporate norms.

Jobs in the primary subordinate segment consist of routine tasks involving little decision making. The vast majority of jobs in the public sector bureaucracies and most production jobs in the monopoly sector of the economy fall under this heading. The chief characteristics required of workers in this sector are dependability, a rules orientation, and responsiveness to authority. In short, conformity to externally imposed norms rather than internalization of norms is the substance of productivity in this sector.

Jobs in the secondary labor market require the minimum of either general or job-specific skills. These are the jobs with the lowest status, lowest wages, and least-secure working conditions. In short, these are jobs anyone could do, but no one would do if they had a choice.

For further explanation of segmentation theory, see Michael A. Carter and Martin Carnoy, "Theories of Labor Markets and Worker Productivity" (Center for Economic Studies, Palo Alto, Calif., August 1974; mimeo.).

8. See Harry Braverman, *Labor and Monopoly Capital* (New

York: Monthly Review Press, 1974), chap. 16, for evidence of the continuing importance of such menial jobs in the overall job structure. Braverman reports that over 12 million workers in menial service and retail trade occupations in 1971 received an average salary of only $91 per week.

9. See Samuel Bowles, "Unequal Education and the Reproduction of the Social Division of Labor" in *Schooling in a Corporate Society*, ed. Martin Carnoy (2nd ed.; New York: David McKay, 1975); Samuel Bowles, "Schooling and Inequality from Generation to Generation," *Journal of Political Economy*, May/June 1972; Samuel Bowles and Herbert Gintis, "I.Q. in the U.S. Class Structure," *Social Policy*, January/February 1973; and Jerome Karabel, "Community Colleges and Social Stratification," *Harvard Educational Review*, November 1972.

10. Bennett Harrison, "Education and Unemployment in the Urban Ghetto," in Martin Carnoy, ed., *Schooling in a Corporate Society*, (2nd ed.; New York: David McKay, 1975).

11. The structural relation of schooling experience to subsequent labor-market experience for women is very complex and does not exactly replicate the relation that obtains for men. For instance, many women achieve good grades, graduate from high school, and still obtain only secondary jobs. To understand the relationship of women to existing job structures, we must consider not only the structure and ideology of the schooling but also the structure and ideology of the family. To avoid confusing the analysis with too many details, we have ignored the circumstances particular to the experience of women. The analysis of women's socialization is a separate area of study under the research grant that sponsored this paper.

12. Fieldwork currently being performed in schools by the Educational Requirements for Industrial Project members will analyze concrete differences in pedagogy, expectations, etc., between schools in high and low SES areas.

13. See J. McVicker Hunt, *The Challenge of Incompetence and Poverty* (Urbana: University of Illinois Press, 1969), for an example of this attitude. Interestingly, Hunt is not a right-wing ideologue but believes that "society" must intervene to create "competence" among the poor.

14. We must analytically distinguish the *technical division of labor*, which tends with the development of technology under the auspices of capital to fragment into a few highly skilled jobs and a large number of routinized jobs, from the *social division of labor*, which comprehends not only these differentiations between jobs but also the institutional mechanisms, relative wage structures, and promotion ladders that regulate the allocation of labor to the various jobs. At this point we are concerned with explaining the functions of the institutions associated primarily with the social division of labor.

Historically, of course, both processes occur simultaneously and both appear to management as complementary methods of cost reduction and labor-process control.

15. We exclude from our analysis of nonroutinized jobs traditional craft jobs such as plumber, carpenter, etc. These are in a sense remnants of an earlier organization of production based in an era before the systematic introduction of high technology and standardized production methods. Of course, these crafts are also currently being subjected to the "rationalization" of standardized production methods and broken down into a number of narrower specialties. These narrower specialities become part of the routinized sector. Unions, by and large, are willing accomplices in fragmentation of jobs and establishment of hierarchy since this is consistent with a strategy of job protection.

16. Although in this sector expense-account padding, use of company cars and phones for personal purposes, and other forms of pilferage are endemic, they are not as much of a threat to profits as similar actions in the primary subordinate market would be, both because there are fewer workers in this sector and because the potential contribution to profits of each employee in this sector is higher.

17. What we do not discuss in this paper is the role schools play in differential socialization to competence. That is, we do not discuss how schools in high SES areas differ from schools in low SES areas; how the former promote the attitudes and values and inculcate the skills that result in relatively large percentages of their students going on to college. Here we merely discuss how the structural/social relations of college correspond to those on nonroutinized jobs and how those of the lower grades correspond to relations on routinized jobs.

18. Paul Sweezy argues in his essay "Toward a Critique of Economics," *Monthly Review*, January 1970, that the underlying paradigm of orthodox economics "takes the existing social order for granted, which means that it assumes, implicitly if not explicitly, that the capitalist system is permanent. Further, it assumes that within this system (a) the interests of individuals, groups, and classes are harmonious (or, if not harmonious, at least reconcilable); (b) tendencies to equilibrium exist and assert themselves in the long run; and (c) change is and will continue to be gradual and adaptive."

19. See Andre Gorz, "Technical Intelligence and the Capitalist Division of Labor," *Telos*, no. 12 (Summer 1972): 27–41.

20. See Andre Gorz, "The Scientist as Worker," *Liberation*, May/June 1974, pp. 12–18.

21. The basic reason for the continued expansion of the educational system and the prolongation of schooling beyond the "needs" of the labor market is the use of schooling credentials to limit access to the most desirable jobs (of course on the other side school ad-

ministrators, teachers, unions, and employees in the educational bureaucracy have lobbied intensely for expanded education). Given this fact, the only way to reduce the demand for schooling would be to cut the links between schooling credentials and high-paying jobs or to increase the cost of higher education dramatically. Either "solution" would pose legitimation problems for society, however.

Martin Carnoy, in his essay "Class Analysis and Investment in Human Resources: A Dynamic Model," *Review of Radical Political Economics* 3, no. 4 (Fall 1971): 56–81, analyzes how the role of a given level of schooling changes (i.e., from socialization-selection to socialization) as the average level of educational attainment of the population increases.

22. See Samuel Bowles, "The Integration of Higher Education in the Wage Labor System," *Review of Radical Political Economics* 6, no. 1 (Spring 1974): 100–133.

23. Educational Requirements for Industrial Democracy project members are currently attempting to collect quantitative evidence on the extent of frustration among young overeducated workers. The Health, Education, and Welfare report, *Work in America* (Cambridge, Mass.: MIT Press, 1973), provides suggestive but not conclusive statistics on the relationship of job dissatisfaction to overeducation.

24. If there is a sharp decline in population growth, this may produce an offsetting reduction in the demand for such jobs. It would also reduce the supply of labor which management draws upon to fill jobs in the secondary labor market.

25. Industrial Democracy refers to forms of work organization which involve significant worker decision making and control over the organization of production extending potentially to affairs of the firm ranging from marketing to investment. For purposes of illustration, we can speak of a continuum of Industrial Democracy bounded at one end by the simple wage contract; at the other, by worker self-management. An analysis of forms of work organization can be found in William Behn, "Classification of Work Organization" (Center for Economic Studies, Palo Alto, Calif., 1975; mimeo.). See also Paul Blumberg, *Industrial Democracy: The Sociology of Participation* (New York: Schocken, 1969); Gerry Hunnius et al., *Workers Control: A Reader on Labor and Social Change* (New York: Vintage, 1973); and David Jenkins, *Job Power* (Baltimore: Penguin, 1974).

4

Henry M. Levin

A Taxonomy of Educational Reforms for Changes in the Nature of Work

According to the "correspondence principle" educational reforms become probable when the existing educational approach and its results are contradicted by changes in the functioning of work organizations.[1] In such an instance educational reform represents a response of the educational system to the contradiction that has arisen. Presumably, if we know the types of contradictions that might arise between the demands of work organizations and the existing educational approach, it should be possible to predict the nature and types of educational reform that will emerge. This chapter constructs a taxonomy of educational reforms that corresponds to a classification scheme of change in the organization of work.[2]

In principle we have assumed a correspondence between the educational process and the work process. From this correspondence we have suggested that the schools and other agencies of socialization serve to reproduce the social relations of production.[3] Educational reform, then, becomes functional only when the social relations of production are altered. Elsewhere we have discussed the process by which these contradictions arise and the role of changes in the organization of work in eliminating them.[4]

It is useful to review briefly a simplified schema of this relation to set the stage for classifying educational reforms. Figure 4.1

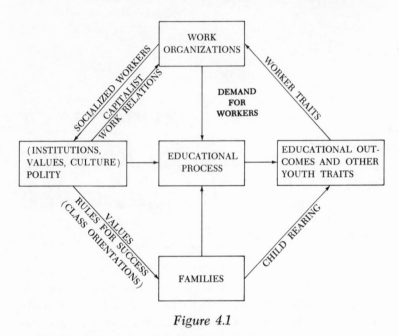

Figure 4.1

Simplified Schematic Description of Relations among Polity,
Family, School, and Work Organizations

provides a very skeletal view of these relations. Essentially, this diagram shows the link between the overall structure of society, the polity, and two institutions of socialization, the family and the school, with respect to work organizations. It is suggested that the overall system of social relationships is imprinted on work organizations, the educational process, and families. Both work organizations and families also mold the educational process. The former create a demand for workers with particular sets of characteristics which are functional to the productive process, and the success of the schools in fulfilling these demands is reflected in the employability and trainability of graduates. Since families have a large influence on the values and knowledge of students who participate in the schools, their impact on the educational process is substantial. The educational outcomes and other youth traits that emerge from the process enter as worker traits into work organizations, and they also serve to reinforce the nature of the polity and the stability of the social system.

But contradictions are constantly arising in these linkages. One type of contradiction that is increasingly in evidence is the failure of work organizations to integrate young persons into traditional work relations. We have suggested reasons for this phenomenon elsewhere,[5] and we have observed a variety of potential and actual changes in the organization of work that are designed to reconcile the contradiction by increasing the amount of worker participation, involvement, and autonomy. But changes in the nature of work will in themselves create new contradictions between work and education because the activities of the schools will correspond more closely with traditional work relations. Accordingly, we would expect to see various pressures exerted on the educational mechanism to alter the preparation of workers. Essentially, there would be a tendency for educational reforms to take place that would be supportive of the new work order. This paper reviews the types of changes in education that might take place in order to reestablish correspondence between changes in the nature of work and the socialization for work.

Organizing a Classification Scheme

A classification scheme for educational reforms must be organized according to some principle. A mere listing of reforms and a description of their character is not very useful. In the context of our project and the diagram in figure 4.1, it is obvious that the focus of organization should be on the degree to which they would reinforce the work reforms that we believe might be in the offing. This correspondence of educational reforms with work reforms might be done in two ways. The first possibility would be to match changes in the organization and manifestation of social relations in work organizations with those in school organizations. The presumption is that the organization of the educational environment would necessarily correspond with that of the work environment whether under the existing modes of work or under their transformation. For example, if teams were to be used more extensively in work, what type of educational reform would also build on the use of teams in problem solving and other educational activities? If greater worker participation with respect to the governance of work organizations were predicted, what changes in the governance of educational organizations would correspond?

A second approach would focus less on the organizational arrangement and more on the actual worker characteristics. We have referred to the linkages between work and schools with respect to the worker characteristics that are formed or supplied by institutions of socialization and those that are demanded or required by work organizations.[6] We have also posited that the existing organization of work with its emphasis on pyramidal capitalist hierarchies requires different worker characteristics than those that would become functional under worker self-management or a variety of reforms of work reorganization that institutionalize greater industrial democracy.[7] Therefore, we should like to know what are the vital characteristics that the present system requires and how they are produced. Second, what changes in worker characteristics will be required, and which educational reforms will be necessary to produce them? If these two issues were resolved, it would be possible to determine what types of potential educational reforms would correspond with changes in work, and it would be useful to compare potential educational modifications with those educational reforms that have been developed for adaptation by the schools.

Actually, the approach that we use here is a combination of both of the preceding methods. It is not possible to use an orthodox version of either approach because of an inadequate empirical base. That is, the first classification scheme would require a fairly detailed list of work reforms with particular attention devoted to the organizational changes that would ensue in the workplace. Since most of these are still on the drawing board, it is not possible to know in any reasonably explicit way how they will be implemented. We can only draw some general dimensions of change that are related to each.

The second classification approach is even more difficult to apply in any precise sense. Our present knowledge of the workers' characteristics that are required for particular work enterprises is quite general, and comprehensive empirical work in this area is severely deficient. Given this lack of data on the present relations, it is then much more difficult to discuss the specific worker characteristics that will be required under the various reforms in the organization of work. Nevertheless, as long as we refer to worker characteristics at a very general level, it should be possible to differentiate among educational changes that will or will not contribute to the changes in the nature of work. For example, it is possible to delineate such changes as increases in cooperative as opposed to competitive behavior, greater equality vs. differentiation in skill requirements, and so on. Even this modest approach will prove valuable in the analysis of the complex nature of contradictions that arise between work and education (or socialization processes more generally).

Changes in the Organizaton of Work

Before proceeding with a discussion of educational reforms and their relevance for changes in the organization of work, we must give a brief picture of the types of alterations in work that are being considered. Two trends exist, and each has quite different implications.

First are the aggregate changes in the nature of jobs created by secular trends in an advanced economy. Specifically we refer to the tendency over time of a shifting emphasis from manufacturing and production jobs to service-oriented ones.[8] In 1950 employment in the United States was divided equally between service and manufacturing jobs, but by 1970 the balance had tilted to 62 percent of the employment in the services and only 38 percent in manufacturing.[9] This inexorable movement toward the service sector has obvious implications for education in that the educational requirements for such jobs are likely to be considerably different than for manufacturing ones. In general, the service sector with its emphasis on white-collar tasks requires greater formal education than does its manufacturing counterpart. Notably, a significant and growing proportion of service employment lies in the public sector.

A second aspect of the aggregate trend in work is the increasing "proletarianization" of white-collar and professional jobs.[10] Increasing dominance of large corporate enterprises and government as well as diminishing opportunities for self-employment have expanded the proportion of the work force subjected to hierarchical control in work experience. "Among a class of occupations notable for their autonomy—managers, officials, and proprietors (excluding farms)—self-employment fell from 50% in 1950 to 37% in 1960."[11] These developments suggest that corresponding educational changes will be oriented to preparing white-collar, managerial, and professional employees for increasingly dependent and relatively narrow positions in large bureaucratic organizations.[12]

But this aggregate picture tends to mask the contradictions that are arising within work organizations. The tendencies toward narrowing of job roles and reduction of independence in combination with increasing educational requirements are creating a variety of work-related problems for government and industry. Among these are apparently rising incidences of worker turnover, worker absenteeism, wildcat strikes, quality control deficiencies, drug use and alcoholism among employees, and sabotage.[13] These difficulties seem to be especially prevalent among young workers, who appear to be less willing to accept the conditions of work that face them.[14] Without changes in the nature of work and the work situation, we believe that the tendency will be toward increasing employer-employee conflict, worker dissatisfaction, work disruptions, and deterioration of work quality. The severity of such problems is well illustrated by the recent events at the Chevrolet Vega plant in Lordstown, Ohio,[15] and we believe that these types of conflicts will do more to mold the nature of changes in work organizations than the aggregate tendencies toward service employment and wage labor that have been noted. Indeed, simple extrapolation of overall employment data will give a misleading impression of changes that will be forth-coming in the workplace; for the reaction by workers to the conditions of work and the employers' response to an associated drop in productivity would appear to be a much more influential predictor of changes in the nature of work than the afore-mentioned trends themselves.[16]

Accordingly, the work reforms to be discussed in this chapter represent those which correspond to the possible responses of employers to the growing labor difficulties we have projected. In order to reduce the threat of disruption, private firms and govern-ment are searching for methods of altering the nature of work to increase worker loyalty and productivity.[17] Possible changes range all the way from cosmetic alterations in the physical environment, more affable managers, a redesign of jobs to reduce boredom, and profit sharing to industrial democracy or worker self-management.[18] Although Behn reviews these modifications in a more thorough way,[19] it is necessary to provide some indication of their direction in order to show how they relate to educational reforms.

Table 4.1 represents an illustrative classification of work re-forms. Reforms are divided into four categories: (1) micro-technical, (2) macro-technical, (3) micro-political, and (4) macro-political. Since this division will also be used in description of educational reforms, a note of clarification is in order. The first category includes those changes that do not require organiza-tional departures from traditional practice. They are narrowly technical and individualistic in implementation. The fourth cate-gory, macro-political, refers to major changes in the governance and technical conception of organization. The changes are more encompassing and political.

The fact that each successive category tends to be more com-prehensive than, and to subsume, the previous category means that there will appear to be some overlap among classifications. The attempt in creating this taxonomy is to provide a conceptual separation that is useful in reviewing changes in both work and education. Accordingly, the subsequent classification of educa-tional reforms also untilizes the four categories. In this way we can compare the classification of changes of both work and

Table 4.1

An Illustrative Classification of Work Reforms

I. *Micro-Technical*
   A. Flexible work schedule
   B. Reduced formality in communication and attire
   C. Job redesign
      1. job enlargement
      2. job rotation
      3. better equipment
      4. technical redesign of task
   D. Changes in physical work environment

II. *Macro-Technical*
   A. Organizational development
      1. new staff configuration
      2. regular meetings among staff
      3. open-door personnel policies with respect to personnel grievances
      4. revitalization through seminars, educational and training opportunities, and sabbaticals
   B. Profit sharing and other incentive payment schemes
   C. Redesign of organizations

III. *Micro-Political*
   A. Job enrichment
   B. Other forms of participative management
      (management consulting, workers' councils, etc.)

IV. *Macro-Political*
   A. Employee ownership
   B. Worker representation on corporate board
   C. Worker self-management

---

education along similar political and technical dimensions. For example, micro-political alterations refers to changes in the internal governance of the organization with respect to decisions on production activities and resource allocation whether we are addressing schools or the workplace. An explicit discussion of each category is in order.

Micro-Technical   Micro-technical changes refer to changes in the nature of particular jobs that have generally been determined by such technical specialists as industrial psychologists, industrial sociologists, human factors engineers, and industrial engineers. They include attempts to improve working relationships among employees and management through more flexible work schedules as well as eliminating much of the formality in communications and attire.[20] Jobs may be redesigned to reduce worker boredom through job enlargement (increasing the number of tasks or activities done by a worker) and job rotation whereby workers exchange tasks on a regular schedule.[21] Such job alterations also include the modification and redesign of the job where it involves intrinsically difficult, fatiguing, and boring work, and the design of better equipment where it fulfills these ends. Another type of micro-technical change is that of changing the work environment to remove hazards to health and safety, as well as to make it more pleasant through the reduction of extraneous noises and through improvements in the visual surroundings and to install such employee amenities as lounges and canteens. These represent the most common forms for changing the nature of work. They can be designed by the technical experts who guide management practices, and they can be done in a piecemeal fashion in those parts of the operation where problems arise without spilling over into other aspects of the organization. Thus, they can localize a problem without affecting the overall operations of the plant, firm, or government agency. Most important, they are controlled by management and carried out at its discretion.

Macro-Technical   In contrast, macro-technical changes are also based upon "technical" changes in production relations that are recommended by the various specialists, but these tend to be wider in scope than the micro-technical ones. Under the previous category, even a single job could be redesigned to eliminate or reduce worker problems, but under the macro-technical aegis the solution will apply to groups of workers and could cover the entire organization. Typical of the macro-technical changes are those which are often cast under the rubric of organizational development.[22] These represent attempts to improve communications and human relations within the organization. Presumably, if workers are listened to and if staffing patterns are deployed appropriately, worker dissatisfaction will diminish. Increases in worker opportunities for training and educational experiences as well as sabbaticals are also expected to contribute to worker satisfaction. Typical of the "reforms" that are instituted in these areas are devices for increasing communication among workers and between workers and management such as regular meetings and open-door policies with respect to personnel grievances. In some cases staffing patterns are altered to improve lines of communication up and down the hierarchy.

A second macro-technical approach is the adoption of profit sharing and other types of work incentive plans. The former scheme is based upon the presumption that if workers share in the profits of the firm, they will tend to be more productive. Actual plans vary from year-end division of a portion of the profits according to salary or seniority to more sophisticated methods that attempt to tie employee shares to productivity. The effectiveness of such plans is problematic and apparently depends crucially on a large number of factors.[23] Other incentive approaches include changes in payment mechanisms ranging from salary to commission and piecework basis as well as vacations and prizes for fulfilling particular work goals (sales and production especially).[24] The principle underlying all these plans is that by changing the structure of external rewards in ways consonant with the objectives of the organization, workers will support these goals through their self-interest.

The other major macro-technical strategy is that of redesigning the production unit itself. This approach entails a combination of assessing the problems entailed by the existing organization or subunit and designing an approach that is likely to reconcile these problems and increase productivity. Such changes include new organizational and new personnel configurations as well as the modification or replacement of plant and equipment to fit the new mode of operation. One of the most notable examples of redesign of the production unit is found in the case of automobile manufacture in Sweden. Both Volvo and Saab-Scandia have moved away from the traditional assembly line in some of their plants. At Saab the engine blocks are produced by a team of workers who work together to organize and schedule production, provide training, and rotate particular tasks. Volvo has carried the team-assembly concept even further by building a plant where the assembly line is eliminated completely. In its place are a number of subassembly shops where teams of workers carry out functions similar to the engine assembly at Saab. Both firms claim improvements in productivity, quality control, and work-force stability.

Micro-Political Micro-political changes represent changes in the internal decision making of the work enterprise that increase the participation of workers in affecting the conditions and relationships that surround their jobs. One category of changes of a micro-political nature is that of job enrichment which implies "vertical job loading"—the integration of planning, execution, and evaluation of tasks into one job—in contrast with the "horizontal job loading" approach inherent in job enlargement or job rotation. The latter change increases the number of jobs performed by individuals at about the same task level in order to reduce worker boredom.[25] Other forms of internal participative management may vary from management consultation with employees about job assignments and scheduling to more formal participation of employees through worker councils. In the latter case the workers would elect or appoint representatives to sit on decision making bodies in the organization. Micro-political changes can also take the form of direct worker participation in determining the organization and scheduling of work, implementation of training programs, and the adoption of new work practices. Remuneration and evaluation of work performance may also be done with the participation of fellow workers. In all these cases some traditional management prerogatives are relinquished or shared with workers.[26] Even though the overall control of the organization is not altered with respect to such issues as which products will be produced, their prices, investment plans, distribution of profits, and similar issues, the internal organization of work tends to be governed by a greater degree of worker participation.[27]

The illustration of changes in Swedish automobile manufacture provides a good example of these types of changes in decision making. While we have described the shift from assembly lines to work teams as one that is based upon technical redesign of the organization, it also represents substantial micro-political changes based upon the ability of groups of workers to determine within reasonably broad limits the organization of their work. The Swedish example also shows the degree to which various work reforms may fit into more than one subcategory of the classification scheme. In particular, the "political" types of reforms almost invariably have technical implications, although the opposite is not necessarily true. Many technical changes in jobs can be carried out without affecting the pattern of decision making.

Macro-Political In contrast with the micro-political work reforms, the macro-political category includes those modifications designed to give workers a greater measure of control and participation in the work enterprise as a whole, rather than just within their own work units. While the micro-political changes include only internal changes in the distribution of decision-making roles, macro-political alterations encompass changes in the governance and direction of the total work organization. In principle such reforms can increase the participation of workers in virtually all the policies of the firm from internal work practices to the selection and marketing of products, determination of prices and investment policies, and allocation of profits or surpluses. At least these are the possibilities represented by such changes in governance.

The specific form of the macro-political reform is crucial in determining the nature of the results. For example, plans for ownership would seem to have very important implications for work organization. Some of these take the form of employees receiving shares of stock or options to purchase stock on the basis of seniority, salary, or position. In other cases, the employees acting as a group purchase the firm by obtaining a loan that is repaid out of profits. It is probably safe to say that in a majority of cases the employees rarely exercise the power inherent in such ownership to change the nature of work. Rather, they seem content to leave these decisions to traditional managerial hierarchies with the tacit belief that professional expertise is necessary to obtain maximum growth and returns to their stock ownership. This result may also derive from the fact that most proposals for employee ownership are management initiated. When this is not true it may produce quite different results.[28]

A second macro-political reform is that of worker representation on corporate boards. For example, in several large industries in West Germany, a policy of codetermination has been adopted whereby from one-third to one-half of the places on the governing board of the firms is delegated to workers.[29] This approach would be somewhat equivalent to requiring that corporate boards of directors in the United States have significant proportions of worker representatives. Yet, it is not clear that the codetermination approach has had much of an impact on the nature of work and work organization, and the policy is exceedingly controversial with respect to its impact.[30]

A third form of macro-political work reform is that of worker self-management. The focus of this approach is on the direct power of the workers to govern their work organization.[31] Again, this mode of control can take many forms. For example, the Yugoslavian version is based upon workers' councils that make the major policy decisions for the firms.[32] Among small enterprises (less than thirty employees), all the workers are members of such councils; and among larger enterprises, the councils are elected by the workforce. The council holds all formal power, and it makes decisions regarding hiring and firing, salaries, investment, and so on.[33]

In contrast, work organizations in countries such as China and Cuba emphasize direct participation in their management and operations, rather than participation through representation. All members of the work enterprise are expected to play active roles in contributing to the formation of the work process. There is a heavy emphasis on study and discussion among workers as a basis for understanding their role in creating a revolutionary society through their work. The Israeli kibbutz, or collective, is another well-known example of workers' control where all decisions about production and the distribution and use of productive surpluses are made by the membership. The traditional work hierarchy is eliminated in favor of a democratic mechanism for making decisions.[34]

In general, macro-political reforms represent the most far-reaching possibilities for changing the nature of work organizations to increase the participation of workers in affecting the nature of their jobs and their work relationships. That is, with major changes in the overall governance, corresponding modifications take place in internal governance and in the technical arrangements of the work organization. Of course, as noted, this hierarchical approach to describing work reforms from micro-technical changes to macro-political ones tends to subsume the former categories under each successive classification, although there may be exceptions to this generalization. For example, employee ownership may change none of the characteristics of the work organization beyond who receives the dividends, and profit-sharing plans may also have no effect on the nature of work. The classification scheme we have described gives some indication of the variety of possible work reforms that might be adopted in response to the problems that appear to be increasingly obvious in the workplace.

Classification of Educational Reforms

Before attempting to classify educational reforms and their relevance to the changes in work, it is important to comment on the problems in identifying the nature of educational changes and their impacts. While many labels refer to changes in the educational process or content, it is very difficult to ascertain any rigorous definition of the change. As a result, a particular type of educational modification may mean different things according to the visions and experience of the beholder. Beyond this problem of definition, there is an enormous heterogeneity of implementation so that the same concept looks even more varied in the applied setting.[35] Sarason has argued that the process of educational change is so nebulous that rarely can one even find descriptive data of what has taken place.[36] Accordingly, the approach taken here is to list illustrative changes that have been suggested or debated for the schools. The descriptions given are approximate, intended only to differentiate them from other changes. Whether they have the intended effects is open to empirical inquiry, and we do not draw firm conclusions on this matter. Nevertheless, we suggest that certain of these reforms could correspond to particular changes in the nature of work.

Table 4.2 shows a categorization of educational reforms that is constructed in a fashion parallel to that of the work taxonomy. The micro-technical label refers to those relatively small technical changes that do not require organizational modifications of schools, such as the addition of new subjects or the adoption of different instructional materials. The macro-technical category includes a more embracing set of technical alterations that affect the organization and content of schooling. These include new staffing models and major curricular reforms that go beyond mere changes in textbooks or teacher retraining. Micro-political reforms entail changes in the internal governance of schools with respect to who makes decisions about curriculum, personnel, and resource allocations as well as the control of the instructional process. Finally, the macro-political reforms comprise major changes in both the governance and control of schooling.

Micro-Technical Micro-technical changes represent those nominal or piecemeal changes in schooling within the context of the existing organizational arrangements. Such modifications may have little to do with the micro-technical work reforms since the latter themselves require no substantial changes in the socialization of workers. Examples of micro-technical changes include the addition of new subjects such as sex education or new approaches to teaching traditional subjects such as the "new math." In these cases the work implications are nominal, but when new vocational subjects are added to the offerings of the community colleges and other institutions of higher education, the connections between new demands in the workplace and the new subject may be direct.

Other micro-technical educational reforms include the adoption of different instructional materials based upon alternative approaches to teaching as well as upon emerging social values

Table 4.2

A Classification of Educational Reforms by Organizational Changes

---

I. *Micro-Technical*
   A. New subjects
   B. Changes in instructional materials—different approaches to teaching reading, purging textbooks of sex stereotypes
   C. Teacher training and retraining
   D. Multicultural and bilingual programs
   E. Educational technology (specific application)

II. *Macro-Technical*
   A. Differentiated staffing
   B. Team teaching
   C. Open classrooms
   D. Flexible modular scheduling
   E. Mastery learning
   F. Educational technology (generalized use)
   G. Work-study
   H. Desegregation and integrated education

III. *Micro-Political*
   A. Changes in internal governance of classroom or school with respect to students, teachers, and administrators
   B. Greater responsibilities to students in operation of instructional process—peer teaching, for example

IV. *Macro-Political*
   A. Community control
   B. Educational vouchers
   C. Deschooling policies
   F. Factory-run schools

---

that have not been adequately represented in earlier materials. Teacher training and retraining for preparing teachers to handle new instructional content also fit into the micro-technical classification as well as the use of educational technology such as language cassettes and programmed instruction or computer-assisted instruction. Finally, the hiring of bilingual teachers and the adoption of multicultural approaches for some subjects represent alterations of the traditional curriculum that fit into this classification. All these changes tend to be compartmentalized into a specific framework that does not have much if any impact on the larger organizational context of schooling.

Macro-Technical   While the previous category of changes referred to a very specific set of actions that were not likely to have a general impact on the larger educational organization, a second set of technical modifications would appear to have widespread implications. Since these alterations can be considered independently of changes in the governance or political control of schools and have been designed by educators and other professionals for modifying the educational process, we have used the technical descriptor. Of course, just as changes in the governance of firms would likely lead to technical changes in operations as well, the same is true of changes in the governance of schools. Thus the distinction between political and technical educational reforms might be blurred in practice.

Typical of macro-technical changes are those designed to alter some aspect of the internal organization of schools. For example, differentiated staffing approaches are based upon analyzing the tasks that are entailed in carrying out instruction, determining personnel requirements and duties for each, and setting scales of remuneration.[37] Staff are hired, trained, utilized, and paid according to the functions set out, and a career ladder is created so that advancement is possible within the school to a much greater degree than is evident in the more traditional staffing model. The result of the approach, if it were fully implemented, would be a much more highly specialized and hierarchical approach to school operations. Evaluations of attempts to alter staffing patterns according to the differentiated staffing model suggest that the approach is both short-lived and ineffective at altering the educational environment.[38]

Another staffing reform is that of team teaching. The terminology of team teaching is apparently very ambiguous and means different things to different observers.[39] In its most visionary form: "Team teaching may be defined as an arrangement whereby two or more teachers, with or without teacher aides, cooperatively plan, instruct, and evaluate one or more class groups in an appropriate instructional space and given length of time, so as to take advantage of the special competencies of the team members."[40] In practice, team teaching may simply mean that more than one teacher instructs a group of children according to the specialization of the teacher or that teachers rotate among classes. According to the definition given above, team teaching could increase the amount of specialization among teachers and reduce the basis for interaction, or it could increase the cooperation by requiring joint planning and implementation of instruction. Empirical evidence on the adoption of specific team-teaching approaches and their effects is not available.

One macro-technical reform that has received a large measure of publicity in recent years is that of the "open classroom" based upon the changes that have taken place in many British primary schools.[41] These schools have discarded the more formal classroom and curriculum structures and replaced them with a rich variety of activities and materials with which children can engage themselves. The emphasis is on a diversity of activities occurring simultaneously in which individual students can pursue their interests and needs. Teachers and other personnel assist students in assessing individual needs and selecting activities that respond to those needs.

There is a great emphasis on both students and staff seeking creative approaches to both teaching and learning, and a great deal of responsibility is placed upon the individual student in discovering and responding to his or her own needs with relatively nominal assistance from adults. The substantial independence that is encouraged among students enables the teachers to spend much of their time working with pupils with particularly intransigent learning problems or designing new instructional approaches. Paramount is the emphasis on student individualism in the selection of activities and in participation in the school environment. This reform requires substantial modifications of the physical structure of the classroom, teacher training and orientation, curriculum, and materials.

Flexible modular scheduling is an approach that has been used at secondary level to "individualize" instruction. While the traditional secondary school relies upon relatively uniform time segments and organizational arrangements for each course, flexible modular scheduling enables the design of classes and other educational experiences in which the amount of time, scheduling, and mode of presentation (e.g., lecture vs. small group) are varied according to the subject matter, student needs, and available facilities.[42] This modification enables a greater individualization of instruction as well as a greater range of student choices.

Mastery learning represents a curriculum approach that assumes that the school and classroom can be organized so that almost all youngsters reach some preset functional or mastery level in each subject.[43] The objective of the strategy is to organize instruction to maximize the number of students who meet the mastery criterion within the time limit set for the task. This is attempted through a combination of individualization of instruction, the sequential assignment of resources from those students who have achieved mastery to those who have not, and the use of students tutoring other students. If mastery learning is successful, there should be greater equality in cognitive educational outcomes with obvious implications for work reforms that require cooperation and teamwork based upon relatively equal skill levels.[44]

Although we noted that educational technology can be a microtechnical modification when it is applied to a specific subject or portion of the curriculum, educational technologies have also been designed and adopted as a pervasive force for educational reform.[45] Probably the most important of these are educational radio and television.[46] In some school systems such as Hagerstown, Maryland, educational television is used for a substantial part of the instructional program. In Samoa, Colombia, El Salvador, Niger, South Korea, Ivory Coast, Mexico, and Brazil nationwide or regional systems of educational television or radio are the principal media for instruction. In these cases the programming is developed centrally and transmitted to all classrooms at a particular grade level. While the motivations for constructing such systems are ostensibly to cut costs, compensate for teacher shortages, and improve the quality of instruction, the use of the medium itself is likely to have unique effects on student socialization.[47] For example, the fact that most of the educational television and radio instructional systems are designed to send information in one direction only, surely has implications for the preparation of youngsters for relatively noninteractive work roles.

In many respects work-study approaches to education fit the macro-technical category. Under this rubric are a variety of plans for combining job experiences with formal schooling. In most cases the student alternates between study and work as part of a daily, weekly, or other periodic pattern. The assumption behind these plans is that education for work specifically and for the world generally cannot be limited to the formal instruction of the classroom, and an effective way of tying theory to practice is through the workplace. The work-study approach also has the advantage of providing financial support which can be used to pay educational expenses. Indeed, such higher educational institutions as Antioch College and Northeastern University have had extensive work-study programs for years that have paid the educational costs of their students.[48]

The thrust toward getting the student into the workplace has had particular impetus recently as a response to the dissatisfaction with existing schools and the belief that students are not being prepared properly for work.[49] The effect of work-study provisions on the work characteristics of students will obviously depend upon the nature of the work experiences. To the degree that these are tied to the traditional work organizations, the results will likely conform to existing approaches to work rather than to work reforms; however, work-study programs can certainly be implemented under revised forms of work organization as well.

A final macro-technical example that could have profound effects on the organization and operations of schools is that of desegregation and integrated education. Such a change requires that schools change many of their policies in order to adapt to the mixture of races and social classes.[50] These alterations may extend from changes in tracking policies to new curricula, instructional materials, and teacher-training approaches. If these attempts are successful in providing fully integrated schooling experiences, the socialization effects in changing the attitudes of representatives of the different races and social classes toward one another may have strong implications for work reforms which would reduce hierarchy and worker stratification.

Micro-Political Micro-political changes include those changes in the internal governance of educational organizations with respect to the rules, regulations, curriculum, personnel selection, and resource allocation as well as control of the educational process. While the overall control may still be vested in boards of directors or trustees as well as government agencies, the internal decisions are normally made by teachers and administrators in traditional schools. Micro-political shifts refer to changes in the distribution of decision-making power among the three groups. Recent years have experienced some movement in the direction of more student and teacher input into the decision-making process. In the university these changes have taken the form of student-initiated course offerings and subject majors as well as the decline of the in loco parentis regulations that enabled higher educational institutions to dominate the private lives of their students.

A more formal mechanism for changing the internal governance of educational institutions is reflected in the official transfer of responsibility from one constituency to another. While often the changes are only cosmetic—for example, the typically ineffectual role of student councils at the secondary level and student associations at the college level—some attempts have been made to alter the formal structures for making decisions at many colleges and universities in the United States by requiring that all internal committees have student members. In many cases the student members are not permitted to vote on important matters; they can only participate in discussions and present a student viewpoint. Even when students do have voting power, they generally constitute a small minority of the committees so that they do not represent a potent force in themselves. Of course, it is possible to build coalitions between students and some faculty members or administrators on particular issues, so student representation can influence the outcome of some deliberations where the student interests coincide with those of enough nonstudent representatives to obtain a majority of the votes. Depending on the actual arrangements for student representation, the device can parallel that of internal worker participation in either an advisory or codetermination type of mode. Again, the scale of participation is quite limited.

It is interesting to note that West Germany is experiencing nationwide demands for increased participation of teachers, parents, and students in the school's internal decision-making process.[51] Similar changes have also taken place in both the macro and micro-governance of the German universities. In the context of our analysis, it is noteworthy that the increase in the demands for greater autonomy of schools and greater participation of teachers, parents, and students in their internal operations has been attributed in part to the corresponding "controversy over co-determination (*Mitbestimmung*) in industrial management."[52]

One final version of an educational change that has micropolitical implications is that of peer teaching or tutoring.[53] This approach has been used among children of the same age in order to emphasize cooperation and to enlist the assistance of high achieving students in improving the proficiencies of slower ones. It has also been used to create "tutorial communities" where older children are expected to assist the younger ones in learning particular skills. There is an obvious parallel between this educational approach and those work reforms that require peer training and cooperation in the work enterprise. Team-oriented work reforms, in particular, seem to demand the proficiencies that might be inculcated through peer teaching. Moreover, this reform tends to challenge the hierarchical assumptions that are normally built in to the teaching-learning process, as well as reducing age segregation in classrooms.

Macro-Political   The final and most comprehensive category of educational reforms are those which alter the external governance and control of schooling organization. Of course the embracing nature of these modifications means that they are also likely to have profound effects upon the micro-political and technical characteristics of schooling as well. Macro-political reforms include changes in the control of the existing school organization and shifts in the provision of education from the existing schools to educational marketplaces and workplace.

Community control of schools represents one of the most important of these approaches. During the last decade black and other minority citizens in large cities have demanded that schools in their neighborhoods be governed by neighborhood school boards with responsibility for personnel, allocation of school budgets, curriculum, and other school policies.[54] They view their existing dissatisfaction with the schools and the fact that many of their children fail to learn even basic reading and arithmetic skills as attributable to the existence of large school bureaucracies dominated by school boards and educational professionals who have little concern for children from low-income and minority families. Accordingly, they have argued that if the families who were most affected by school policies had responsibility for the operations of their schools, the present outcomes could not be tolerated.

While many large-city school districts have responded by proclaiming official plans of administrative decentralization with citizen advisory boards, actual control of the decision making process has not been altered in most cases. In New York City, a somewhat more extensive plan has been adopted, but major concessions were granted to the educational professionals in formulating the plan so that the changes in control have probably transferred greater power to teachers than to citizens. It would appear that community control of schools could have profound effects on the participation of students, parents, and staff if such plans were fully adopted. This arrangement would be likely to have its major impacts on raising the collective consciousness and participative experiences that are necessary for a greater involvement in molding the major institutions that affect the lives of the members of the community. In this respect there are likely to be strong similarities between the participative requirements for control of work organizations and schools.

In contrast with the collective decision-making orientation of community control, educational vouchers would focus on individual choice. According to this strategy, the control of education would shift from the state to the consumer by establishing a market for educational services. Parents would be given a tuition voucher that could be used for schooling at any approved educational institution.[55] The state would set out eligibility requirements for participation of schools, and educational enterprises would be encouraged to enter the marketplace to compete for vouchers that would be redeemed by the state. In principle, the profit motive would operate to make schools responsive to the wishes of parents and students and to create diversity; and educational clientele would be able to exercise control over their education by selecting that school that best fit their needs. Schools that were unable to attract enough vouchers would not survive.

Critics of the voucher approach have argued that the marketplace has always provided better results for upper-income groups than for lower ones and that a system of market choice will tend to lead to increased social class and racial segregation among schools.[56] It is further asserted that the results of such a plan would be to increase the intergenerational transmission of social class. Nevertheless, the federal government has attempted to promote voucher demonstrations in order to test their feasibility,[57] and one approach that is based on the voucher concept is being tried currently in a school district in San Jose, California.[58] While the community-control option would increase the collective power of parents and perhaps students vis-à-vis the teachers and administrators, the voucher approach would tend to increase only the individual options available to them, rather than their political power and participation.

A different perspective to macro-political educational reform is provided by the deschooling proposal of Illich.[59] This approach would reduce the dependency on formal schooling and substitute educational opportunities in other forms such as access to libraries, other informational and educational technologies, on-the-job training, peer training, and other nonformal educational alternatives. Since the institution of formal schooling would decline, the control of education and its effects on youth would be determined by the availability of "nonformal" opportunities that arose.

At the present such opportunities seem to be a function of the "connections" and social-class position of the family, and there is nothing in the deschooling approach that would appear to change this pattern. Traditionally, when children from poor and minority families have deschooled themselves by dropping out, few training alternatives have arisen to replace the role of formal schooling. Middle-class and upper-middle-class youngsters have had only to rely upon their parents' contacts or the "free" schools that have arisen to serve their needs. Accordingly, the emphasis on individual choice and options is likely to have a similar effect on youth socialization as the market approach represented by educational vouchers. It seems reasonable to view the deschooling approach by Illich as a particular variant of the move toward the educational marketplace, just as vouchers are another version of this thrust.

A final macro-political reform of education is that of shifting education from the schools to the workplace. This change can take the form of increased on-the-job training as a substitute for formal schooling, or it can encompass a more profound shift where even literacy and other basic socialization are organized and transmitted through the workplace. In such revolutionary societies as Cuba, China, and Tanzania, attempts have been made to bring schooling to the fields and factories.[60] While most of the formal educational endeavors in such societies still take place in schools, there appears to be an increasing focus on the provision of basic literacy skills, cultural experiences, and scientific and technical training in the workplace.

Applying the Classification Scheme

In order to relate changes in the organization of work to those that will be required in education, we have constructed parallel taxonomies of work reforms and educational reforms. We have suggested that modifications in work may require workers with different skills, attitudes, and behaviors and that it is desirable to develop a classification of educational reforms that will be likely to correspond to such changes. The preceding discussion has been general, for its purpose has been only to develop a provocative context within which the very specific changes in work can be traced to particular needs in the alteration of education.

A useful concluding note would be to illustrate how the approach might be used. One way in which this can be done would be to differentiate between two types of work reforms, those which emphasize greater individuality on the part of the workers and those which emphasize greater participation and cooperation.[61] One path toward changing the nature of work and improving the status of the worker has been to stress greater individuality in work reforms.[62] Examples of such proposals include enabling the employee to choose his own work schedule (flexible hours); individualization of training programs, often with educational technology such as audio cassettes and programmed instruction; redesign of individual jobs to make them less burdensome; increasing choices among job assignments and job rotation; individual counseling; and enhancing the personal incentives for achieving particular goals in production, sales, and quality control. In contrast, other work reforms have been oriented toward greater participation, cooperation, and human interaction. Among these are many of the human relations approaches, the use of teams, internal participative management, and worker self-management.

Table 4.3 shows the educational reforms that are consistent with these two types of work reforms, those that correspond to a greater emphasis on worker individuality and those that focus on greater worker participation and cooperation. Among the educational modifications that would appear to be consistent with the first type of work reform are the uses of educational technology, particularly those that permit the student to proceed at his own pace and at his own convenience such as audio cassettes, programmed instruction, and computer-assisted instruction, differentiated staffing and flexible modular scheduling with their emphasis on individualization of instruction, open schools with their focus on diversity and choice of activities, and both vouchers and deschooling with their orientations toward alternative school and learning environments.

Work reforms that emphasize greater cooperation and

Table 4.3

*Educational Reforms That Are Consistent
with Two Types of Work Reforms*

Work Reforms

	Emphasis on Individuality	Emphasis on Cooperation and Participation
Educational Reforms	1. educational technology	1. team teaching
	2. differentiated staffing	2. mastery learning
	3. flexible modular scheduling	3. desegregation
	4. open schooling	4. micro-political changes
	5. educational vouchers	5. community control
	6. deschooling	6. factory-run schools

participation would be consistent with the adoption of team teaching where adults are expected to cooperate in the instructional process; mastery learning with its concern for equalizing skill levels and guaranteeing that all students meet mastery requirements; desegregation of schools with its attempt to improve human relationships among races and social classes; micropolitical reforms that would increase the participation of students and teachers in the instructional process; community control with its stress on governance and control of schools by the community which they serve; and factory-run schools with "on-the-job" training in teamwork, sharing, and cooperation as part of the work enterprise.

The exact form of each educational response must depend upon the specific detail of work reforms. Accordingly, two interesting explorations would seem to be in order. First, it would be useful to review a set of particular work reforms that seem to be under consideration in order to establish more precisely the possible educational adaptations that would be necessary to prepare workers for their new job orientation. Second, it would be helpful to predict on the basis of political, technological, social, and economic criteria which reforms are most likely to be adopted in order to ascertain the most probable changes in educational responses that will have to be made. The present framework represents only a sketch of the overall context in which such explorations might be analyzed.

In addition, it is necessary to examine more fully the nature of contradictions between education and work in order to obtain a better perspective on the nature of educational reforms that would become functional. Certainly our knowledge of how contradictions arise and the process by which they are resolved to obtain correspondence and continued reproduction of the social relations and skills of production is limited. This is a dynamic relationship which can only be studied in an historical context, and the richness and complexity of the phenomenon is obscured by the study of static correspondence between education and work. These are difficult areas of inquiry, but they should be undertaken in order to augment our understanding of the more practical aspects of this scenario.

Notes

1. Henry M. Levin, "Educational Reform and Social Change," *Journal of Applied Behavioral Science* 10, no. 3 (August 1974): 304–20, and chapter 2 in this volume.

2. William Behn, "Classification of Work Organization" (Menlo Park, Calif.: Portola Institute, 1974). Mimeographed.

3. David Gold, "Socialization to Occupational Roles" (Menlo Park, Calif.: Portola Institute, 1974), mimeographed; Marilyn Power Goldberg, "Sex Role Socialization and Work Rules: The Experience of Women" (Menlo Park, Calif.: Portola Institute, 1974), mimeographed; William H. Behn, Martin Carnoy, Michael A. Carter, Joyce C. Crain, and Henry M. Levin, "School Is Bad; Work Is Worse," chapter 9 in this volume.

4. Levin, "Educational Reform and Social Change."

5. Ibid.; see also chapter 9 in this volume.

6. See chapter 9 in this volume; Michael A. Carter and Martin

Carnoy, "Theories of Labor Markets and Worker Productivity" (Menlo Park, Calif.: Portola Institute, 1974); Samuel Bowles, "Unequal Education and the Reproduction of the Social Division of Labor," in *Schooling in a Corporate Society*, ed. Martin Carnoy (New York: David McKay, 1972), pp. 36–64; Samuel Bowles, "Understanding Unequal Economic Opportunity," *American Economic Review* 63, no. 2 (May 1973): 346–56.

7. Levin, "Educational Reform and Social Change"; see also chapter 9 in this volume.

8. Victor R. Fuchs, *The Service Economy* (New York: National Bureau of Economic Research, 1968).

9. U.S. Department of Health, Education, and Welfare, *Work in America* (Cambridge, Mass.: MIT Press, 1973), p. 22.

10. Stanley Aronowitz, *False Promises* (New York: McGraw-Hill, 1973), chap. 6; David Jenkins, *Job Power* (Baltimore: Penguin Books, 1974), pp. 49–51; HEW, *Work in America*, pp. 38–40.

11. HEW, *Work in America*, p. 21.

12. Daniel Bell, "Labor in the Post-Industrial Society," *Dissent*, Winter 1972, pp. 163–89.

13. Levin, "Educational Reform and Social Change"; Peter Henle, "The Economic Effects: Reviewing the Evidence," in *The Worker and the Job*, ed. Jerome M. Rosow (Englewood Cliffs, N.J.: Prentice-Hall, 1974), pp. 118–44; Bennett Kremen, "No Pride in This Dust," *Dissent*, Winter 1972, pp. 21–28.

14. Aronowitz, *False Promises*, chap. 8; HEW, *Work in America*, pp. 43–51.

15. Aronowitz, *False Promises*, chap. 2.

16. Levin, "Educational Reform and Social Change"; Herbert Gintis, "The New Working Class and Revolutionary Youth," in *Schooling in a Corporate Society*, ed. Martin Carnoy (2nd ed.; New York: David McKay, 1975).

17. Jenkins, *Job Power*.

18. HEW, *Work in America*, chaps. 4–7; Jenkins, *Job Power*; Gerry Hunnius, David Garson, and John Case, eds., *Workers' Control: A Reader on Labor and Social Change* (New York: Vintage Books, 1973); Louis Davis and James Taylor, *Design of Jobs* (Middlesex, England: Penguin Books, 1972).

19. Behn, "Classification of Work Organization."

20. Jenkins, *Job Power*, chap. 10.

21. Davis and Taylor, *Design of Jobs*; Harold M. F. Rush, *Job Design for Motivation: Experiments in Job Enlargement and Job Enrichment* (New York: Conference Board, 1971).

22. Harold M. F. Rush, *Organizational Development: A Reconnaissance* (New York: Conference Board, 1973).

23. HEW, *Work in America*, pp. 105–10.

24. Tom Lupton, ed., *Payment Systems* (Middlesex, England: Penguin Books, 1972).

25. Rush, *Job Design for Motivation.*

26. Jenkins, *Job Power.*

27. Hunnius, Garson, and Case, *Workers' Control.*

28. Paul Bernstein, "Run Your Own Business: Worker-Owned Plywood Firms," *Working Papers* 2, no. 2 (Summer 1974): 24–34.

29. Jenkins, *Job Power*, chap. 8.

30. Helmut Schauer, "Critique of Co-Determination," in Hunnius, Garson, and Case, *Workers' Control*, pp. 210–24.

31. Paul Blumberg, *Industrial Democracy: The Sociology of Participation* (New York: Schocken Books, 1969).

32. Jenkins, *Job Power*, chap. 7; I. Adizes, *Industrial Democracy: Yugoslav Style* (New York: Free Press, 1971).

33. Jaroslav Vanek, *A General Theory of Labor-Managed Market Economies* (Ithaca, N.Y.: Cornell University Press, 1970); Jaroslav Vanek, *The Participatory Economy* (Ithaca, N.Y.: Cornell University Press, 1971); Hunnius, Garson, and Case, *Workers' Control.*

34. Jenkins, *Job Power*, chap. 6; Keitha Sapsin Fine, "Worker Participation in Israel," in Hunnius, Garson, and Case, *Workers' Control*, pp. 226–64.

35. Neal Gross, Joseph B. Giacquinta, and Marilyn Bernstein, *Implementing Organizational Innovations* (New York: Basic Books, 1971); W. W. Charters, Jr., *Measuring the Implementation of Differentiated Staffing* (Eugene, Ore.: Center for the Advanced Study of Educational Administration, 1973).

36. Seymour B. Sarason, *The Culture of the School and the Problem of Change* (Boston: Allyn & Bacon, 1971).

37. Dwight Allen and Robert Bush, *A New Design for High School Education* (New York: McGraw-Hill, 1964).

38. Charters, *Measuring the Implementation of Differentiated Staffing*; Ronald J. Pelligrin, "Administrative Assumptions Underlying Major Innovation: A Case Study in the Introduction of Differentiated Staffiing," in *The Process of Planned Change in the School's Instructional Organization*, ed. W. W. Charters, Jr., et al. (Eugene, Ore.: Study of Educational Administration, 1973), pp. 13–34; C. Thompson Wacaster, "The Life and Death of Differentiated Staffing at Columbia High School," in ibid., pp. 35–51.

39. J. Goodlad and K. Rehage, "Unscrambling the Vocabulary of School Organization," in *Change and Innovation in Elementary Organization*, ed. M. Hillson and R. Karlson (New York: Holt, Rinehart & Winston, 1965), p. 10.

40. David W. Beggs, ed., *Team Teaching, Bold New Venture* (Bloomington: Indiana University Press, 1964), p. 16.

41. Joseph Featherstone, *Schools Where Children Learn* (New

York: Liveright, 1971); Charles Silberman, *Crisis in the Classroom* (New York: Random House, 1970), chaps. 6 and 7; Elliot W. Eisner, *English Primary Schools: Some Observations and Assessments* (Stanford, Calif.: Stanford University Press, 1973).

42. Gaynor Petrequin, *Individualizing Learning Through Modular-Flexible Programming* (New York: McGraw-Hill, 1968).

43. Benjamin S. Bloom, "Learning for Mastery," *Evaluation Comment* 1, no. 2 (1968); James H. Block, ed., *Mastery Learning: Theory and Practice* (New York: Holt, Rinehart, & Winston, 1971).

44. Henry M. Levin, "The Economic Implications of Mastery Learning," in *Schools, Society, and Mastery Learning*, ed. James H. Block (New York: Holt, Rinehart, & Winston, 1974), pp. 75–88.

45. Robert Arnove, ed., *Educational Television: A Policy Critique and Guide for Developing Countries* (Stanford, Calif.: Stanford University Press, 1973).

46. Wilbur Schramm et al., *The New Media: Memo to Educational Planners* (Paris: UNESCO, International Institute for Educational Planning, 1967).

47. Aimee Dorr Leifer et al., "Children's Television More Than Mere Enterainment," *Harvard Educational Review* 44, no. 2 (May 1974): 213–45.

48. Asa E. Knowles and associates, *Handbook of Cooperative Education* (San Francisco: Jossey-Bass, 1972).

49. James S. Coleman et al., *Youth: Transition to Adulthood* (Chicago: University of Chicago Press, 1974).

50. Gary Orfield, "Implications for School Desegregation for Changes in the Educational Process" (Paper presented at the Conference on the Courts, Social Service, and School Desegegration, Hilton Head Island, S.C., 18–21 August 1974).

51. Hans N. Weiler, *The Politics of Educational Innovation: Recent Developments in West German School Reform* (Stanford, Calif.: Stanford University Press, 1973), pp. 52–56.

52. Weiler, *Politics of Educational Innovation*, p. 53.

53. Ralph J. Melaragno and Gerald Newmark, "The Tutorial Community Concept," in *New Models for American Education*, ed. James W. Guthrie and Edward Wynne (Englewood Cliffs, N.J.: Prentice-Hall, 1971), pp. 98–113.

54. Henry M. Levin, ed., *Community Control of Schools* (Washington, D.C.: Brookings Institution, 1970).

55. Milton Friedman, *Capitalism and Freedom* (Chicago: University of Chicago Press, 1962).

56. Henry M. Levin, "Educational Vouchers and Educational Equity," in *Schooling in a Corporate Society*, ed. Martin Carnoy (2nd ed.; New York: David McKay, 1975).

57. Center for the Study of Public Policy, *Education Vouchers, A Report on Financing Elementary Education by Grants to Parents* (Cambridge, Mass.: The Center, December 1970).

58. Daniel Weiler et al., *A Public School Voucher Demonstration: The First Year at Alum Rock* (Santa Monica, Calif.: Rand Corporation, June 1974).

59. Ivan Illich, *Deschooling Society* (New York: Harper & Row, 1971).

60. Richard R. Fagen, *The Transformation of Political Culture in Cuba* (Stanford, Calif.: Stanford University Press, 1969); Marvin Leiner, "Major Developments in Cuban Education," Warner Publications Module 264 (1973), pp. 1–21; Stewart E. Fraser and Kuang Liang Hsu, *Chinese Education and Society* (White Plains, N.Y.: International Arts and Science Press, 1972); John N. Hawkins, *Mao Tse-tung and Education* (Hamden, Conn.: Shoe String Press, 1974).

61. David W. Johnson and Roger T. Johnson, "Instructional Goal Structure: Cooperative, Competitive, or Individualistic," *Review of Educational Research* 44, no. 2 (Spring 1974): 213–40.

62. Frederick Herzberg, *Work and the Nature of Man* (London: Staples Press, 1968).

5

Martin Carnoy

Educational Reform and Social Control in the United States, 1830-1970

Introduction

The operation of the principles of correspondence and contradiction (particularly correspondence) is nowhere clearer than in periods of societal transition. In *Education as Cultural Imperialism* (1974), we showed how British and French attempts to incorporate their colonies into the needs of an expanding metropole capitalism were accompanied by the development of formal school systems in the colonies which corresponded to the role those colonies were to play in the British and French economies. In that case, the transition represented a change from precapitalist economies to increasingly penetrated capitalist dependencies operating at the fringe of metropole industrial structures. Similarly, we try to show in this essay that within industrializing metropoles like the United States important changes were taking place *during* capitalist expansion, and the school system was altered to meet changing needs for labor skills, for the incorporation of labor into the industrial system, and for the exploitation of labor in that system.

We suggest that the U.S. economy went through two major alterations during the nineteenth century, each of which required corresponding changes in the education of youth to better fit into the new organization of work. The first began to take place in the 1820s and 1830s in the northeastern part of the country—the early textile mills and shoe factories were the first examples in the United States of what was to be the *factory system* of industrial production. The growth of the factory system was accompanied by a major school reform. By the end of the century, the factory system had spread to the production of many other goods, and production of some of these began to be concentrated in a few *large corporations*. Monopoly corporations, we contend, developed new ways of organizing labor in the factories, a division of labor that soon influenced the organization of schooling. They were also able to develop new ways of exploiting labor, primarily through a system of "scientific management."

In the early nineteenth century, the United States was an agrarian society where manufactured goods were produced by artisan masters and journeymen. Even though the capitalist intermediary (usually a merchant or a master artisan) had already intervened in the production/marketing process by becoming a wholesaler, production was still carried out in small shops and by men who controlled their time and their tools. The factory system changed all this: the amount of time people worked in the factories was greatly extended; women and children were brought into the manufacturing process at much lower wages than men. Thus, factory production reduced the cost of labor through greater hours worked per week and lower average wages paid per week with hourly wages dropping drastically. But successful factory production required the socialization of labor (used to keeping their own hours on the farm and in the shop) into a regimented work schedule. Absenteeism in the early factories was rampant, and labor turnover was also high. Industrialists in Massachusetts saw the need for a social institution, controlled by the state, which would develop proper "industrial" attitudes in young people. The "common school" became that institution.

By the end of the century, the development of large corporations that controlled a significant percentage of particular product markets changed the nature of capitalist production and the internal and external relations of the firm. Once the competitive phase of capitalist expansion in the United States waned and the transition to monopoly capitalism began, a series of important changes took place in the organization of work, and these changes took place in each sector as it became monopolized. Corporate managers were conditioned by the nature of the monopoly firm's position in the market to take a different view from that of the competitive entrepreneur of how best to maximize the firm's profit and devise work structures that fit this view. Unlike the early factory owners, monopoly corporations had to contend with large labor organizations, militant workers, and a growing class consciousness and anticapitalist movement in the working class.

Throughout the competitive capitalist period, the introduction to machinery *reduced* the average skills necessary to produce a particular product. New technology was often developed specifically to eliminate the control of skilled workers over the work process and to lower labor costs by reducing or eliminating the skilled (high wage) component in production. The factory system increased production by lengthening the working day; but by the 1890s, workers had gained enough political power to limit the length of the legal working day in factories. All firms therefore had to be concerned with the production per hour of work. But it was the large corporations, because of their long-term production horizons and greater economic power, that had the freedom to plan longer term management strategies which would effectively control labor and raise productivity. The large firms were able to institute a new division of labor, not based necessarily on difficulty of task, but on wage and promotion incentives which raised productivity in the short run and, in the longer run, pitted workers against one another in the quest for more wages and higher positions on the job ladders. The growth of the corporation also created the beginnings of a supervisory bureaucracy which had to control markets, finances, and labor. This white-collar labor force had different entry points into the firm with different educational requirements: managerial workers had to be inculcated with responsibility to the corporation, not to the working class—they had to identify with capital, not with wage labor.

The drive to increase productivity also led to the adoption by larger corporations of scientific management, or "Taylorism," a means of using particularly productive workers as "rate-busters," —as examples to other workers of how much work could be done per hour. Scientific management attempted to break down work into a series of distinct tasks, which could then be speeded up or, in the case of highly skilled workers, assigned to a less-skilled (lower paid) worker who would do only the single component of the work rather than the whole job.

The development of new hierarchies and scientific management in the organization of production was soon reflected in the school system. The second major reform in American education took place after the turn of the century and was characterized by testing, tracking, counseling, and the introduction of new school management techniques loosely based on Taylor's "scientific" principles. The homogenous labor force requirements of competitive capitalism gave way to multiple entry points and job ladders of large corporations. This required a varied school system and a sophisticated selection process to determine who was going to fit where in the production process. It also meant the beginning of a focus on school "efficiency" (through testing) in assuring that students were in the "correct" place in the system and were learning a curriculum appropriate to producers' requirements.

This chapter describes in detail the nature of these two major educational reforms and how they responded, not to the needs of those who went to school, but the industrialists who promulgated them.

What is now the United States was one of several colonies (among others, Argentina, Canada, and Australia) that were virtual extensions of European society, with (eventually) a European immigrant majority and industrial growth parallel to that of many European countries. The original U.S. colonies were in many ways separate societies, and they developed separately until the early nineteenth century. The northern colonies were populated by small landholders who raised food products largely for consumption in the colony. Artisans also produced for local consumption, and traders brought goods such as molasses from the West Indies to be processed into rum and exported to Europe and Africa. The southern colonies, on the other hand, after an initial period in the seventeenth century of small holdings, rapidly became dominated by large plantations, tobacco and cotton exports, and the import of manufactured consumption goods and African slaves. Thus, the northern colonies began early to take on the economic and social structures of their parent metropoles, while the South developed a plantation economy similar to that of the West Indies and Brazil.

The evolution of education closely followed these economic and social structures. Both in the North and in the South, educational systems were decentralized: each colony, and usually each community, was in charge of its own children's schooling. As in England, schools were usually established privately, although some colonies passed laws in the seventeenth century governing primary school provision by communities; after independence different states treated schooling differently. Nevertheless, certain educational trends are apparent. Until the end of the Civil War (1865), southern schooling was limited to the formation of an elite white society. Schooling was private and provided the small number of professionals needed for a plantation economy. Since the South remained agricultural and precapitalist, relying on England and the North for industrial goods, an institution such as public schooling was not necessary to maintain societal order. There was little social change. Much of the labor force were slaves, kept away from schools and even from churches because owners believed that any gathering of blacks bred sedition. Poor whites lived on small holdings in rural areas, as they had before independence. Only with the northern victory in 1865 was public education imposed on the South.

But in the northern states, primary education—although it consisted of little more than learning how to read and write and religious instruction—became an important issue as early as the beginning of the nineteenth century. Besides the New England community schools and the private primary schools for wealthier children preparing for university education, church groups organized public school societies for educating the poor. These public school societies paralleled similar groups in England, all of which formed the model for British (and American) missionary efforts in Africa and Asia.

> With minimal administrative expense, scrupulous financial integrity, and commendable efficiency, the [New York Public School] [s]ociety maintained for decades an extensive network of schools that taught thousands of children a year.
>
> But make no mistake about it: This was a class system of education. It provided a vehicle for the efforts of one class to civilize another and thereby insure that society would remain tolerable, orderly, and safe.[1]

The public school societies made poverty a condition of free schooling, a stipulation that clashed with the interests of those who wanted to extend primary schooling to all. As long as public schooling was associated with being poor, the children of those who were neither wealthy nor paupers would not attend. Wage earners were a rapidly growing group in the North, and social change wrought by industrialization and the immigration of large numbers of Irish into northern cities threatened social order in the young Republic. Visionaries such as Horace Mann saw schools as the means to produce economic change without disruption and chaos. With Adam Smith, he believed that state support (and control) of public schooling would help maintain morality and decent behavior, and would contribute to economic growth. But to achieve this, it was necessary to get everyone in school. The Public School Society, or "paternalistic voluntarism," as Katz calls the Society's organization of schooling, was not suitable for the task. It stood in the way of universal public schooling because it set the condition of poverty for access to it. Decentralized control in the districts was also not suitable because it often left the conduct and curriculum of schools in the hands of the very working class that had to be transformed into moral and decent members of an industrializing economy.

In the place of the Public School Society and the decentralized district control of schools, reformers like Mann—beginning with the Massachusetts Board of Education in the 1840s and '50s—organized public education centrally under their control and their philosophy. This was the first major reform in U.S. education and it set the pattern for school expansion for the next two generations. By that time, another wave of immigrants was entering the United States and large enterprises were in the process of consolidating their position in the economy. To meet these new conditions, a second important period of educational reform took place between 1900 and 1920. But that reform was an *extension* of earlier structures built in Massachusetts, and simply reinforced trends established earlier.

Thus, the movement for public education in the United States began in the industrializing northern states under pressure from reformers who represented the views of a growing bourgeoisie.[2] Local industrialists saw schooling as a means to offset the disruptive social conditions of factory life; some institution was necessary to provide the moral guidance and control which the family and church had supplied in precapitalist society.[3] Schooling was imposed on a working class who viewed schooling (correctly) as largely serving the children of higher-income groups.[4] The South did not participate in this movement until northern capital took control of its institutions.[5] Public education as it developed in the United States was the reformers' answer to the growth of industry and the crisis it caused in the traditional social structure. Schooling was seen by reformers and industrialists alike as promoting their common vision of an ordered, purposeful, and progressive society. In conjunction with this view, it also helped preserve a class structure in the face of economic and social change.

Since Massachusetts was the first state with state-run public education, and since that case served as the model for others and is so well documented, we use it as a detailed example of mid-eighteenth-century educational reform. The chapter then discusses the reform period around World War I and the present problems in American education.

The Early Reform Era: Public Schooling
in Massachusetts

The most detailed analysis of early school reform in America is found in Michael Katz's work.[6] Katz shows how the first generation of professional educators, who emerged in the northern, industrializing states, faced a society in the process of rapid social change. The agrarian economy that had characterized the colonial and immediate postcolonial period was being transformed into an urban one. Even more important, children of small farmers came into the towns to become wage earners. They were joined by a wave of Irish immigrants. Decision making in production passed from the one-family farmers and artisans to capitalists with many workers in their factories. The extended-family system which pervaded rural life began to break down, and with it, control on social behavior.

One answer to the feelings of powerlessness and dislocation caused by capitalist industrialization was to adapt rural institutions to urban conditions. "Democratic localism," as Katz calls it, was a movement which tried to bring the district or community school into the cities. The people of the district would have the right to provide any kind of education they wished and they could not be overridden by the state. The democratic localists wanted to keep American government decentralized; they emphasized the virtues of variety and adaptability. They believed in public education for all, but also believed that each individual community (even within a city) should control its schools:

> The case of the democratic localist, then, rested ultimately on a combination of faith in the people and a point of view about the sources of social change. . . . The imposition of social change would never work; changes in society, in habits and attitudes, came only from within the people themselves as they slowly, haltingly, but surely exercised their innate common sense and intelligence. By being left

to their own devices, by perhaps being encouraged, cajoled, and softly educated, but not by being forced, the people would become roused to the importance of universal education and the regular school attendance of their children.[7]

The professional educators rejected this way of organizing the schools and opted for a centralized model in which a state-level bureaucracy, run by educator-reformers, would organize education, setting norms and enforcing them. The reformers argued that democratic localism was in fact undemocratic since 51 percent of the local parents could dictate the religious, moral, and political ideas taught to the children of the remainder. Katz adds that democratic localism also failed on other grounds: it was a rural transplant and could not function properly in the heterogeneous urban setting.

But the professionals' opposition to democratic localism was much more profound than their critique of its democracy. Their view of future American society was centralized, under the control of those who would transform it from agriculture to industry, avoiding the problems of crime and poverty prevalent in English cities. Because they perceived schools as the "key agencies for uplifting the quality of city life by stemming diffusion of the poverty, crime, and immorality that were thought to accompany urban and industrial development,"[8] professionals argued for raising the quality of education by centralizing power over the educational system. Through that central bureaucracy, they could systematize and standardize structure, curricula, and teacher certification.

In order to achieve their goal, it was necessary to break the hold of the districts and masters (schoolteachers) over the schools. Once the Massachusetts Board of Education was created, Mann and his fellow members began their attack on district control by establishing and promoting public high schools, whose administration cut across district lines.

All their plans had certain characteristics in common, most important among them centralization. This had two principal components: first, the modification and eventual elimination of the bastion of democratic localism, the district system, whereby each section of a town or city managed its own schools with a great deal of autonomy. . . . The ultimate remedy was the replacement of the district by one central board of education. In most cases, however, that was politically impossible, and reformers consequently turned to an interim measure, the establishment of high schools. In Massachusetts, for example, both the law and practical considerations required the high school to be a town school. . . . It was thus an administrative device for undercutting the power of the district.[9]

The reformers argued that the high school promoted mobility, contributed to economic growth and communal wealth, and saved the towns from "disintegrating into an immoral and degenerate chaos."[10] They were backed, not surprisingly, by the bourgeoisie, which had the same vision of society and perceived the same solution to the ills which the realization of that vision was creating.[11] Katz shows that in the vote on the abolition of Beverly High School in Massachusetts in 1860, the people of most wealth and prestige in the community, joined by those of middle-level position, supported the high school. They shared the view that cities and factories were good and should be promoted. The high school, they believed, would foster industrial growth by increasing communal wealth and creating a skilled labor force through replacing the apprenticeship system. At the same time, the high school would fight the accompanying social and family disintegration caused by industrial growth by civilizing the community and providing guidance to children usually lacking in the working-class family situation. With the reformers, these wealthier members of the community looked to the state to "sponsor education that would help build modern industrial cities permeated by the values and features of an idealized rural life."[12]

Thus, the reforms were not the result of majority consensus, even though the educators' most important argument against democratic localism was that it fostered the tyranny of some of the parents over the education of all the children. The very reformers, such as Horace Mann, who proposed to protect the interests of all the people, *imposed* a system of education which served minority interests. The working class in Beverly opposed the high school and voted it down. Artisans saw in the new industrialization the destruction of their position in the community. The high school represented to them that new order. The artisans were the propertied, moderately well-off groups whose life was being altered by technological development. They were joined by citizens without children who protested the raising of taxes to finance the schools. Finally, many working-class people felt that the high school would not benefit their children.

> The underlying cause of both the establishment and abolition of Beverly High School was the shifting economic base and the consequent social division in both the town and the state. It was to keep pace with these changes that promoters urged an extension of the educational system; it was to assure opportunity for the individual within an altered economy that the high school was argued; it was to reunite a splintering community that a high school was necessary.[13]

Despite the Beverly case, the reformers prevailed. By 1861, Massachusetts had 103 high schools, one for every three towns and cities. Public high school became the symbol and reality of the first major school reform in America, beginning in the 1820s and continuing into the 1880s and '90s. It represented the victory of the professional educators and the industrialists over the local power structures which had their base in rural areas and in the wards of the larger towns. Through the high school, the reformers effectively imposed their view of what Massachusetts and the rest of the industrializing North would be like in the coming generations. Other states developed high schools as they industrialized and urbanized, for the high schools accompanied the need to combat the destruction of preindustrial, agrarian social structures by large-scale capitalist enterprise. The impact of the reform was predictable: although the reformers had promised that the high school would promote social mobility and civilized communities, it did neither. Like other institutions associated with industrialization, it exacerbated divisions in the community by serving the well-to-do. Nor was it able to overcome the problems of poverty and crime which plagued industrial towns.[14]

One of the most important objectives of the centralized state school system was to form a new working class for industrial growth. Schools had to inculcate behavior patterns relevant to working in factories instead of on self-owned farms or as artisans. Crucial to factory work patterns was a sense of time and authority. Reformers realized that if children could be taught to attend school regularly and be taught the importance of punctuality, they would come on time to work. If they could be taught to respond to the reward system in the classroom and to submit to the authority of the teacher, they would be obedient workers. Industrialists also recognized that the school served as a means of preparing a disciplined work force:

> ". . . by diligence and a willing acquiescence in necessary regulations, to merit the good opinion of their employers and the community"; they "secure . . . by the same means, the respect and confidence of their fellows," and "oftentimes exert a conservative influence in periods of excitement of great value pecuniarily and morally."[15]

The main task of the educators, then, was to get the children into the schools. With the opposition of working-class parents to schools that did not serve their needs, truancy was rampant. If schools were to incorporate all children into the new society, school had to make schooling more appealing to children. This was a main purpose of the pedagogical reforms which accompanied the structural reform. The pedagogical reform was concentrated at the primary level, and it consisted of changing teaching methodology to excite the children's interest in learning. The reformers wanted to develop in students the "necessary intrinsic self-controls through leading them to internalize a love for knowledge."[16]

Simply enough, the reform was designed to make school a more pleasant place, so that children would be induced to like school. At the same time, however, the reform reflected changed views of the relation of the adult to the authority structure. "Soft-line" educators, as Katz calls them, could have pushed for less authoritarian structure in the schools, with more peer group reinforcement. But they wanted to replace the old style of teaching, which stressed *direct* obedience to external authority, with teaching which stressed obedience to *abstract* authority through internal controls. This change reflected the reality of the times. With the gradual destruction of the old authority structures—the family and the tight-knit community—which controlled members directly, the old forms of external authority were disappearing. Factory managers could not afford to hire new people every week and teach them their jobs; nor could they constantly watch the workers to make sure they were performing correct tasks. Urban communities were not cohesive enough to control directly the actions of individuals living in them. Also, large numbers of immigrants, particularly the Irish, represented an "untamed" group who had to be incorporated into new social values and norms without the benefit of a well-organized community to teach them. A new authority was needed to fulfill all these functions, but it had to be indirect. Thus, the soft-line educators wanted to reform the schools so that children would be taught to *internalize* external authority and become individuals who would follow rules because of society's reward for doing so rather than the fear of being punished. Although the soft-line educators claimed that they were concerned with the spiritual values of life, the stress on responding to external reward was precisely translated into the response to material gain, the quality most needed to succeed in the competitive capitalist society.

The pedagogical controversy had one other important aspect. It pitted the centrist reformers against local primary school teachers, who argued for strong discipline in the classroom and for teaching methods that were not particularly designed to try to interest the child. The teachers believed in an "absolute" curriculum which taught the child how to discharge the "duties of life."[17] But the curriculum issue represented the fight of the teachers against control by the state Board of Education, a fight for local autonomy against the state bureaucracy. In order for Mann and his fellow reformers to organize the educational system under their jurisdiction, they had to demonstrate their power over the teachers. The Board did this by changing the required curriculum and therefore changing how the teachers taught.

Other changes were pushed in schools in line with changes in the organization of society, particularly the organization of the production of goods. Just as processes in manufacturing were being increasingly subdivided, so the teaching process was subdivided in the high schools. Teachers, ideally, would be responsible for students' education, and the teachers would be trained in the new normal schools. Larger schools formed to eliminate overlap and to gain efficiency. Furthermore, partially because it was believed that women were better teachers for younger children, and mainly because they cost much less to employ than men, the feminization which occurred in U.S. industry between 1840 and 1860 was matched by a feminization of the schools. According to Katz's data, in that period, the percentage of males teaching in Massachusetts schools dropped from 60 to 14 percent.[18] In order to bring the large numbers of immigrant children into the schools—since their parents contributed little to taxes—it was necessary to cut down on the cost of schooling; this was done by hiring women. Thus, the same scarcity of labor that brought women into manufacturing and put pressure on manufacturers to increase efficiency, brought them into schools and put pressure on the schools to avoid duplication of effort and promote division of labor.

Soon after their establishment, it became clear that public high schools benefited the middle class. Boys gained entrance either into college or the business world from the high school while it prepared girls primarily for teaching. In theory, the high schools competed with the private academies, which had been established in the eighteenth century to prepare boys for university. But in practice, the academies drew their boys from a wealthier class than attended the public schools. Public education also offered nonacademic courses (some academies did too). Such nonacademic courses were the beginning of the tracking system which became prevalent after the turn of the century. Far from being a "thoroughly democratic institution since it fostered equality of opportunity,"[19] the high school instituted a hierarchy of access to education which corresponded to the social hierarchy associated with capitalist industrialization. There were important socioreligious overtones to this hierarchy. The reformers had argued against democratic localism on the grounds that Catholics could impose their will on non-Catholics in the wards. The reformers' view was that the schools should be religiously and politically neutral. In practice, the schools were not neutral at all. "Protestant ministers, as David Tyack has shown, played active and important roles in common school promotion and management, and it is in fact impossible to disentangle Protestantism from the early history of the common school."[20] For the most part, the wealthy Protestants in the preindustrial order retained their positions in the new order. Catholics, at least in Massachusetts, were the immigrants, and they filled the new working classes. Schooling contributed to establishing the new social structure.

Once the high school was established, the children of wealthy parents continued to attend academies to prepare themselves in classic education, with the possibility of going on to university. Middle-class children gained entrance to public high schools (and some who could afford it also went to academies) and were tracked either into a college preparatory course or a nonacademic (business) course. Working-class children generally did not get into high school or their parents were not sufficiently convinced of the value of education to want them to go. The significant change introduced by the high school was that a free higher level of schooling now existed which, unlike the academies, did not require fees. The only criterion for entrance was *achievement*. Mann and his contemporaries probably believed that simply making a higher level of school *available* would guarantee equal access to all classes of society, as soon as all parents could be convinced of the value of education. Of course, this is not what happened. The stress on achievement is a fundamental criterion for reward in bourgeois democratic theory, and was an important part of the shift in the basis of social valuation from ascriptive (traits handed down from father to son) to universalistic ("objectively" measured achievement) norms. But when achievement in school became a measure of potential achievement in the economy, the class structure was preserved rather than democratized.

> Schoolmen who thought they were promoting a neutral and classless—indeed, a *common*—school education remained unwilling to perceive the extent of cultural bias inherent in their own writing and activity. However, the bias was central and not incidental to the standardization and administrative rationalization of public education. For in the last analysis, the rejection of democratic localism rested only partly on its inefficiency and violation of parental prerogative. It stemmed equally from a gut fear of the cultural divisiveness inherent in the increasing religious and ethnic diversity of American life.[21]

It is this class structure of the schools, the incorporation of white immigrant groups into the lower rungs of the education and economic ladder, and the growing centralization and bureaucratization of urban schools that marks American educational history in the rest of the century. In the 1880s and '90s, for example, the second generation of educational reformers were becoming superintendents of large-city school systems, after they, together with the leading industrialists and professionals of the cities, moved successfully to take control of urban schools away from political wards dominated by politicians and working-class ethnics and to transfer it to city-wide elected school boards controlled by business interests.[22]

Well before 1900, then, the schools were organized to promote capitalist industrial development—to produce a working class with desired behavior patterns, particularly the internalization of an authoritarian work structure and loyalty to a society which was run by the bourgeoisie. Reformers, industrialists, and the wealthier segments of northern society combined to impose centralized control on school systems; democratic localism, which tried to retain this control at the local level even in the cities, failed in this political and philosophical power struggle. Once their control over school systems was achieved, the reformers turned to the second phase of reform: helping the schools to serve these social and economic functions more *efficiently*.

The Consolidation of Capitalism and
Twentieth-century Educational Reform

Important changes occurred in the United States after the Civil War. First, northern industry grew phenomenally as a result of the war, and by the turn of the century, cities began to dominate American life. There was also a great immigration to these cities from Eastern and Southern Europe. As the population grew and industry expanded, schools had an increasingly more important role in preparing people for incorporation into the industrial structure. As industry became more complex, the schools also had to change to meet its needs. Furthermore, enrollment in the schools increased and the percentage of primary school graduates going on to high school grew markedly. Compulsory schooling became more accepted by the working class, especially the new immigrants, and compulsory schooling age rose. The socio-economic composition of the high schools therefore changed, creating serious conflict in the purpose and structure of public education.

Educators (and other "leading" citizens) met this crisis by gaining increased political power over urban schools, and then differentiating the high school curriculum to make it vocationally oriented. As we shall show, they accentuated the class bias of public education through striving for greater efficiency in preparing children for occupational roles in the expanding economy. Reform at the end of the nineteenth and beginning of the twentieth century has been named Progressivism, paralleling the so-called Progressive movement in politics. Yet, like its political counterpart, it was basically conservative, supporting industrial monopolies' (corporate capitalism's) influence on American life by using public institutions to help consolidate their power.[23]

The reform movement at the turn of the century built on the philosophy and structures established by Massachusetts fifty years before. As with earlier reform, it had strong class overtones, and was based on the attempt "to socialize the urban poor to behavior that will decrease crime, diminish expenditures on public welfare, promote safety on the streets and contribute to industrial productivity."[24] Later in the century, schools took on the added function of helping to find nonsocialist approaches to educational reform. With the new waves of migration, the growth of manufacturing, and socialist movements in Europe, schools had to ensure that the free-enterprise system worked: workers had to be made to identify with the growth and health of that system, even though it was inequitable, and not very healthy. People had to be sold on the idea that getting education would solve the problems of poverty and unemployment.

> The prescription, for one thing, unleashes a flurry of seemingly purposeful activity and, for another, requires no tampering with basic social structural or economic characteristics, only with the attitudes of poor people, and that has caused hardly a quiver.[25]

Despite the reforms in Massachusetts and the spread of high schools to many other industrializing states, democratic localism still flourished after the Civil War. The big-city political machines were based on control of political wards; municipal education systems were run by city school boards elected from the wards, and the wards got patronage from the city bosses in the form of educational jobs, contracts and supplies. Thus, through political muscle people in wards continued to control the kind of education their children got. This system was corrupt and led to very uneven schooling, but it had the advantage of decentralized community control. The reformers attacked the boss and patronage systems in the 1880s and 1890s, and as part of that attack, they proposed the centralization of power in a small school board with members elected at large. A small board representative of the whole city, they felt, would be freer of political influence; it would standardize education throughout the city and would provide higher quality schooling more efficiently.

By 1900, the reformers were successful in almost every large city. The educators who led this movement often became big-city school superintendents. The new boards were controlled by old-stock first citizens, often professionals and big businessmen. They did standardize education, but as we shall see, standardized education was geared to differentiate children by the adult occupational roles they were measured to be fit for. The professionals and businessmen had an antiimmigrant and antiworking-class attitude which underlay most of their municipal reform.

> Their aim remained similar to earlier reformers: inculcating the poor with acceptable political attitudes. This has had important political implications. It has meant that the government of school systems has continued to rest on disdain for a large portion of students and their families. This has only widened the gulf between working class communities and schools that mid-century reformers had helped to create.[26]

One of the most important results of the alliance between the educational reformers and businessmen—an alliance that stemmed from the common vision that the two groups held of societal progress and their common class values (going back to the 1830s and '40s)—was an emphasis on school efficiency and the introduction of business-oriented curricula in high schools.[27] Efficiency was interpreted by schools as the effectiveness with which they prepared children for future work. Since schooling was conceived as preparation for work, schoolmen turned to factory efficiency studies and models to organize the schools.[28] "School superintendents saw themselves as plant managers, and proposed to treat education as a production process in which children were the raw materials."[29]

But as Michelson points out,[30] the application of "scientific management to factories and schools had less effect on workers and students than the introduction of industrialization with its "fragmentation of jobs and life styles" had had fifty years earlier. Nevertheless, scientific management in industry did differentiate production further, and schools followed suit by differentiating courses. Differentiated courses meant that educators were giving up the concept of equality of opportunity. In that concept, rich and poor would attend high school together exposed to a common curriculum and would participate equally in the upward mobility of the community. Of course, as we have seen, the poor generally did not go to high school until the end of the century, just when course differentiation began in earnest. The new concept of equal opportunity, developed to resolve the conflict between equality and efficiency, was the "opportunity for all to receive such education as will fit them *equally well* for their particular life work."[31] Thus, as the differentiation of schooling spread, the notion of equal school achievement for equal ability emerged. "Differentiation was justified as a way of organizing education to conform with social and economic realities, and this in turn was presented as a way of providing meaningful equality of educational opportunity."[32]

This aspect of Progressivism was appealing because the single academic track in high school led to retardation and dropouts. Working-class and immigrant children could not meet the difficult regimen of the middle-class-oriented program, for which standards had been set at a time when only a small percentage of children went to high school. Rather than change the nature of academic (or college preparatory) training—a move which would have been inconsistent with the class bias in the schools and in the work place—the reformers stratified the curriculum so that working-class children would not drop out but neither would they receive academic instruction. Once this system of "equal opportunity" was implemented, its success could be measured by the number of pupils who were kept in school, and how well the schools trained people for available jobs.[33] The incorporation of vocational training in the high schools alongside academic and business courses during and after the First World War was the triumph of the comprehensive high school.[34]

The National Education Association's 1910 *Report of the Committee on the Place of Industries in Public Education* summarized the rationale for educational differentiation:

1. Industry, as a controlling factor in social progress, has for education a fundamental and permanent significance.
2. Educational standards, applicable in an age of handicraft, presumably need radical change in the present day of complex and highly specialized industrial development.
3. The social aims of education and the psychological

needs of childhood alike require that industrial (manual-constructive) activities form an important part of school occupations. . . .

4. The differences among children as to aptitudes, interests, economic resources, and prospective careers furnish the basis for a rational as opposed to a merely formal distinction between elementary, secondary, and higher education.[35]

Ultimately, in the 1920s, testing led to ability tracking in junior high and even primary schools. Because truancy and dropouts continued to be a problem even with vocational training tracks in high school, a new way had to be found at lower levels of school to keep children in school and more fully "individualize" their instruction. Thus, children were classified into ability groupings where members were fairly homogeneous in ability. L. M. Terman, the author of the Stanford-Binet IQ test, and one of the leaders of the testing movement, was also one of the founders of tracking. Terman and others believed that tracking ensured "educational democracy." By fitting the curriculum to the child, they thought that every child could be brought closer to the maximum achievement consistent with individual ability.[36] Proponents of tracking argued:

> It is not social segregation. It is not a caste stratification. It is not an attempt to point out those who are worthwhile and those who are not. It is not a move to separate the leaders from the followers.[37]

But fifty years later, Judge Skelly Wright, in reviewing tracking in the Washington, D.C., school system,[38] concluded that "while in theory the tests which presumably measured ability and the track which were supposed to serve individual needs actually, in practice, measured past socio-economic advantage as much as presumed ability while the curricular track served to lock the child into the socio-economic class from which he came. Few children ever crossed tracks."[39] Once the child was tracked, the court found, he worked at the level expected from the requirements of the track. In fact, there is evidence that pupils' performance actually declines when they are in a low track. Since tracking was progressively moved downward from junior high to primary school, many pupils were (and are) locked into a prescribed pattern before they had (or have) a chance to develop their full mental abilities.

To function properly, differentiation among students needed an effiecient mechanism to allocate them among the various course levels. There were two stages to this mechanism. The first stemmed from a dogmatic belief that adult success depends on school achievement. If the schools were in the business of transforming children into successful adults, they should—to be efficient—differentiate them on the basis of their achievement in school. Thus, the development and popularization of testing instruments that measured the educator's definition of school achievement contributed to the scientific management of the schools. Armed with a battery of tests, the educator could ensure that each student fit into his or her proper place in the school and, by inference, into the proper adult occupation. "Thorndike and his students developed scales for measuring achievement in arithmetic (1908), handwriting (1910), spelling (1913), drawing (1913), reading (1914), and language ability 1916)."[40]

The Alpha Test developed by the army during World War I to identify officer potential and those unfit for service showed a clear correlation between measured intelligence and occupational attainment.[41] At the same time, testing in school showed that people who had higher IQ completed more years in school. All these results reinforced educators' notions on the relationships between achievement and success, and helped rationalize the use of testing to achieve greater school efficiency, as defined by the successful incorporation of children into the differentiated school structure. By 1932, when President Hoover called a White House Conference on vocational education, about three-quarters of the 150 large cities surveyed were using intelligence tests to classify students.[42]

Vocational guidance represented the second aspect of the classification mechanism. Vocational guidance and the junior high school were, like the differentiated high school, a response to the increased complexity of American industry by the turn of the century. Skills were more diverse and skilled workers more mobile. Firms were less willing to invest in the more general skills that they needed, because workers could move to other establishments which could also use their general training. Schools were given the task of providing this general training. To carry out this task efficiently, the schools had to differentiate students according to vocational goals.

> The early vocational guidance leaders attempted to function as human engineers who matched and shaped individual abilities to fit a particular slot in the social organism. This gave them the dual responsibility of analyzing personal talents and character and planning educational programs in terms of future vocation. Junior high schools were designed to make educational planning and guidance possible at an early age. The original purpose of the junior high school was to divide students into separate courses of study in the hope that with proper guidance they would choose vocations early and follow a directed educational program through high school to the occupation.[43]

The guidance counselor was therefore an intermediary between corporate needs and students. In that role he classified students for the labor market. Armed with a variety of tests, the counselor decided which occupations the student was suited for. The student then was channeled into the high school program most relevant to his or her career. It was in junior high school that this testing and channeling began, so that by the time a student completed the ninth grade, it was determined whether he or she would follow an academic, business, or vocational career. High school courses were geared to prepare the student for his counseled occupation.

All this differentiation was class biased. The school "meritocracy" first depended on all children being able to do high school academic work which was oriented to middle-class culture and norms. The college preparatory curriculum (which included Latin and Greek) required behavior patterns alien to working-class children. Many working-class families, as Katz shows, chose not to send their children to high school at all. Once business courses were introduced, it was natural that those who were not "suited" to the academic track were prepared for lower occupational strata. Finally, with the advent of vocational courses, testing, and guidance, the efficiency of selecting the greatly expanded number of enrollees for the various courses increased. The schools' methods of measuring merit were therefore seriously biased by inherited status and culture. According to Bowles and Gintis, who have done work on recent data,

> . . . while one's economic status tends strongly to resemble that of one's parents, only a minor portion of this association can be attributed to social class differences in childhood IQ, and a virtually negligible proportion to social class differences in genetic endowments—even accepting the Jensen estimates of heritability. Thus, a perfect equalization of IQ's across social classes would reduce the intergenerational transmission of economic status by a negligible amount.[44]

Thus, there is evidence that the rating systems used by the schools were (and are) only in part related to childhood IQ. They differentiate children more on class-associated information and forms of expression, as well as behavior patterns. In designing the Stanford-Binet intelligence test,

> Terman developed questions which were based on presumed progressive difficulty in performing tasks which he believed were necessary for achievement in ascending the hierarchical occupational structure. He then proceeded to find that according to the results of his tests the intelligence of different occupational classes fit his ascending hierarchy. It was little wonder that IQ [as measured by this test] reflected social class bias. It was, in fact, based on the social class order. Terman believed that, for the most part, people were at that level because of heredity and not social environment.[45]

The Progressives therefore contributed to a system of schools which divided children, mostly on the basis of their class, into occupation-oriented course streams, and to a system that used (and still uses) ability tracks even at the elementary level. The schools prepared children for future work roles defined by class-biased "ability" tests and by the vocational guidance counselor. The tests and guidance served to "objectify" selection processes in a way that made people think that they were being given the fairest deal possible within *their own limitations*. Merit selection shifted the responsibility for an individual's productive capability to the individual himself and away from the structure and organization of the economy. If a person is convinced that he is *not able to do well*, he is less likely to rise up against the social system than if the person believes that the system is unfair and based on class. The Progressives institutionalized meritocracy as a means for social control, to insure that those with the "correct" characteristics got the highest positions in the society and that those who were not as suitable believed in the objectivity and fairness of the decision which put them in their place. America was the land of opportunity, where the best excelled and the inferior found themselves in the lowest status (and paid) occupation. The definition of democracy had changed from rule by the people to rule by the intelligent. The intelligent, as defined by the designers of tests and vocational guidance counselors, were those of higher social classes, who were at the same time more "moral" and had the characteristics necessary for leadership in America.[46]

It is worth discussing one other part of the Progressive education movement because it is so identified with the philosophy of the period. Already in the earlier reform era, the "soft-line" educators had argued for child-centered curriculum. In the first decades of this century, the child-centered wing of American education were advocates of play in schooling. They generally opposed market-oriented, extrinsic criteria of educational merit, although some justified play as the child's natural work and therefore as the most efficient method for producing good workers. It was this latter argument that permitted the formation of kindergartens and, later, nursery schools—primarily for middle- and upper-class children—during a period when the public schools were moving toward an increased occupational orientation. Nevertheless, public school personnel often argued that kindergarten children came to school poorly prepared either to learn or to behave properly.[47]

John Dewey rejected the work-play dichotomy. He believed that work and play were part of a continuum, and they differed only in that work required a longer period of concentration and a greater goal commitment. The lack of goal commitment in play made it an intrinsic activity, carried out for its own ends, thus keeping alive a creative and constructive attitude in the child. But Dewey's view of work and play could be consistent only if the nature of work in the society changed. He realized this and called for a change in the organization of work from an orientation to the needs of the economy—that is, the production of more goods—to the needs of the individual or society. Given the nature of work, Dewey wanted the school to provide a period for the child in which he could live and learn without economic pressure, carrying out activities for their intrinsic value. This would enable the young to learn for learning's sake, internalizing the joy of intellectual experience.[48]

Although Dewey's philosophy of education gave a boost to the child-centered orientation in education, it had little impact on public education until important changes occurred in the kind of work done within corporations in the 1950s and '60s. The movement to bring play into the classroom had its greatest following in middle-class private schools, where this type of education fit in with the trend in middle-class child rearing "away from repression and externally imposed discipline, towards greater freedom," and the idea that "happiness in learning seemed to be linked with higher levels of achievement."[49] While industry needed specialized and well-disciplined workers, and societal "leaders" saw schooling as a means to control social change (especially during a period of rapid immigration and urban poverty), it was not likely that public schools would stress intrinsic experiences as a form of learning.

The failure of Dewey's philosophy to have an effect on the nature of schooling at the time of his Chicago Laboratory School points out the flaw in those histories of societal institutions like schooling which stress the "man in history" view of institutional change. Dewey was obviously an important intellectual force in American education, but it was those educators who rationalized and made more efficient the role of the school as a provider of specialized and socialize labor to industries and as an agent of social control who made the greatest impact on the educational system during their time. Educators who worked to make the capitalist economic and social system—with its class structure and hierarchic organization—function more smoothly were the principal reformers of the early twentieth century. Thus, it was a particular economic and social system which shaped reform, not John Dewey.

This reform was not the result of conspiracy between business leaders and schoolmen, although there is ample evidence that business interests did control the schools through pressures on schoolmen and that schoolmen *were* businessmen.[50] It was the result of the same kind of sharing of societal views as occurred in Horace Mann's time. The key to understanding why schools were organized for the benefit of the few and the repression of the many is *enlightened self-interest*. Both reformers and business leaders were interested in maintaining a social order in which those who shared their view of societal change, not the immigrant and working-class rabble, came to power in the next generation.

The Problems of U.S. Education in the 1970s

The description of these two earlier reform periods should make clear that the structure of U.S. schools today is not an accident or the result of inefficiencies or of conservative administrators and teachers. Rather, schools are the way they are today because of *successful* reforms between 1850 and 1920, reforms which were designed to meet the needs of capitalist industrialization. The objective of schoolmen was to inculcate faith in the capitalist system, especially in its objectivity and rationality, and to prepare people to take their *proper* place in that system. This objective was derived from a particular and hierarchical view of society which in turn was derived from a particular and hierarchical economic philosophy: the rich and powerful are cleverer than the poor and weak, and therefore have the *right* to be rich and powerful. And society is better off for that division and ordering of power.

Alongside this view, however, there has always been an undeniable concern with equality in American society. Horace Mann saw the public high school as equally accessible to all, a place where different social classes would mix freely, exposed to the same curriculum and experiences, and with the same opportunities for success in a growing economy. The later reformers gave up this idea partly because all children were not getting into or finishing high school. They considered it more important to get all children into school and keep them there longer than to have children take the same courses. Of course, the differentiation of schooling also served changing industrial needs, and the necessity for stricter social control during a period of heavy immigration, labor organizing, and left-wing agitation in the labor movement. To satisfy the concern with social unity while preserving the class structure, differentiation was organized within the same school. As Spring points out, the concept of equality as interpreted by the reformers included the ideal of democracy which brought people from different classes together in the same institution —the comprehensive high school—to give them "common ideas, common ideals, and common modes of thought, feeling, and action that made for cooperation, social cohesion, and social solidarity."[51] Since students were separated into different courses, other means of creating a sense of unity and equality among the groups was necessary; thus different social classes of students were mixed through extracurricular activities, such as athletics, social clubs, and school government.

But equality was only a façade and had little to do with the reality of the school or the reality of the economic and social structure. Once out of school, the sharing of common experiences by members of different social groups ceased. Furthermore, with the large internal migration of blacks and Mexican-Americans to Northern and Western urban areas after World War II, racial and ethnic conflicts became too great to overcome with a false sense of unity in schools.

The school system as reformed in the early twentieth century began running into serious problems in the 1960s. Twenty years of rapid postwar economic growth had produced little change in income distribution. Education was still distributed along class and racial lines, a situation that became increasingly unacceptable to blacks, Chicanos, Puerto Ricans, and American Indians, whom the Progressive definition of "equal opportunity" left at the bottom of the vocational ladder. To them, centralized control by Anglo school boards was to blame, and in some communities a struggle began for community control of schools—the democratic localism movement all over again. But in the 1960s, many upper-middle-class whites were not satisfied with schools either: they rejected the corporate structure and the transmission of that structure and its values through the school. Those parents pushed for child-centered schools which stressed interpersonal relations rather than extrinsic rewards.

> In a more general framework, we see two significant challenges to the existing social order. First there are demands that the schools satisfy their rhetorical goals of providing equal educational opportunities (read as equal educational outcomes) for all groups in the society, rich and poor, black and white, Chicano and Anglo. This objective has implications for the financing, heterogeneity of enrollments, and educational offerings of the schools. Second, the schools are being pressured to be client-oriented rather than professionally oriented, child-centered rather than adult-centered. This goal has implications for the number and nature of alternatives that must be available to satisfy the needs of students with substantially different talents, personalities, abilities, and interests.[52]

Most blacks, Chicanos, and Puerto Ricans, as well as some Indians are demanding that the schools make them more *employable* in the present economic structure; that the schools increase their status within the colonial structure. Much of the community control movement fits into the challenge of equal school outcomes: minority groups believe correctly that white Anglo control has created schools in which their children *cannot* do as well as those of the controlling interest; therefore, control is essential to equal opportunity to learn in schools. "Control," however, is a tricky, many-leveled word. Where blacks have gained control of the boards of ghetto schools, for example, they have found that they do not control the state legislature, which distributes state aid to education and sets curriculum and other requirements. But even if blacks could get equal funds out of the legislature, even if they could alter curriculum, even if they could produce equal outcomes through community control, they still would not control the economy and requirements for jobs. They would remain dependent for the definition of social roles on a society that has continually ensured them the bottom rung on its ladder.

Winning at least some control over one's own destiny, however, especially for a people who have been oppressed during their entire history in this country, does have important psychological effects. Political and social learning as a result of community control may not be the end point of a liberation period, but the beginning of something much more extensive and profound, depending upon who controls the community control movement. Cooptation by establishment blacks and Chicanos would ensure that the building of self-identity and the use of the schools for real community social change and political development be subverted to the needs of the corporate structure. In that case, oppressed minorities would successfully maintain their undesirable social roles through their "own" school boards. The results of community control of schools, then, are inexorably tied to the dependency of the community on decisions presently out of its control.

Since most poor still believe that more and better schooling can get them out of poverty, both individually and *as a class*, the role of liberal reformers is to try to provide minorities (who have been most militant and most threatening to societal order) more mobility *without* giving them more control over the economic and social structure. Again, reformers in the 1960s turned to the schools to meet the challenge of serious disruption of the social order. In this most recent attempt at reform, "disadvantaged" children—children who come from homes that do not prepare them properly for middle-class education and hence, for college-level vocations—were to get (1) expenditures per pupil in their schools equal to middle-class children's schools, and (2) "compensatory" education—extra schooling such as Head Start and higher-quality instruction during the normal course of their schooling. The ultimate objective of the reform was to equalize the *school* (*test*) *performance* of all *groups* of children going to school: pupils entering with, on the average, different "endowments" in the first grade would leave high school with, on the average, equal endowments. The function of the state and the schools would be to allocate resources in a way which would fulfill this compensatory objective.

But, like Horace Mann's belief in equal opportunity, the underlying assumptions of compensatory education have fatal flaws:

1. It is assumed that the instruments used to measure equalization—for example, reading, verbal, or math test scores—are not class-, race-, or sex-biased, and at the same time, reflect employers' hiring criteria and society's status criteria. But in a society that practices racial, sex, or ethnic discrimination, tests will be better predictors of future economic success, if the tests are biased in the same way the labor market is. Terman's Stanford-Binet test (1960 version) reflected the reality of the economic system's class structure: those children who could identify the Nordic Anglo-Saxon child as the correct answer to the question, "Which is prettier?" best understand the values of their society.[53] If the tests are unbiased and the labor market is discriminatory, it is less likely that the test score will be correlated with economic success. The equalization of test scores in the face of a labor market that has a different set of rules from the school will not do much to equalize social and economic roles. Clearly, equal test scores for women and men does not translate into equal opportunity for women in the economy and society. Neither will blacks or Mexican-Americans coming out of school with scores equal to those of whites necessarily gain equal pay or status.

2. It is assumed that the choice of future roles among graduates with equal test scores is equal. The perception of "desirable" vocations for lower and higher socioeconomic class students may be very different at the end of high school despite equal test scores for the two groups. Women's test scores are equal to men's, but their choice of occupations has been clearly different: social-

role perception correlated with social origin, race, and sex is reinforced by schools even if test scores are equalized. From this standpoint alone, public schools, organized by the state to service the goals of the state, cannot equalize different social, ethnic, racial, or sex groups' life possibilities at the end of a given period of schooling unless the society is itself egalitarian. Public schools, as we have seen, reflect and reinforce rather than counteract the prejudices and perceptions of the outside world.

3. It is assumed that the relationship between the teachers and students in the school is such that improving the "quality" of the teacher will result in compensating low-performance pupils. Compensatory education models in the United States assume that this relation is capable of producing equal performance on the part of different groups of pupils. But most teachers use learning models that expect pupils to *behave* in certain ways while absorbing cognitive knowledge. Under the track system, lower-class children are usually in the lowest tracks, so they are expected to learn less than the higher-class children in the higher tracks. Even in tracks, however, lower-class children are supposed to learn in the same way (they may have to be more disciplined) as higher-class children, even though they come from different cultures. The learning environment in the classroom leads the teachers to treat much better those children with whom they can communicate well (and reward them more often) than children with whom they are having difficulty. Even today, with all our understanding of cultural differences and an increasing sensitivity to cultural pluralism, schools are preparing different social classes of students for different economic and social roles. Discipline is much stricter in lower-class high schools than in higher-class schools, and the hierarchical relationship in all the schools leaves the child no recourse but to take rewards and punishment from the teacher.

There is almost no evidence that increasing the dollar resources per student or the "quality" of teachers for "disadvantaged" pupils will equalize performance of "disadvantaged" and "advantaged" pupils. However, there is a growing body of empirical results which shows that compensatory education within the present societal and school structures will *not* equalize school outcomes even if more school resources are devoted to the poor than the rich.[54] The supposition that more resources would be devoted to poor children than to rich is obviously hypothetical, since if U.S. education followed that course, the state's decision would have to be preceded by a radical change in the state's view of inequality. Its decision would probably also imply a change in the organization of production, since it is unlikely that wealthy managers and industrialists would be willing to have public education organized in a way that favored the poor over their own children (and their own class) unless formal schooling had become an unimportant allocator of socio-economic roles. In fact, to have schooling reorganized in favor of the poor would mean that those who are at the head of the economic hierarchy would have to lose their political power, both their direct power and the implicit power that their class holds over the values and norms of U.S. society.

Reformers always believed in merit selection because they believed that they could reduce economic and social inequality through individual mobility. They reasoned that as more and more people got schooling—any kind of schooling that helped them to get work—the less unequal the income distribution would be. The notion that increasing the average level of education and other social services is a substitute for direct redistributive social change is the foundation of American liberalism.[55] Liberal reformers are committed to the idea that significant redistribution of income, wealth and power can occur in a society without confronting the distribution and ownership of property nor the organization of production.

The challenge to the liberal position is now devastating. Income distribution in the United States has not changed significantly since 1944, despite a rapid increase in the average level of schooling in the labor force and a significant decrease in the variance of years of schooling received.[56] Kolko argues that income inequality has not decreased significantly since 1910.[57] Chiswick and Mincer show that the decrease in income inequality they observe between 1939 and 1965 was the result of a large decrease in the dispersion of weeks of unemployment in the labor force, which occurred primarily in the five years between 1939 and

1944. Furthermore, they predict that even with full employment, income distribution will not change significantly between 1965 and 1985, assuming that the structural relationships estimated for the 1949–69 period continue to hold true.[58]

Yet it could be argued that although income distribution does not change, the people getting high incomes and low incomes change from generation to generation. Since there is a significant relationship between the number of years of schooling an individual has had and income earned (especially in younger age groups), we can easily check how the amount of schooling taken by those with low-education fathers has changed relative to the mean education of the adult population. Table 5.1 shows that *white* males whose fathers had less than eight years of school have not improved their position relative to the mean number of years of schooling since the early 1920s.[59]

Table 5.1

United States: Absolute and Relative Years of School Completed, White Males, by Age and Father's Education, March 1962

Years of Schooling Completed by Father

Age of Son (years)	<8	8–11	12	College 1–3	≧4	Total Mean
20–24	10.6 (0.78)	11.8 (0.89)	12.8 (0.96)	13.4 (1.01)	14.1 (1.06)	13.3
25–34	10.8 (0.89)	12.1 (1.00)	13.0 (1.07)	14.3 (1.18)	15.3 (1.26)	12.1
35–44	10.6 (0.92)	11.6 (1.01)	13.0 (1.13)	14.0 (1.22)	15.1 (1.31)	11.5
45–54	9.9 (0.92)	11.6 (1.07)	12.4 (1.15)	13.0 (1.20)	14.2 (1.31)	10.8
55–64	9.1 (0.91)	10.4 (1.04)	11.8 (1.18)	11.9 (1.19)	13.6 (1.36)	10.0

Source: Bureau of the Census, *Current Population Reports*, Series P-20, no. 132, September 1964, table 4.

Even if we ignore the 20–24 age group, many of whom have not completed their college training, and even if we recognize that there is some bias in the average number of years completed by those with low-education fathers, it appears that those lowest two groups have not improved significantly relative to the mean years of schooling. Distribution of schooling years has improved over time, but children of fathers with less than high school education still find themselves in a disadvantageous job-market position.

Table 5.2 shows that the greatest percentage increase in those who attended college between the mid-1920s and the mid-1950s came from families where the father had attended college, even though this group is much smaller than the group of fathers who had not attended college. Although of those who went to college in the 1920s an equal percentage were sons of fathers who had completed high school or attended some college, in the 1950s, sons with fathers who completed high school had a 30 percentage point lower probability of attending college than those with fathers who had attended some years (but not completed) college. Since at least some college in the 1950s was already considered necessary for entrance into the white-collar occupa-

Table 5.2

United States: Absolute Probability of Attending College, White Males, by Age and Father's Education, March 1962

Years of Schooling Completed by Father

Age of Son (years)	<8	8–11	12	College 1–3	College ≧4	Total Mean
25–34	0.174	0.282	0.445	0.724	0.896	0.323
35–44	0.164	0.225	0.457	0.618	0.810	0.262
45–54	0.130	0.195	0.336	0.524	0.732	0.204
55–64	0.091	0.150	0.329	0.351	0.602	0.157

Source: See table 5.1.

tions, this spreading probability of access to college between those from families where the father had completed high school or less and where the father had completed some years of college indicates the kind of class division that still characterizes the public school system. Also, these tables are only for *white* males, which means that a high percentage of the lowest income groups in the United States are excluded. For example, in 1962, only 13.9 percent of nonwhite males 25–34 years old completed one or more years of college, compared with 32.3 percent of white males.[60]

The schools are also being attacked from another direction: by high-income whites. Alienation within this group, when it occurs, is not concerned with opportunity but with the *meaning* of opportunity. To this segment of the affluent, liberation means rejecting the employment mentality, rejecting the accouterments of success, and rejecting the concept that increasing the complexity and technification of society is progress. The "free schools" are the result of this white "liberation." The cost to affluent parents of experimenting with new educational forms is hardly high; surrounded by a learning environment outside the school, parents and children can always change their minds and be successful in traditional ways. Although no real research has been done on what happens to children after they leave the free schools, the desired result is to increase their propensity to choose life rather than death.[61] This choice would manifest itself in the ways in which an individual works and lives, especially in the relations he has with those around him, as well as the kinds of products and services he produces and consumes, and the way he produces them.

As in the case of community control, however, the full impact of free schooling in its experimental and innovative forms may never be felt. Professional educators, along with foundations and industries, are incorporating elements of free-school style (child-centered classrooms) into the public schools. Silberman's interest in English open classrooms and the North Dakota "experiment" of child-centered classrooms as the solution to our schooling problem show the direction professional educators are taking to maintain control of the schools.[62] Children can undoubtedly gain as a result of North Dakota-type schools, with their sensitized teachers and more joyful atmosphere. But the end result will still be competitive achievement tests and socialization into capitalist, alienating economic organizations—organizations with needs that are somewhat less rigid than in the past, but which still require workers who respond to extrinsic rewards and who will follow implicit rules and regulations.

> . . . when the rhetoric becomes so heated that people can be heard suggesting that we do away with the system or radically change it, Carnegie Foundation supported James Conant (1964), who, in effect, said the system was basically sound but then co-opted the rhetoric of the attackers to recommend limited change. It was, after all, the survival of the system which Conant had in mind when he spoke of social dynamite in the ghettoes. By the 1970's when most manpower projections clearly indicated surplus of labor for the next decade, the educational reform rhetoric shifted from training scientists and engineers to open classrooms. Again, critics could be heard suggesting that the system be radically altered if not abolished, and once again, the Carnegie Foundation supported a study by Silberman which, in effect said that the system was basically sound but needed some reforming.[63]

In concluding this chapter, it is worth noting that, as in the past, today's educational problems in the United States are a manifestation of a much more profound malaise in the economic and social order, particularly the hierarchical relations in production-consumption brought on by large-scale capitalist industrialization. In the past, educational reformers, many idealistic and with good intentions, imposed on the mass of urban workers an educational system which contributed to preserving social order, but did so while maintaining an inequitable class structure. In the 1970s, professional educators continue to try to rejuvenate this same educational system because they continue to believe in the existing economic and social structure, and in the corporations' view of America's future.

Notes

1. Michael Katz, *Class, Bureaucracy, and Schools* (New York: Praeger, 1971), p. 9.

2. Samuel Bowles, "Unequal Education and the Reproduction of the Social Division of Labor," in *Schooling in a Corporate Society,* ed. Martin Carnoy (New York: David McKay, 1972).

3. Michael Katz, *The Irony of Early School Reform* (Boston: Beacon Press, 1970), pp. 93–112.

4. Ibid., pp. 48–50.

5. For an analysis of black education in the South after the Civil War, see Carnoy: *Education as Cultural Imperialism,* chapter 6.

6. Katz, *Irony of Early School Reform* and *Class, Bureaucracy, and Schools.*

7. Katz, *Class, Bureaucracy, and Schools,* pp. 19–20.

8. Ibid., p. 30.

9. Ibid., p. 33.

10. Katz, *Irony of Early School Reform,* p. 47.

11. The relation went the other way as well. Horace Mann helped push through the legislative bills supporting and assisting railroad construction. Ibid., p. 35.

12. Ibid., pp. 49–50.

13. Ibid., p. 85.

14. It is possible to take a Schumpeterian view of schooling's failure to solve the social crisis in the cities: perhaps it was obstacles already present in the towns before the advent of large scale industrialization which could be blamed. On the basis of this analysis, the reformers attempted to create a new city, Lawrence, Massachusetts, which would avoid the problems of European industrial towns. A school system was part of this dream. Yet even the best possible schools "failed to maintain prosperity, social harmony, and morality" (Katz, *Irony of Early School Reform,* p. 97). Lawrence was subject to the same economic fluctuations as any other industrial town, and these fluctuations caused the same immorality and poverty as elsewhere. The reformers could not overcome the harsh realities of capitalist development; they could only foster an uneven economic growth.

15. William B. Whiting, a Massachusetts manufacturer, quoted in ibid., p. 88.

16. Ibid., p. 132.

17. Ibid., p. 139.

18. Ibid., p. 58.

19. Ibid., p. 53. This was the argument the reformers used against the academies having a monopoly on high school education.

20. Katz, *Class, Bureaucracy, and Schools,* p. 37.

21. Ibid., p. 39.

22. David Tyack, "Centralization of Control in City Schools at the Turn of the Century," in *The Organizational Society*, ed. Jerry Israel (Chicago: Quadrangle Books, 1971).

23. For a reinterpretation of the Progressive era in American politics, see Gabriel Kolko, *The Triumph of Conservatism* (Glencoe, Ill.: Free Press, 1963).

24. Katz, *Class, Bureaucracy, and Schools*, pp. 108–9.

25. Ibid., p. 109.

26. Ibid., p. 116.

27. "Equally interesting, especially after 1900, were changes in the actual content of the subjects themselves. The influences of commercialism and industrialism appeared throughout the curriculum. Commercial and business arithmetic, for example, began to receive extensive attention in the mathematics curriculum" (R. Freeman Butts and Lawrence Cremin, *A History of Education in American Culture* [New York: Henry Holt, 1953], p. 441).

28. David Cohen and Marvin Lazerson, "Education and the Corporate Order," *Socialist Revolution*, no. 8 (March/April 1972): 47–72.

29. Ibid., p. 51.

30. Stephan Michelson, "The Political Economy of Public School Finance," in *Schooling in a Corporate Society*, ed. Martin Carnoy (New York: David McKay, 1972).

31. Boston school superintendent (1908) quoted in ibid., p. 69.

32. Ibid., p. 68.

33. The parallel to the present-day measurement of educational success in nonindustrialized countries should be obvious. See Philip Coombs, *The World Educational Crisis* (New York: Oxford University Press, 1968).

34. "The classic statement for the comprehensive high school was the Cardinal Principles of Secondary Education issued by a special committee of the National Educational Association in 1918. . . . The report proposed that 'differentiation should be in the broad sense of the term vocational . . . such as agricultural, business clerical, industrial, fine-arts, and household arts curriculums.' It supported the idea of a junior high school but limited its functions to exploration of vocations and prevocational guidance. This meant that a systematic and organized differentiation of students would not take place in the junior high school but would be postponed to senior high school. The junior high was defined as a period of exploration while the senior high was one of training. . . . The comprehensive high school also allowed for what the committee called the two components of democracy, specialization and unification. . . . The specialized and differentiated curriculum of the school was to train the individual to perform

some task that would be good for the society. . . . Unification was that part of the ideal of democracy that brought people together and gave them 'common ideas, common ideals, and common modes of thought, feeling, and action that made for cooperation, social cohesion, and social solidarity'" (Joel Spring, "Education and the Corporate State," *Socialist Revolution*, no. 8 [March/April 1972]: 84–85).

35. Cohen and Lazerson, "Education and the Social Order," pp. 54–55.

36. Clarence Karier, "Testing for Order and Control in the Corporate Liberal State" (University of Illinois, 1972), p. 25. Mimeographed.

37. Heber Hinds Ryan and Philipine Crecelius, *Ability Grouping in the Junior High School* (New York: Harcourt Brace, 1927), quoted in Paul Lauter and Florence Howe, "How the School System Is Rigged for Failure," *New York Review of Books*, 18 June 1970, p. 16.

38. *Hobson* v. *Hansen*, Civil Action, no. 82–66. *Federal Supplement*, V. 269.

39. Karier, "Testing for Order and Control," p. 26. This is Karier's summary of the Court decision.

40. Cremin, quoted in Michelson, "Public School Finance," p. 150.

41. Cohen and Lazerson, "Education and the Social Order," p. 52.

42. Ibid., p. 54.

43. Joel Spring, "Education and the Corporate State," *Socialist Revolution*, no. 8 (March/April 1972): 76.

44. Samuel Bowles and Herbert Gintis, "IQ in the U.S. Class Structure," *Social Policy*, January/February 1973.

45. Karier, "Testing for Order and Control," pp. 13–14.

46. Ibid., p. 16.

47. Cohen and Lazerson, "Education and the Social Order," p. 59.

48. Ibid., p. 60; and John Dewey, *Democracy and Education* (New York: Macmillan, 1961).

49. Cohen and Lazerson, "Education and the Social Order," p. 61.

50. Raymond Callahan, *Education and the Cult of Efficiency* (Chicago: University of Chicago Press, 1962); and G. S. Counts, *The Social Composition of Boards of Education: Schools and Society in Chicago* (Chicago: University of Chicago Press, 1927).

51. Spring, "Education and the Corporate State," p. 85.

52. Henry M. Levin, *An Economic Analysis of Education Vouchers* (Papers in the Economic and Politics of Education, Stanford University School of Education, 1972). Mimeographed.

53. This example comes from the latest revision (1960) of the

Stanford-Binet Intelligence Test as illustrated in Karier, "Testing for Order and Control," p. 18.

54. See Martin Carnoy, "Is Compensatory Education Possible?" in *Schooling in a Corporate Society*, ed. Martin Carnoy (New York: David McKay, 1972); also, Christopher Jencks, *Inequality* (New York: Basic Books, 1972).

55. Simon Kuznets extrapolated this argument to postulate that capitalist development produced a tendency toward more equal income distribution. For a discussion of his argument and others related to income distribution, see Martin Bronfenbrenner, *Income Distribution Theory* (Chicago: Aldine, 1971), pp. 67–75.

56. In 1939, the average level of schooling in the labor force was 8.8 years while in 1965, it was 11.16 years. Variance dropped from 3.7 to 3.4.

57. Gabriel Kolko, *Wealth and Power in America* (New York: Praeger, 1965), p. 13.

58. Barry Chiswick and Jacob Mincer, "Time Series Changes in Personal Income Inequality in the United States," *Journal of Political Economy* 80, no. 3, pt. 2 (May/June, 1972): S56.

59. These mean years of schooling for sons are calculated from a table showing the probability of completing different levels of schooling given father's education. I took the mean of the less than eight years of schooling category as six years, which biases downward the mean years of schooling taken by younger age groups relative to older, since this open-ended category probably had a lot more sons with no schooling in it in the 1920s than in the 1950s. Thus, in general, we tend to underestimate the average number of years of schooling in the lowest age categories of sons relative to the highest age categories, especially for those with fathers who had less than eight or eight-to-eleven years of school.

60. Bureau of the Census.

61. For a discussion of life choices versus death choices, see Erich Fromm, *The Revolution of Hope* (New York: Harper & Row, 1970).

62. Charles Silberman, *Crisis in the Classroom* (New York: Random House, 1970), pp. 284–97.

63. Karier, "Testing for Order and Control," p. 33.

6

Henry M. Levin

The Economic Implications of Mastery Learning

Any attempt to describe the economic implications of mastery learning is necessarily audacious. Since its initial formulation by Bloom in the late 1960s,[1] based upon the work of Carroll,[2] it has stimulated a wide variety of applications, and the individual projects and programs that are linked by the mastery-learning banner are so diverse that they defy easy generalization.[3] Moreover, little attention has been devoted to costs or other types of data that might represent the basis for economic evaluation. Given the lack of a data base and the diversity of applications, one is handicapped in making any generalizable assertions about the economic implications of mastery learning. Accordingly, it is necessary to proceed by making a number of assumptions about the nature, processes, and outcomes of the mastery-learning approach. To the degree that readers disagree with these assumptions, they are also likely to question the subsequent analysis.

In this commentary I view mastery learning as an instructional strategy characterized by the following traits: First, it is presumed that learning tasks are related to specific and unambiguous goals, and that success in achieving these goals can be assessed adequately by a criterion-based test. Second, it is assumed that it is possible for a legitimately constituted group of decision makers to select the "mastery level of attainment" in such a way that this level of attainment is indicative of functional competence in the specific area of concern. Third, the vast majority of students can attain mastery, so defined, if enough time is permitted for achieving it. Fourth, the objective of the mastery-learning strategy is to maximize the number of students achieving mastery subject to the overall constraints on the magnitude of resources and the aggregate amount of time, but there will be no constraints on the distribution of time and resources among students within those aggregates. Finally, the principal educational treatments that will be utilized to achieve this objective are the differentiation of instruction according to learner aptitudes and the sequential allocation of resources from those students who have achieved mastery to those who have not. The process continues until all students have achieved mastery or until the aggregate time boundaries allocated to the learning task are exceeded. The aim of both the learner-differentiated instruction and the assignment of resources to those who need them most is to reduce the time differential between the fastest and slowest learners for attaining mastery.

Several aspects of the mastery-learning approach make it particularly amenable to economic evaluation. For any particular task, one should be able to observe specific outcomes as well as measures of time and resource allocations. Moreover, the strategy has an explicit theoretical model underlying it so that data can be interpreted within the structure of that paradigm. Finally, the mastery-learning technique is concerned as much with equality of results as it is with the level of cognitive proficiency. Thus, both the outcome and its distribution among students are taken into account. All these characteristics make the mastery-learning approach considerably more susceptible to economic analysis than traditional modes of educational organization since the latter are usually characterized by vague objectives, ambiguous theories, and inadequately elaborated instructional processes.

Economic Criteria

There are two general guidelines for examining the economic implications of an educational strategy. The first type of evaluation addresses the internal efficiency of the approach with regard to its cost-effectiveness at producing a given result.[4] A specific method is considered to be efficient according to internal criteria if it is able to attain a given set of educational goals at lower cost than other alternatives.

The criterion of external efficiency considers not only the costs relative to results, but also the value to society of the results. Attempts are made to estimate the monetary value of both the costs and the benefits in order to compare that ratio with the costs and benefits of other educational approaches as well as with investments in areas of social concern outside the educational arena.[5] In order for a strategy to satisfy the criterion of external efficiency, it must provide at least as great a social benefit per unit of cost as other social investments.

While the evaluation of internal efficiency is devoted only to ascertaining the costs of a specific outcome—for example, 80 percent of students attaining mastery—the evaluation of external efficiency requires that the outcome itself has high benefits relative to its costs. In summary, comparisons of internal efficiency are essentially comparisons of the costs for attaining a given result; in contrast, comparisons of external efficiency require the assessment of both the costs and social benefits that might emanate from a given activity.[6]

According to both internal and external efficiency criteria, it is difficult to make empirically based statements about the relative economic efficiency of mastery learning. The reason for this lack is twofold. First, mastery learning has different goals than traditional instruction, so it is not possible to compare the costs of attaining the same result. Second, no adequate cost data exist from either conventional instruction or mastery learning that enable one to attempt even a rough comparison of efficiency. Accordingly, the remainder of this analysis attempts to develop the economic implications of mastery learning by analyzing the cost aspects and benefit aspects of the technique. In some cases we are able to draw comparative inferences on the economic properties of mastery learning, and in other cases we are not.

Internal Efficiency of Mastery Learning

According to advocates of mastery learning, the approach can increase the average level of knowledge for a particular group of students and simultaneously reduce the variance in the levels of knowledge within the group.[7] If we can assume that both increases in cognitive attainments and greater equality in their distribution are of positive value, and this can be done within the same time and resource constraint as for the conventional framework, then the mastery technique is superior to the traditional organization on grounds of internal efficiency. That is, more can be accomplished by applying resources through mastery learning than through the traditional approach. But, we have no supporting experimental or quasi-experimental evidence at this time since most of the testing of mastery techniques has taken place outside of the economic framework.[8] Yet, the various components of the mastery "technology" can be scrutinized in order to observe their cost implications with regard to a given outcome.

At least four aspects of mastery learning appear to be related to the internal efficiency question: (1) learner-differentiated treatments; (2) sequential transfer of resources from students who have attained mastery to those who have not; (3) coordination of curriculum and mastery attainments so that students are prepared for successive levels of instruction; and (4) possible changes in the affective outcomes of schooling. Each of these will be reviewed briefly, and the nature of their effects on the relationship of costs to outcomes examined. In all four cases we will assume that the criterion of effectiveness will be the number of students achieving mastery at each level.

The use of learner-differentiated instructional treatments would seem intuitively to improve the internal efficiency of the schools. That is, if resources can be reorganized in such a way as to capitalize on the different aptitudes of students, it seems plausible that learning outcomes will improve.[9] Certainly, there is a strong conceptual basis for this expected outcome in the "aptitude-treatment-interaction" literature. The principle underlying this approach is that different students enter the classroom situation with different aptitudes for learning particular material, and instructional treatments should be differentiated to capitalize on such differences in aptitudes.

What is unrecognized in this argument is that while learner-differentiated instruction may produce gains in the number of children achieving mastery, such an approach has added costs as well (relative to traditional instructional approaches). These costs are of three types: diagnosis and screening, allocating fixed costs of treatments over fewer students, and lost time in moving from treatment to treatment.

The diagnosis and screening requirements for identifying students with different aptitudes and determining the appropriate instructional treatments are likely to be substantial. Information that is obtained on an individual student basis for each learning task is exceedingly costly, and the knowledge of instructional treatments consonant with aptitude classifications is speculative at best.[10] To the degree that a substantial number of learning-related aptitudes exist among a typical group of students, the cost problem is compounded. Both costs and probable results rise with the number of aptitude-treatment classifications implemented, but it is likely that the additional costs exceed the gains beyond a relatively small number of aptitude differentiations.[11] It is important to note that the cost of obtaining information on student differences and appropriate instructional approaches can be substantial, even in the two-aptitude cases, especially when aptitudes and treatments are not generalizable across subject areas.

A closely related area of added cost is that each treatment will be divided over fewer students under a learner-differentiated approach. To the degree that instructional treatments have fixed costs, the allocation of such costs to fewer students means a higher cost per pupil. Indeed, to the degree that there will be fixed staffing requirements for each instructional treatment—regardless of the number of students involved—learner-differentiated approaches will require a greater expenditure on personnel. This assumption is particularly warranted if we assume that the different instructional approaches must be applied concurrently in order to minimize the aggregate amount of time allocated to the task.

Finally, that portion of learner-differentiated instruction that uses the same personnel and physical resources for each instructional group faces a loss in efficiency and time in the shift from one group to another. There are two reasons for such a loss. First, the physical movement of groups and personnel takes time, but more important is the loss of continuity as resources are shifted around from group to group. One of the important gains from specialization of function is that which is attributable to the continuity of task in contrast to the shift from one task to the next. This assertion would seem equally valid in the classroom.

In summary, there appear to be both added cognitive gains and costs to utilizing the learner-differentiated approach. It would appear that cognitive gains would emerge from designing instruction to capitalize on differences in aptitudes, but such a policy would also entail the added costs of diagnosis and screening, fewer students per treatment, and loss of resource efficiency in moving among instructional tasks. Without a data base and a specific task it is impossible to set out the conditions under which the costs of learner-differentiated instruction would be justified by results, so it is not possible to determine a priori whether this aspect of mastery learning will improve the efficiency of educational resource use.

In contrast, a second aspect of mastery learning would appear to improve the internal efficiency of resource application in the schools. This aspect is the sequential transfer of resources from students who have attained mastery to those who have not. In the traditional classroom, students who have mastered the subject matter are exposed to the same instructional treatments as those who have not. Such an approach has two negative consequences with regard to the effective use of educational resources. First, it wastes resources by subjecting students who have already mastered material to redundant exercises. This repetition may also have the effect of oppressing and "turning off" those students. Second, it does not give the students who have not yet achieved mastery the benefit of concentrated resources. By shifting resources sequentially from those students who have achieved mastery to those who have not, the faster students can be encouraged to inquire into enrichment areas which would not otherwise be covered, and the slower pupils will benefit from an increasingly higher concentration of resources assisting them as the other students attain mastery. Such an approach also enables the quicker students to tutor the slower ones in order to assist the latter group to attain mastery. This is an advantage which is difficult to implement in the conventional classroom setting with its teacher-dominated approach.

A third aspect of the mastery-learning approach is also likely to increase the internal efficiency of the educational enterprise. Since mastery learning seeks to maximize the number of students attaining mastery of a given task, successful results mean that a higher proportion of students will be ready for the subsequent learning task. Under the present normative-based approach, it is expected that a substantial number of students will not succeed. As the curriculum progresses to more difficult material, these students find themselves farther and farther behind until "contact" is lost completely. By ensuring that a maximum number of students achieve mastery at each level, a maximum number will be ready to move to the next level. This aspect of the mastery approach has important implications for increasing resource effectiveness.

A final aspect of the mastery-learning approach that has implications for internal efficiency is that which deals with the affective outcomes of instruction. According to Benjamin Bloom and James Block,[12] preliminary data suggest that mastery approaches have noticeable positive effects on students' interest and attitudes. Not only are improvements in such outcomes as students' attitudes about their capabilities and interest in their studies valuable on their own merits, but such affective improvements are likely also to contribute to cognitive gains. While the present data are not adequate to assert that mastery learning generally produces better affective outcomes than traditional instruction, it seems reasonable that this might occur because of the emphasis on maximizing the number of students who achieve mastery rather than utilizing the normative-based treadmill where only the "leaders" can feel confident of their success.[13]

Summary of Internal Efficiency   Given the criterion of the number of children achieving mastery as the measure of effectiveness, there appear to be several ways in which the internal efficiency of schools might be increased through mastery learning. The first of these, learner-differentiated instruction, is likely to improve learning outcomes, but it is not likely that this strategy can be attempted without an increase in resource costs. Whether these additional costs are offset by the larger number of children who attain mastery is problematic. Specific empirical data are needed in order to evaluate the issue, and such data are not presently available.

The effects of other aspects of the mastery approach on internal economic efficiency are less ambiguous. These include the sequential transfer of resources from students who have attained mastery to those who have not (including the use of student tutors); the coordination of curriculum and mastery attainments so that students are prepared for successive levels of instruction; and possible improvements in the affective outcomes of schooling. To the degree that these can be derived independent of the learner-differentiated instruction, they do not imply higher costs, and they would appear to increase the number of students attaining mastery.

The preceding discussion was based completely on conceptual differences between traditional modes of instruction and mastery approaches. The lack of cost-effectiveness data on all types of instruction prevents any further generalization. Also, any specific application of any particular mode of instruction may vary so much from setting to setting that any generalization is hazardous at best. Given these cautions, however, I suspect that empirical data will show that mastery learning approaches are somewhat more efficient relative to costs in increasing cognitive attainments and reducing the variance in results when compared with more traditional instructional approaches. I doubt that the differences in relative efficiency are dramatic since there are many other factors influencing both the level and distribution of cognitive outcomes that are quite independent of the organization of formal instructional activities.

External Efficiency of Mastery Learning

In order to ascertain the relative external efficiency of mastery learning, we must consider the relative social benefits as well as the costs of the approach. While a study of internal efficiency might just review the costs and cognitive effectiveness of different approaches, the evaluation of external efficiency requires that these effects be translated into measurable social benefits for comparison with costs and benefits from other types of social investments. In theory, then, we would be able to compare investments in traditional instruction and mastery with investments in health, highways, welfare, recreation, and so on, in order to see which one yields the largest returns to society for each additional dollar of expenditure.[14]

Obviously, if we do not have adequate data on comparisons of internal efficiency questions, we are even more handicapped with regard to our evaluation of external efficiency. Yet, the possible sources of improvement in educational effectiveness can be examined in order to see how these might translate into social benefits. In so doing, it is best to start off with the most optimistic assumptions about the internal efficiency of mastery learning and to proceed from there. Accordingly, we will assume that mastery learning will raise the average level of cognitive attainments for any group of students while simultaneously reducing the cognitive variance or inequality among those students. We must now ask how these effects will be converted into social benefits.

It is, of course, appealing to believe that increases in the level of and improvements in the distribution of cognitive proficiencies will lead to improvements in the amounts and distribution of social attainments. For example, the literature on human capital would suggest that improvements in skill levels as reflected in mastery attainments might raise social productivity and income as well as upgrade occupational attainments.[15] Moreover, it might be assumed that by reducing the disparity in cognitive accomplishments among students, there will also be a corresponding reduction in inequality of income and occupational status. Such theories assume tacitly that: (1) income and occupational attainments are determined primarily by cognitive proficiencies; and (2) that educational reform leads to social reform.

Each of these assumptions must be questioned. That is, very little empirical evidence supports the view that cognitive proficiencies are an important determinant of income and earnings or occupational status, and no body of evidence supports the proposition that educational reform leads to social reform. In the first case, an increasing body of literature is emerging which relates test scores, socioeconomic background, educational attainments, and a host of social-psychological variables to earnings and occupational status. The somewhat surprising result in virtually all these studies is the exceedingly modest relationship between cognitive proficiencies measured by standardized test scores and measures of earnings and occupational status.[16] Indeed, recent excursions into the relations between education, occupation, and income have found increasing evidence of the role played by noncognitive outcomes in both the educational and mobility processes. Accordingly, there is no assurance, given the present social and economic structure of society, that improvements in the level of and distribution of cognitive outcomes will change substantially the nature of social outcomes.

The important point is that the schools correspond to their host society in that they fulfill the requirements for socializing persons into adult roles.[17] In a society characterized by substantial inequalities in adult roles, the schools will function purposively to socialize differentially the population to fill the occupational and income hierarchy.[18] Thus, it is hardly a mindless endeavor of the schools to sort, stratify, and track youngsters in such a way that at the end of the process their places in the hierarchy of production are legitimated and certified.[19] That is, the reproduction of the social relations of production is an important function of the schools, and schools will continue to show unequal results as long as there exist large inequalities in the production, occupational, and earnings hierarchy.[20]

Without changes in the nature of production and its accompanying social relations, any strategy that will more nearly equalize cognitive outcomes will have little effect on the distribution of opportunity since the opportunities themselves are so unequal. There are only a limited number of rewards at each level in the existing social structure, and there is neither a conceptual nor an empirical tie between more equal cognitive outcomes and greater social equality.

The crux of the matter is that the fairness or social justice inherent in the mastery learning concept is not reflected in a corresponding set of social institutions. To go somewhat further, this lack of correspondence would tend to support the following predictions: (1) the mastery-learning strategy will not be adopted in any systematic sense; or (2) if adopted, the outcomes for which mastery learning will be implemented will not be important ones with regard to the social selection process. That is, if mastery learning is successful in being adopted and in equalizing certain educational outcomes, the outcomes themselves will lack importance with regard to the social process of selecting individuals for filling roles within the occupational and income hierarchy. Cognitive characteristics which the schools equalize will not be functional traits for the allocation of the very unequal set of social rewards, and schools will continue to differentiate their students on important dimensions of the social selection process.

Summary of Economic Implications of Mastery Learning

The economic evaluation of mastery learning can be carried out at two levels, internal and external. According to the internal efficiency criterion, there are a number of characteristics of the mastery-learning strategy that suggests it might obtain better cognitive outcomes relative to costs than traditional methods of instruction. In contrast, it was argued that according to the external efficiency criterion the mastery-learning strategy did not seem to have an advantage. The greater equality of cognitive outcomes is not likely to change the distribution of social outcomes such as the distribution of earnings and the occupational structure. Moreover, it was asserted that even changes in the overall level of cognitive performance are not likely to be reflected in significant increases in aggregate productivity and earnings.

What we have not examined are two aspects of mastery learning that are probably far more important in the long run than the narrow questions raised by economic efficiency criteria in the present context. First, is there anything intrinsically worthwhile about mastery learning that is desirable regardless of its economic benefits? And second, are there changes in the social and economic structure that will make the mastery-learning approach increasingly functional? In my view the answers to both of these questions are yes.

The mastery-learning approach has a very humane quality in its concern with equalizing outcomes. Although the term equality resounds throughout the philosophical literature on American education, I would maintain that the traditional educational strategy is designed to deliberately separate and differentiate students by performance rather than to equalize them. School organizations devote an enormous amount of energy to testing, grouping, curriculum, and counseling practices that are designed inherently to sort and socialize children differentially. Although these procedures are rationalized educationally on the most pious of grounds, they serve to cull out systematically the children from poorer backgrounds. The existent system of financing education also discriminates systematically against the poor.[21] It is precisely the contradiction to this programed inequality that represents both the strengths and weaknesses of mastery learning. The concern of the mastery-learning conception with equality and fairness in the achievement of educational outcomes is worthy of great praise. Paradoxically, this virtue is also its Achilles' heel since such values are not implicit in the social, political, and economic organization of the larger society.

More optimistically, there are important societal changes in the offing that will increase the functionality of the mastery learning approach even though at the present time it is contradicted by the larger set of social institutions. The present system of production in both the public and private sectors is becoming increasingly beset by events that threaten to create severe disruptions. As a recent report produced by the Department of

Health, Education, and Welfare emphasized, the increasing alienation of the American worker with the circumstances of his job is responsible for rising incidences of wildcat strikes, alcoholism and drug problems on the job, breakdowns in quality control, worker turnover and absenteeism, and employee sabotage.[22] In order to safeguard production and the control of capital, business firms and government agencies are seeking ways to reorganize work in order to decrease worker alienation and increase worker loyalty.

While there are many different changes in work organization, all of them attempt to reduce the alienation and dissatisfaction of workers while increasing productivity by changing the nature of workers' relationships to the firm, to fellow workers, and to the decision-making mechanisms.[23] Some approaches would allow workers to organize into production teams that would rotate specific jobs, set production schedules, and monitor quality-control functions. Other proposals would replace hierarchical lines of authority and bureaucratic organization with worker self-management. This broad family of alternatives can be thought of as attempts to increase the degree of "industrial democracy." Recent experiments in the United States and abroad suggest that this phenomenon will become increasingly important as a strategy for improving worker satisfaction while reducing the threat of disruptions.

If these predicted changes take place, then mastery learning will become increasingly functional for training workers. Under most proposals for reorganizing work, there would be a much greater emphasis on cooperation and on the universal mastery of particular skills so that workers could rotate jobs and share particular duties. In order to satisfy these needs, an educational strategy that attempts to bring all persons up to requisite levels of mastery is needed. Although the mastery approach does not correspond to the demands of the present production organizations, it does fulfill many of the educational requirements that will be demanded by proposed changes. Accordingly, I expect that the economic importance of the mastery-learning strategy will rise substantially over the foreseeable future.

Notes

1. Benjamin S. Bloom, "Learning for Mastery," *Evaluation Comment* 1, no. 2 (1968).

2. John B. Carroll, "A Model of School Learning," *Teachers College Record* 64 (1963): 723–33.

3. James H. Block, ed., *Mastery Learning: Theory and Practice* (New York: Holt, Rinehart & Winston, 1971); James H. Block, "Mastery Learning in the Classroom: An Overview of Recent Research" (Paper presented at the annual meeting of the American Educational Research Association, New Orleans, Louisiana, February 1973).

4. J. Alan Thomas, *The Productive School* (New York: Wiley, 1971).

5. Thomas I. Ribich, *Education and Poverty* (Washington, D.C.: Brookings Institution, 1968).

6. Henry M. Levin, "The Effect of Different Levels of Expenditure on Educational Output," in *Economic Factors Affecting the Financing of Education*, ed. R. L. Johns et al. (Gainesville, Fla.: National Educational Finance Project, 1971).

7. Block, *Mastery Learning* and "Mastery Learning in the Classroom."

8. The exceptions are N. O. Christoffersson, *The Economics of Time in Learning*, Special Topic Bulletin 34, Department of Educational and Psychological Research (Malmo, Sweden: School of Education, 1971), and W. T. Garner, "The Identification of an Educational Production by Experimental Means" (Paper presented at the annual meeting of the American Educational Research Association, New Orleans, Louisiana, February 1973), who view mastery learning with regard to the economics of time. However, they do not consider the human and physical resources that enter the educational process.

9. L. J. Cronbach and R. E. Snow, *Individual Differences in Learning Ability as a Function of Instructional Variables* (Bethesda, Md.: ERIC Documentation Reproduction Service, 1969).

10. A theoretical base on the economics of information is found in George Stigler, "The Economics of Information," *Journal of Political Economy* 69 (1961): 213–25. Heuristic issues on the costs of additional testing vs. its utility are found in L. J. Cronbach and G. C. Gleser, *Psychological Tests and Personnel Decisions* (Urbana: University of Illinois Press, 1965).

11. See Cronbach and Gleser, *Psychological Tests and Personnel Decisions*, for a similar problem regarding the use of tests for personnel selection.

12. Benjamin S. Bloom, "Affective Consequences of School

Achievement," in Block, *Mastery Learning* and "Mastery Learning in the Classroom."

13. Block, "Mastery Learning in the Classroom."

14. A. R. Prest and R. Turvey, "Cost-Benefit Analysis: A Survey," *Economic Journal* 75 (1968): 683–735.

15. Gary S. Becker, *Human Capital* (New York: Columbia University Press, 1964).

16. Samuel Bowles and Herbert Gintis, "IQ in the U.S. Class Structure," *Social Policy* 3, no. 5 (January/February 1973): 1–27; Z. Griliches and W. Mason, "Education, Income, and Ability," *Journal of Political Economy* 80, no. 3 (1972): 219–52; Paul J. Taubman and Terence J. Wales, "Higher Education, Mental Ability, and Screening," *Journal of Political Economy* 81, no. 1 (1973): 28–55.

17. Alex Inkeles, "The Socialization of Competence," *Harvard Educational Review* 36 (1966): 265–83.

18. Samuel Bowles, "Unequal Education and the Reproduction of the Social Division of Labor," in *Schooling in a Corporate Society*, ed. Martin Carnoy (New York: David McKay, 1972); Herbert Gintis, "Toward a Political Economy of Education," *Harvard Educational Review* 42 (1972): 70–96; Henry M. Levin, "Educational Reform: Its Meaning?" chapter 2 in this volume.

19. Such characteristics of schools are discussed in Robert Dreeben, *On What Is Learned in School* (Reading, Mass.: Addison-Wesley, 1968), and their links to production are reviewed in Herbert Gintis, "Education, Technology, and the Characteristics of Worker Productivity," *American Economic Review* 61 (1971): 266–79; and in Bowles, "Unequal Education."

20. Louis Althusser, *Lenin and Philosophy and Other Essays* (New York: Monthly Review Press, 1971); Bowles, "Unequal Education"; Martin Carnoy, *Schooling in a Corporate Society* (New York: David McKay, 1972); Levin, "Educational Reform."

21. John E. Coons et al., *Private Wealth and Public Education* (Cambridge, Mass.: Harvard University Press, 1970).

22. U.S. Department of Health, Education, and Welfare, *Work in America* (Cambridge, Mass.: MIT Press, 1973).

23. Carole Pateman, *Participation and Democratic Theory* (New York: Cambridge University Press, 1970); Gerry Hunnius, David Garson, and John Case, eds., *Workers' Control: A Reader on Labor and Social Change* (New York: Vintage Books, 1973).

7

Henry M. Levin

Effects of Expenditure Increases on Educational Resource Allocation and Effectiveness

Can court-mandated edicts change deeply rooted social and political behavior? Such a question must surely haunt the historian who would review the record of school segregation following the 1954 *Brown* decision. In 1972 the schools of the nation were more highly stratified racially than in 1954, despite almost twenty years of litigation, moral suasion, and social agitation over the issue. In this chapter it will be argued that *Serrano* and similar suits aimed at equalizing educational opportunity will result in a similar fate with little change in the educational fortunes of those students for whom the equal protection "victories" were allegedly intended. Unless a redistribution of expenditures is accompanied by a substantial redistribution of decision-making authority, the educational outcomes and life chances of those who are the ostensible recipients of higher expenditures will hardly be affected. In short, without massive changes in the political structure of our society, the *Serrano* decision has all the earmarks of a bold and humanitarian gesture that will not produce the ultimate result that the court had in mind.[1]

For the last seventy years or so the schools have relied heavily on the local property tax for a major share of their support. Differences in the local property tax bases among geographic entities have resulted in substantially lower financial support for schools in some areas than others, and even assistance from state treasuries has not come close to equalizing expenditures among school districts. The result is that children who reside in property-tax-poor school districts have substantially less spent upon their schooling than those in richer districts; and paradoxically, the tax rates are often higher in the poor communities.[2] In essence, the California Supreme Court attacked this pattern in the *Serrano* decision by declaring that "this funding scheme insidiously discriminates against the poor because it makes the quality of a child's education a function of the wealth of his parents and neighbors."[3]

It is important to note that the court was concerned with the "quality of a child's education" and not expenditures per se. That is, the court operated on the tacit belief that a fairer system of educational support would lead to a more equal distribution of educational opportunities and outcomes. Thus *Serrano* and similar decisions can be approached at two levels: First, what kind of funding arrangement is consistent with the assertion of the court that the educational expenditures on a child should not be a function of the wealth of his parents and neighbors? And, second, what kind of administrative arrangement will translate increases in educational expenditures into concomitant improvements in the educational welfare of the intended beneficiaries?

Most of the responses to *Serrano* deal only with the first issue, equity in the distribution of expenditures and in the school tax system.[4] But *Serrano* and similar cases are ultimately concerned with a redistribution of educational opportunities among children, not just the redistribution of dollars among school districts. Accordingly, one should ask how the additional monies will be transformed into school services that will improve the educational and social outcomes for the target groups.

This chapter describes these linkages and scrutinizes their implications for increases in educational expenditures. First, I suggest what must be done to improve educational outcomes. Second, I review how the present structure for providing well educational services satisfies those requirements. Third, I explore a decision model and empirical evidence relating increased funding from higher levels of government to educational operations and outcomes. Finally, I describe policy conclusions from this analysis.

Linking Dollars and Schooling Outcomes

The necessary and sufficient conditions for school budgets to be transformed into improved educational results are indicated in figure 7.1, a simple flow diagram of the stages by which budgets are established and converted into educational resources and outcomes.[5] First, the polity determines through its governmental processes what budget will be provided for school purposes. In practice these decisions are made by the federal and state governments, and the thousands of local school districts or educational agencies that are responsible for existing funding arrangements. This diagram ignores such complexities by aggregating all of these decisions under the heading of a general polity.

Budgetary resources represent funding available for the general support of school services, but the monies themselves must be translated into specific resources that can be used in the schooling process. Thus, at the next stage the budget is used to pay for personnel services, facilities, instructional materials, and other educational resources. The marketplaces supply specific inputs— for teachers, administrators, special personnel, building and construction, and so on. Often these decisions are made in consultation with or through direct negotiations with the major personnel organizations; acting in behalf of their constituencies to influence employment levels, salaries, employee mobility, and other personnel policies.

The selected resources are combined into the schooling process to produce such outcomes as changes in attitudes, knowledge, reading and numerical proficiencies, values, and other aspects of student development. This process refers to the organization of

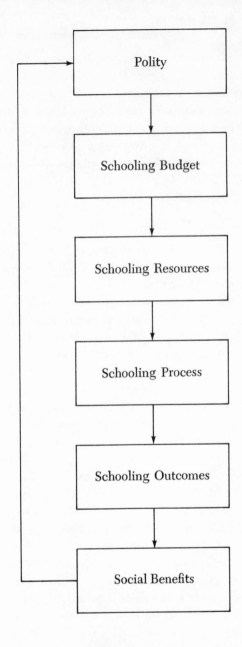

Figure 7.1

*Translating Expenditures into Educational Outcomes
and Social Benefits*

schools, classes, and personnel configurations, as well as to the methods (curriculum) by which resources are brought together to obtain educational results. In this phase, attempts to improve schooling productivity are made through changes in the ways resources are used as well as by increasing the amount of resources in the process.

The application of the resources in schooling results in a variety of outcomes, notably increases in knowledge and skills, which have been the object of extensive documentation through achievement testing. Schools also have an effect on the development of values and personality factors. For example, in our society the educational process heavily emphasizes extrinsic rewards, such as gold stars, social approval, and grades rather than internal satisfaction. The process socializes young people to be less concerned about the nature of the work that they are performing than the external rewards (grades, status, wages, pensions, vacations, and so on) they will obtain for performing it.[6] Such outcomes represent the less-discussed aspects of schools, but they represent outcomes nevertheless.

Society finds it worthwhile to invest in the educational process, not because of the educational outcomes per se but because it is believed that these results yield social benefits.[7] Accordingly, the last stage of the transformation is the translation of educational outcomes into social benefits. Outputs of the schools such as increased knowledge and reading scores are useful only to the degree that they improve the level of welfare of the individuals who have achieved these results or of the society generally. It is claimed that the schooling sector increases national income through enhancing the productivity of workers,[8] improving the functioning of democratic society by raising political literacy and understanding of complex issues,[9] increasing technological advance and cultural attainments through the discovery and encouragement of latent talent,[10] and so on.

In recent years the assumption that schools produce this wide range of social benefits has been seriously questioned.[11] The existence of the schools is justified on the basis of social benefits rather than schooling outcomes per se. Since the social benefits are often far removed in time and space from the schooling outcomes, it is difficult to evaluate the role of different school policies on them. Thus, our evaluations often analyze the observable effects of schools on immediately measurable outcomes, such as achievement tests, and we assume that these outcomes are ultimately translated into social benefits. The analysis that follows is also handicapped by the lack of knowledge on ultimate social effects, so I limit my scrutiny of budgetary effectiveness to schooling outcomes rather than their ultimate social benefits.

In summary, the schema suggests that additional funding will affect schooling outcomes by providing more or different resources that will enter the schooling process, and that these additional resources will result in improvements in schooling outcomes. Thus, an analysis of the effects of higher spending should raise at least three questions: (1) How will additional budget dollars be allocated? (2) What changes will these allocations make in the schooling process? (3) What changes in schooling outcomes will take place? Any effort to enhance school outcomes should be reflected in the responses to these questions.

Under what conditions are additional monies likely to be transformed into improved school outcomes? In the past it has always been assumed that school decision makers would make financial decisions that would normally improve the effectiveness of their educational programs, but recent research and evaluation on the subject have not upheld this assumption.[12] Since efforts to equalize the finances available to school districts would necessarily provide considerably more dollar support for low-wealth and high-cost jurisdictions, one might ask how this money will be allocated. More specifically, what assumptions are necessary for the state to expect that additional financial support will have a powerful effect on educational results?

The conditions under which educational expenditures will translate into improved educational outcomes are fairly stringent. First, there must be substantial agreement on which outcomes are important; second, there must be knowledge of how added resources can be used to improve those outcomes; and third, those who are responsible for the educational process must have incentives to maximize the socially desirable outcomes. In each case, the actual situation seems to contrast with the assumptions that are necessary for added dollars to improve educational results.[13]

There are many divergent views on what constitutes good education. While there is general agreement that basic skills such as reading and arithmetic are important, some citizens view the primary role of schools as that of providing discipline and order in the lives of children, stimulating competition, and increasing respect for authority in order to prepare youngsters for the world of work. Still other groups view the role of the schools as helping children to become aware of their values and needs, to learn how to learn, and to increase interactions with viewpoints and persons with whom they would normally not have contact in a society that is highly segregated, both socially and racially. To the degree that these goals are in conflict, decisions must be made that will favor one set of objectives over another.

Even if agreement could be reached on goals, there is no body of knowledge that would guide decision makers in converting additional resources into improved outcomes. For example, it is asserted that most supplementary educational funding for children from low-income families is applied to improving academic performances of such children, a view that will be challenged below.[14] Yet, even if we accept the improvement of reading scores as one of the prime objectives, there is no body of literature that can describe with any reliability how changes in the amounts and organizations of inputs will raise reading levels. There is not even evidence to support the contention that reducing class size will improve such outcomes, even though that is the most common application of additional schooling dollars.[15]

Finally, it is difficult to see any direct relationship between the incentives provided to those responsible for the educational process and such educational outcomes as improved reading scores. Personnel in schools that fail to teach basic skills or motivate their students are not penalized in any way. They receive salary increases and seniority according to their longevity in the system rather than according to their accomplishments. Accordingly they have little incentive to conform to the aims of external school constituencies. Indeed, the lack of incentives for improving schooling outcomes also explains why schools are reluctant to innovate and experiment to discover new approaches that are more effective than the older ones.

The Actual Decision-Making Framework

There is no agreement on educational priorities, no body of knowledge that can predict the effects of different school policies on educational outcomes, and no relation between staff incentives and the rhetorical goals of schools. This all suggests that school budgets are not likely to be translated efficiently into improved educational outcomes. Rather, the actual application of the increased support is likely to be determined by the power and interests of the decision makers themselves, and the factors determining these outcomes may be completely devoid of the educational concerns cited above.

It is useful, then, to review the decision-making scenario of the local educational agency (school district) with respect to the allocation of funds from higher levels of government. To see if the model we posit has good explanatory value, it is important to be able to apply it to an existing source of data. Accordingly, the following analysis refers to a model of decision making that can be applied specifically to the experience derived from Title I allocations under the Elementary and Secondary Education Act of 1965.[16] Under this Act appropriations were distributed to the states to provide supplemental educational support for the schooling of children from low-income backgrounds. The applications from local educational agencies for these funds, as well as the subsequent audits and evaluations, provide reasonably good knowledge of how the money was allocated and which groups benefited.

The Model The following model is designed to explain how local educational agencies spend money provided to them by state and federal governments. In this example, they are provided with an additional sum of money from state and federal sources to improve educational outcomes for disadvantaged children. We wish to raise several questions: Who are the major constituencies at the local level that have a strong interest in how the money is allocated? What are the goals of each of these constituencies? What is the relative power of each group, and what kinds of coalitions seem probable? Finally, what is the likely outcome of this scenario? That is, which goals are actually attained and which are sacrificed?[17]

Table 7.1 attempts to provide a heuristic approach to answering these questions. Six major constituencies are denoted, and

Table 7.1

*Local Constituencies and the Decision for Allocating
Increased Revenues from State or Federal Government*

Constituency	Goal	Power	Coalition	Outcome
1. Local taxpayer	Minimize local burden	Moderate	With 4	Substitution of outside money for local
2. Disadvantaged parent	Improve educational outcomes for dis-advantaged children	Low	No	No change
3. Disadvantaged student	Improve educational environment	Low	No	No change
4. School board	Minimize conflict	High	With 1 and 6	Low conflict
5. Teachers	Increase employment and job benefits	High	With 6	More employment
6. Administrators	Increase employment and minimize conflict	High	With 4 and 5	More employment low conflict

their goals, relative power, and abilities to form coalitions are posited. In each case, constituency refers to a group with a common interest. This does not mean that every member of a group shares this interest—that is, there are many diverse views represented within a particular constituency—but if that group exhibits a consistent behavior that obscures these underlying diversities, then we assume that the consistencies adequately summarize the behavior of the group.

Constituencies, Goals, and Power   The six major constituencies in our model include: (1) local taxpayers; (2) parents of disadvantaged students; (3) disadvantaged students; (4) the school board; (5) teachers; and (6) administrators (see table 7.1). Each of these groups has a legitimate interest in the allocation of revenues designated for the schooling of disadvantaged students.

1. Local taxpayers.   The local taxpayers have an interest in transferring to higher levels of government as much of the responsibility as possible for a function that might otherwise be provided, partly or fully, by local revenue sources. In particular, it is in the interest of local taxpayers to reduce or minimize the local tax burden for any particular level of educational services. To the degree that state and federal monies might be used for services that would otherwise be supported by the local taxpayers, this goal can be satisfied. For example, if funds for the education of the disadvantaged simply supplant funds that would have been allocated to such students, then the burden of the local taxpayer for supporting such services has been reduced. This goal has become especially important in recent years in light of highly visible and substantial rises in property tax burdens, the major source of local school support.

Although the goal of local taxpayers can be viewed reasonably as that of minimizing their tax burden, their power to effect that outcome is only moderate in the sense that they are not a direct party to the allocation decision. Instead, the elected or appointed school board must do their bidding. Not only is the taxpayer somewhat removed from the actual decision negotiations but the sanction of electing different school board members or recalling the present ones is not very powerful because taxes are just one of many issues in school board elections.

2. *Disadvantaged parents.* Parents of disadvantaged students represent a second constituency that has a direct interest in the allocation of state and federal funds for schooling disadvantaged youngsters. It seems reasonable to assume that their principal concerns are addressed to improving educational outcomes for their children, particularly proficiencies on standardized tests, and reducing the probabilities that their children will drop out. This goal derives from the widespread belief that these educational outcomes are related to economic and social success in the world at large; and if disadvantaged students are to raise their status, they must improve their educational attainments.

But the parents of disadvantaged students are themselves disadvantaged with regard to political and economic power; and they are not a first party to the allocation decision either. If taxpayers as a group lack substantial power in the allocation decision, the disadvantaged parent constituency is almost outside of the influence arena completely. They are not highly organized; they usually represent only a minority of the population; and for a variety of reasons (of which one is their own low educational attainment) their vote is disproportionately small even in relation to their numbers. Often they are represented by school boards who are elected at large, and they are very unlikely to win a majority of proponents under such conditions. Accordingly, they have little if any power to affect the allocation decision.

3. *Disadvantaged student.* The disadvantaged student is central—in theory—to the decision to allocate increased revenues to his education. Although his parents are more likely concerned with the end results of the educational process, he is likely to be more concerned with the process itself. Silberman characterized the schools as "grim joyless places. . . . How oppressive and petty are the rules by which they are governed, how intellectually sterile and esthetically barren the atmosphere, what an appalling lack of civility obtains on the part of teachers and principals, what contempt they unconsciously display for children as children."[18] Although Silberman viewed this description as characterizing most schools, its most poignant aspects seem to be

especially applicable to schools attended by youngsters from low-income families, especially those drawn from minority backgrounds. For many, if not most, of these children, schools are just not very enjoyable places to be, and this fact is reflected in the lower attendance rates for such children as well as higher dropout statistics.

What power do disadvantaged students have to get funds channeled toward improving the educational environment? In most respects they are in the same relatively powerless position as their parents, only they are disenfranchised as well. Indeed, their only sanctions are those of cutting school, dropping out, disruption, and vandalism; and these actions can often lead to greater repression in the schools' never-ending quest to maintain control.

4. *School board.* In theory it is the school board that is responsible for making the decision for allocating increased revenues from state and federal goverments to the schooling of disadvantaged youngsters. That is, the school board represents the legally sanctioned arm of the state for governing the local school district. But school boards are beset by many conflicting pressures and a substantial amount of administrative trivia without the resources and information to perceive clearly the educational implications of their decisions.[19] The immediate pressures are on the resolution of existing conflicts and claims among a variety of parent groups, taxpayer groups, employee groups, and various educational agencies, while they attempt to ameliorate future conflicts. Indeed, it appears that the principal goal of the school board is to minimize conflict, because the avoidance of obvious clashes implies a high degree of control and competence in guiding the rudder of school policy.[20]

The school board has a substantial amount of power to avoid or minimize conflict on allocation matters. It can limit the items that appear on the agenda; it can refer potential problems to the bureaucracy to resolve; it can fail to provide information on school performance to the public when such information is likely to spur a controversy; it can be "selective" in determining whether parent complainants truly represent the interests of the segments of the community that they claim to;[21] and most of all it can ratify agreements worked out between the other two powerful constituencies—the teachers and administrators.

In addition, the school board is a first party to the allocation decision and can insulate its pronouncements from public criticism by claiming special expertise on the budgetary questions (even though most school boards are completely dependent on the school administrators for "interpretations," "explanations," and "rationale" for budgetary allocations).

5. *Teachers.* The teachers represent both the easiest and most difficult constituency to characterize. They are easy to characterize because their priorities have been asserted loudly and consistently over time in both their public pronouncements and in their negotiations with the school boards. Specifically, the goal of the teacher organizations has been to increase the employment and job benefits of teachers through reductions in average class size, increases in remedial specialists, extra pay for planning time, narrowing the scope of normal duties to increase the number of tasks that require extra remuneration, and so on.[22] These concessions represent top priorities in the bargaining packages of teacher organizations, and they also represent the crucial portions of the recommendations for "educational quality" that are advocated by the state and national teacher associations and unions.

The goal of the teachers appears to be to allocate increased revenues for the schooling of disadvantaged children to increased employment and job benefits for teachers. Of course, such strategies are couched in the terminology of raising educational quality, but this claim requires supportive empirical evidence rather than rhetorical justification.

Teachers' interests are not always easy to characterize. Probably no other group shares such a wide diversity of individual viewpoints about how the schooling of the disadvantaged might be improved. Certainly, informal discussions with individual teachers indicate that many thoughtful teachers do not feel increases in personnel and benefits per se will make much difference in educational outcomes for children.[23] But as long as

teacher organizations push so hard for the "teacher benefits" solution to spending additional money, this diversity of viewpoints
is obscured by the overall behavior of the group.

The teacher group has a powerful influence on the decision for
allocating additional revenues for the schooling of the disadvantaged. First, they represent a first party to the decision by virtue
of their ability to negotiate directly with the school board on how
additional funds will be spent. Second, they have many sanctions
at their disposal including subtle acts of noncooperation; the
refusal to perform what they might define arbitrarily as duties
that require additional remuneration; and the ultimate sanction,
the strike. They also have heavy support for their position at the
state levels where legislatures have shown a willingness to support the special pleadings of the educational professionals for
laws that require added personnel.[24]

6. *Administrators.* The last constituency in the model is the
school administrators. In theory, they serve the role of carrying
out the policies established by the school board. Conceptually
the school board sets educational policy, and the administrators
manage the schools in a manner consistent with those guidelines.
In fact, studies of school boards and administrators have suggested that the reverse is often the case—the school board is
charged with processing minutia while the administrators set
policy by their daily actions.[25]

Administrators appear to have two goals with regard to the
expenditure of additional state and federal revenues for schooling
disadvantaged children. First, the school board has the authority
to reward and sanction administrators, meaning that there will
be a desire to pursue the school board's objective of minimizing
conflict. To the degree that administrators can defuse potential
conflict situations that might arise in allocating additional funding, they have spared the school board such anguish, and school
boards will look favorably on administrators who prevent such
conflicts from emerging at the school board level. Second, administrator status and mobility is closely tied to the size and
financial magnitude of the organization that he is administering.
In large measure, the remuneration of principals, superintendents, and other administrators is linked to the number of

employees whom they supervise and the salaries of their subordinates. Increases in the numbers and salaries of teachers and
other employees will tend to push up the salaries of administrators.

Accordingly it is reasonable to believe that administrators
would wish to allocate such compensatory funds to increasing
employment and job benefits for school district employees generally, while attempting to minimize conflict over the decision.
School administrators, too, appear to be in an especially powerful
position to effect their goals. They are a first party to the allocation decision by virtue of their role as the bargaining agent for
the school board, and they can make recommendations that favor
their own interests under the guise of "professional" negotiations.
That is, like the teachers, they can clothe their own motives in the
rhetoric of educational improvement, and the school board and
second-party constituencies have neither the resources, the information, nor the professional status to challenge them.

Coalitions and Outcomes   Obviously, policy outcomes cannot
be predicted from this information unless the possibilities of coalitions among constituencies are considered. The most likely coalitions appear to be the following. The school board has an interest
in keeping the local taxpayer quiescent while minimizing conflict. Any change in tax burdens is highly visible, and taxpayers
tend to be a very vocal group, so the school board will wish to
maintain the existing tax burden or even be prone to using
"outside" money to support services that would otherwise be
provided by local funds so as not to increase the strain on local
taxpayers. Likewise the school board and the administrators have
common interests in minimizing conflict. Accordingly, the school
board would appear to coalesce most closely with the administrators and the local taxpayers.

Teachers' and administrators' goals often overlap. Both groups
benefit from increased employment and higher job benefits. The
traditional view is that teachers and administrators sit on opposite
sides of the bargaining table; but both have a common set of
incentives on the major issue of how to allocate additional school
revenues, and the administrators are constrained in their conces-

sions only by the requirement of minimizing conflict (which means that they must avoid increases in the tax burden if at all possible).[26] No possible coalitions appear to exist for disadvantaged parents and students, either with each other or with other constituencies.

The policy outcomes predicted by this model are straightforward. There would be a tendency to use state and federal funds to supplant local tax support for the provision of school services. That is, outside money would be used, in part, to reduce the local tax burden for school programs that would have been offered even in the absence of such external funding.

Because the administrator-teacher coalition is strong, almost all the external funding would be devoted to benefits for teachers and administrators rather than to disadvantaged children. The revenues would be devoted to increased employment and job benefits for educational professionals, and the decision would be one based on their interests. That is, there would be little evidence that this decision derived from a thoughtful and extensive plan to improve the education of disadvantaged youngsters, even though these allocations would be rationalized on their alleged contribution to the welfare of disadvantaged children rather than to advantaged adults.

This solution would also satisfy the school board's need to minimize conflict. The generous treatment of the local taxpayer would keep him quiescent, while the decision would be closed off effectively to other "outside" constituencies. Finally, the model suggests that it is unlikely that the educational environment or educational outcomes for disadvantaged children will improve unless the increases in employment and employee benefits can themselves effect such changes. As noted, this possibility is subject to empirical verification, and we should not assume, a priori, that benefits that improve the status of professional educators are necessarily the same as those that improve the status of disadvantaged youngsters.

In summary, the following groups would be most likely to benefit from additional state and federal revenues for schooling the disadvantaged: teachers, administrators, school boards, and local taxpayers. The groups that would not appear to benefit are the disadvantaged students and their parents.

Is the Model Predictive? The model presented here can be compared with the actual experience encountered under Title I or the Elementary and Secondary Education Act of 1965. Under this legislation the federal government has been providing about $1.1 billion a year to the states to distribute to school districts to provide additional educational services for children from low-income families. In applying for the money, local school districts were required to state the purposes and design of their Title I programs, and they were required to evaluate the results of their efforts. Thus, we can assume that the school districts understood well the focus of the program, and we can accept at face value the goals that they claimed they were attempting to achieve: for example, increasing reading proficiencies.

During the last seven years, approximately $8 billion has been allocated to Title I programs, and the results of these programs have been summarized in the form of local, state, and national evaluations as well as "special" studies on specific aspects of the Title I experience.[27] Accordingly, there is substantial information that can be drawn upon for testing the predictive power of our model for describing local expenditure allocations of Title I funds. A review of that literature suggests: (1) Title I funds were commonly used to supplant the use of local monies rather than to supplement them as the law intended; (2) most of the Title I funds went toward larger and better paid staffs; (3) there was very little conflict over the local utilization of Title I monies since the information dissemination and community participation provisions of the law were consistently violated by local educational agencies, and the decisions were made by the professionals themselves; and (4) extensive evaluations of Title I programs have found that on the average there were no changes in educational outcomes for disadvantaged children. The next paragraphs take up these points one by one.

1. An extensive analysis and audit of Title I expenditures found that Title I revenues have been commonly used by local school districts to supplant state and locally raised revenues so that the latter could be reallocated to nondisadvantaged children or to tax relief.[28]   Although such use violates the guidelines for the Title I program, the infractions were so common that in 1970 the Department of Health, Education, and Welfare convened a task force whose efforts were devoted largely to setting out a monitoring and enforcement system that would prevent such supplantation. Even with the advent of a new reporting system and threats to cut off Title I aid if such funds were substituted for state and local support, there is every indication that supplantation continues to be a serious problem.[29]

2. *The available data suggest that about 90 percent of Title I funds spent in recent years have been allotted to personnel benefits.*[30]   The principal expenditure strategies have been those of reductions in class size; the hiring of more supervisory and remedial specialists; the employment of more administrators, evaluators, curriculum specialists, teaching aides, and consultants; and the provision of extra pay for "planning" time and other duties that are considered to be a part of the program. The schools allocated almost as much Title I support to truant officers and other attendance services as they did to health services for disadvantaged children, even though children from low-income backgrounds are likely to suffer from a large variety of untreated health problems that will surely affect their educational proficiencies.[31]

3. *Very little overt conflict emerged over the allocation of Title I funds.*   Spending decisions were generally made in a closed setting among the educational personnel and school boards without the involvement of groups from the communities whose schools were allegedly to be the recipients of Title I expenditures. Again, the enacting legislation and Title I regulations were violated; since they stipulated that "to encourage intelligent involvement, regulations require that terms and provisions of each project be made available for public inspection"; that appropriate vehicles for community involvement be established by school systems, such as Title I advisory committees; and that at least half of the members on such committees be representatives of the poor community.[32] In contrast, The National Advisory

Council on the Education of Disadvantaged Children found that out of 116 programs observed by its consultants, only 2 reflected an attempt to involve parents.[33] In the extensive study of Title I carried out by the Washington Research Project, the authors reported:

> Most school officials whom we interviewed indicated that decisions concerning the needs of children and the allocation of funds were made by a few school personnel with little or no consultation with poor white, black, or brown people.[34]

Even where such advisory committees existed it was found that they were often improperly constituted and in some cases were composed entirely of school personnel.[35] Moreover, they were normally used to "rubber stamp" the proposals drawn up by school officials.[36] Finally, it was found that many parents and community leaders were unaware of the Title I projects in their schools and that citizen requests for information were commonly denied.[37] In short, school boards and administrators have tended to minimize conflict over the allocation of Title I monies by closing off the decision and withholding information about Title I from persons outside of their closely guarded province.[38]

Such behavior on the part of the school boards and administrators is in violation of the law, but enforcement of both the spirit and the letter of this regulation is very difficult. The Title I Task Force that was convened by the Department of Health, Education, and Welfare in 1970 placed a top priority on increasing the community involvement component of Title I. Unfortunately, it appears that these regulations continue to be violated.

4. *Extensive evaluations of Title I programs have found that on the average there were no changes in cognitive educational outcomes for disadvantaged children.* Title I regulations require that all projects be evaluated at the end of each school year, and the results of such evaluations are to be sent to the state. The states are required to review these evaluations for their annual reports, and the Office of Education then studies both the state reports and selected reports from school districts (particularly

those districts who report "substantial successes" and the very large school districts). In addition, several overall evaluations have been undertaken by the U.S. Office of Education in order to characterize the national performance of Title I programs and to select exemplary programs.

Unfortunately, the sum total of all of these evaluations seems to be that few of the benefits of Title I expenditures are received by disadvantaged children. Since most of the programs concentrated on reading skills, it is useful to examine the effect of Title I funds on that outcome. In evaluating the 1966–67 and 1967–68 reading programs funded under the Act, the U.S. Office of Education concluded that on the basis of reading test scores, "a child who participated in a Title I project had only a 19 percent chance of a significant achievement gain, a 13 percent chance of a significant achievement loss, and a 68 percent chance of no change at all (relative to the national norms)."[39] Further, the projects included in the investigation were "most likely to be representative of projects in which there was a higher than average investment in resources. Therefore, more significant achievement gains should be found here than in a more representative sample of Title I projects."[40]

The inability of Title I funds to create even a nominal direct effect on reading test scores for children appears to be endemic. Among many thousands of Title I project evaluations and a few other compensatory programs, the U.S. Office of Education selected the 1,000 most promising for purposes of further scrutiny by an independent research contractor. Of these, only 21 seemed to have shown sufficient evidence of significant pupil achievement gains in language or numerical skills.[41] Not only are these results discouraging in themselves, but they also reflect the evaluation bias evident in reports on compensatory education when the persons who are responsible for the program are asked to evaluate their own results. The evaluation claims are rarely supported by the evidence.

The U.S. Office of Education recently commissioned a study that reviewed all the representative data on educational effects of Title I as well as compensatory education projects that had been identified as "exemplary."[42] Based on the data obtained from Title I projects through 1970, this study could find no evidence that states were closing the achievement gap between advantaged and disadvantaged children.[43] Yet, because some individual projects had reported such successes, an attempt was made to scrutinize more closely the specific evaluations of those projects. Of some 1750 projects that were identified as appearing to meet the criteria of success in improving the cognitive functioning of disadvantaged children, only 41 (or 2.3 percent) were found to be successful when evaluated in a systematic way.[44] Of these, only half appeared to be supported by Title I funds; yet each year about 11,000 school districts have been receiving money under the program.

In summary, although there is a great deal of evidence that Title I money has helped the local taxpayer and school-district employees, there is little evidence that it has substantially improved the educational outcomes for disadvantaged children. Moreover, the political model used to explain the allocation decision suggests that without substantial realignments of political constituencies and decision-making structures, the same outcomes can be predicted for the future. Stated more strongly, educational personnel will *always* benefit from the expenditure of additional money on the schooling of disadvantaged youngsters, but only *rarely* will the children themselves benefit.

Serrano and the Effects of Increased Funds   In the preceding section a model of local allocation of state and federal revenues for schooling the disadvantaged was posited, and applied to the evidence provided by the Title I experience. But how applicable is this model of local decision making to increases in school-district expenditures generated by the *Serrano* decision? Since the proposed fiscal responses to *Serrano* and similar decisions would have their major effects on increasing spending in the most impoverished school districts and those educating high proportions of disadvantaged students, the previous analysis is directly applicable to the *Serrano* situation.[45]

As long as the present governing structures and political alignments prevail at the local level, increases in spending are unlikely to have much of an effect on improving the relative educational standing of children residing in the districts that will receive increased allocations from the state. In contrast, the additional funds will have a powerful effect on employment and benefits for school district personnel. In both cases the educational interests of disadvantaged children will be forced to compete with the employment and financial interests of middle-class educational professionals, and the latter group will prevail. Paradoxically, a social reform carried out in the name of increasing opportunity for the poor will have its principal effect in improving the opportunities of middle-class educators.

Although this conclusion is consistent with that of statistical studies that find little or no relationship between resource inputs and educational outcomes, there is a distinct difference in the implications that arise. The statistical studies suggest that educational outcomes for disadvantaged children have not been shown to be sensitive to variations in resources;[46] therefore, increasing expenditures on the schooling of disadvantaged children is not likely to raise educational proficiencies. Unfortunately, the methodology underlying these studies assumes tacitly that school districts are attempting to maximize the educational performances of disadvantaged youngsters, but regardless of their efforts the effects are minimal.[47] In contrast, the theory propounded here suggests that school districts are not attempting to maximize the educational status of disadvantaged students; rather, the resources that are allotted for such purposes are being used to maximize the status and employment of educational personnel while being packaged in the rhetoric of helping children.[48]

In short, the failure of additional funding to improve educational outcomes is not a technical failure of the schooling process as much as it is a technical by-product of the political process. This diagnosis is consistent with the view that so-called compensatory education has not failed; it has never been tried. Nor is it likely to be tried. Only a movement at the state level to change the governing structure of school districts so that the parents of the educationally disadvantaged and the students themselves will have a greater share of decision-making power is likely to move funds in an educationally productive direction for lower-class students.[49] But increasing the relative power of the less-advantaged groups of our society has never been a high-priority item in the political arena, particularly when such an action would conflict with the interests of a well-organized middle-class cadre.[50]

The power of the educational professionals can be illustrated by the fact that it took four years of effort for the California legislature to pass a rather timid enabling act to permit an OEO experiment for testing educational vouchers within the state. That is, one of the reasons for rejecting even a modest experiment financed by federal funds has been the implication that it will improve the relative power of the disadvantaged in making decisions about their schooling.[51] Moreover, the ability of the organizations representing the educational personnel to influence legislation is reflected in the December 1972 passage in California of Senate Bill (SB) 90, which would double minimum expenditure levels guaranteed by the state with no changes in the mechanism by which local allocation decisions would be made. (SB 90 raises the guaranteed support from $355 to $765 for each child in elementary grades and from $488 to $950 per student in high schools.) SB 90 was known as the educational lobby's version of school finance reform, and no attempt was made to exact a quid pro quo that might assure children educational benefits from the expenditure increases.

The power of the school personnel lobby to write its own legislative ticket is likely to rise over time. Although in the late 1960s the power of the educators seemed to be at an ebb, there was an enormous resurgence of political energy and success in 1972 as the educational organizations adopted a new political style. Although "teachers tended to be discreet in their political action avoiding overt electoral activities and maintaining their independence from political parties and action groups," times have changed.[52] In the 1972 elections the political arm of the California Teachers Association (the Association for Better Citizenship, or ABC) gave campaign contributions to fifty-four assembly candidates and seventeen state senate candidates.[53] More surprising is that thirty of the seventy-one candidates received contributions of between $500 and $8,000, very hefty amounts in state electoral races. Also surprising was that apparently the ABC was the most generous contributor among all of the political interest groups. In fact, the group that appeared to be second in its generosity, the real estate interests, showed average contributions only half the size of those of the ABC.

A Personal Postscript   The model and data presented in this chapter suggest that spending increases will have a much greater effect on the economic status and employment of educational professionals than they will have on the educational proficiencies of children. Although a fairer distribution of educational expenditures among school districts is a necessary condition for a fairer distribution of educational outcomes among children, it is not a sufficient condition. The sufficient condition requires that the additional revenues be devoted to the needs of children rather than those of school-district employees, and that condition is violated by the present political institutions.

Yet I have supported the *Serrano* principle, and I will continue to do so for two reasons. First, although *Serrano*-generated spending increases are not likely, on balance, to improve the relative educational standing of the children for whom they were intended, they will have a positive effect in a few isolated instances; specifically, the most impoverished districts may be able in some degree to improve the quality of the school environment in a way that will at least make their schools more pleasant places to be. Second, it seems absurd to refuse to more nearly equalize the educational investment allocated to disadvantaged children simply because they and their families lack the power to assure that such funds will be allocated to improving their educational status. On moral grounds I believe we would be derelict to use the political model as grounds for systematically providing less educational support for the disadvantaged than for the advantaged. Thus I feel obligated to support the *Serrano* principle, even though I am not optimistic about the educational or social outcomes.

Perhaps it is useful once again to draw a parallel with the 1954 *Brown* decision. Even though it has not produced the extensive school desegregation that many of its proponents hoped for, it is still based upon a loftier principle than the "separate but equal doctrine" of *Plessy* v. *Ferguson*.[54] With all of the disappointments of the *Brown* aftermath, I still think it was the correct path. Today we stand at another crossroad. The *Serrano* decision is also based upon a sound moral principle; and even if it fails to deliver the goods, it is important to support the tenet for its own sake rather than the doctrine represented by the existing methods of financing the schools.[55]

Notes

1. For a discussion of the limits of the courts, see Alexander M. Bickel, *The Supreme Court and the Idea of Progress* (New York: Harper & Row, 1970); and Philip B. Kurland, "Equal Educational Opportunity, or the Limits of Constitutional Jurisprudence Undefined," in *The Quality of Inequality: Urban and Suburban Public Schools*, ed. Charles U. Daly (Chicago: University of Chicago Press, 1968), pp. 47–72.

2. See John E. Coons, William H. Clune III, and Stephen D. Sugarman, *Private Wealth and Public Education* (Cambridge, Mass.: Harvard University Press, 1970).

3. *Serano* v. *Priest*, 5 Cal. 3d 584, 487 P. 2d 1241 (1971).

4. For example, see Citizens Commission of Maryland Government, "A Responsible Plan for the Financing, Governance and Evaluation of Maryland's Schools" (Baltimore, 1971); *Report of the New York State Commission on the Quality, Cost and Financing of Elementary and Secondary Education* (New York, 1972), vol. 1, chap. 2; and Charles S. Benson et al., *Final Report to the [California] Senate Select Committee on School District Finance*, vol. 1 (Sacramento, 1972).

5. This process is described in greater detail in Henry M. Levin, "The Effect of Different Levels of Expenditure on Educational Output," in R. L. Johns et al., *Economic Factors Affecting the Financing of Education* (Gainesville, Fla.: National Educational Finance Project, 1971), chap. 6.

6. See Herbert Gintis, "Education, Technology and the Character-

istics of Worker Productivity," *American Economic Review* 61 (May 1971): 266–79.

7. I refer to education in an industrialized and Western context. In other cultures education is considered a way of life. See Carlos Castañeda, *The Teachings of Don Juan* (New York: Ballantine, 1968).

8. Gary S. Becker, *Human Capital* (New York: Columbia University Press, 1964).

9. For an example, see Angus Campbell, Phillip Converse, Warren Miller, and Donald Stokes, *The American Voter* (New York: Wiley, 1960), p. 491.

10. Howard R. Bowen, "Finance and the Aims of American Higher Education," in *Financing Higher Education: Alternatives for the Federal Government*, ed. M. D. Orweg (Iowa City: American College Testing Service, 1971), pp. 155–70.

11. Compare the criticisms in Ivan Illich, *Deschooling Society* (New York: Harper & Row, 1971); Herbert Gintis, "Toward a Political Economy of Education," *Harvard Educational Review* 42 (February 1972): 70–96; and Christopher Jencks et al., *Inequality: A Reassessment of the Effect of Family Schooling in America* (New York: Basic Books, 1972).

12. See the recent review in Harvey Averch, Stephen Carroll, Theodore Donaldson, Herbert Kiesling, and John Pincus, *How Effective Is Schooling? A Critical Review and Synthesis of Research Findings*, R-956-PCSF (Santa Monica: Rand Corporation, 1972).

13. An extensive exploration of these issues is found in Henry M. Levin, "Concepts of Economic Efficiency and Educational Production" (Paper presented at the Conference on Education as an Industry, National Bureau of Economic Research, June 1971). These contradictions are also evident in the movement for "educational accountability." See Henry M. Levin, "A Conceptual Framework for Accountability in Education" (Report Prepared for the Task Force on Accountability and Performance Reporting of the National Academy of Education, Occasional Paper in the Economics and Politics of Education 72-10, School of Education, Stanford University, September 1972).

14. See the summary of data in Michael J. Wargo, Kasten Tallmadge, Debbra D. Michaels, Dewey Lipe, and Sarah J. Morris, "ESEA Title I: A Re-Analysis and Synthesis of Evaluation Data from Fiscal Year 1965 through 1970" (Palo Alto: American Institutes for Research, March 1972), pp. 144–64.

15. Refer to the critical survey of school effectiveness in Averch et al., *How Effective Is Schooling?*

16. For a critical survey of the act, see Stephen K. Bailey and Edith K. Mosher, *ESEA: The Office of Education Administers a Law* (Syracuse: Syracuse University Press, 1968).

17. A more general analysis of the political relationships is found in Frederick M. Wirt and Michael W. Kirst, *The Political Web of American Schools* (Boston: Little, Brown, 1972).

18. Charles Silberman, *Crisis in the Classroom* (New York: Random House, 1970), p. 10.

19. See David Minar, "Educational Decision Making in Suburban Communities," in *The Politics of Education*, ed. M. W. Kirst (Berkeley: McCutchan, 1970), pp. 167–83.

20. See M. Kent Jennings and Harmon Zeigler, "Interest Representation in School Governance" (Paper delivered at the 1970 meetings of the American Political Science Association, Los Angeles, 1970); and Wirt and Kirst, *Political Web of American Schools*, pp. 79–84.

21. Robert F. Lyke, "Representation and Urban School Boards," in *Community Control of Schools*, ed. H. M. Levin (Washington: Brookings Institution, 1970), pp. 138–68.

22. For example, the program that has been heavily promoted by the American Federation of Teachers, the so-called More Effective Schools (MES), would drastically decrease class size and provide backup teachers and additional professionals. In New York City the MES program translates into a doubling or more of "normal" per pupil expenditures.

23. That is, it is likely that strategies to improve educational outcomes for disadvantaged children would necessitate the hiring of additional personnel. Yet, in that case, it is the planning and program that would emerge first and the personnel needs that would follow. In the present instance it appears that the personnel demands emerge first, and the program always seems to be an afterthought that is asserted in order to rationalize the higher employment and benefits.

24. James Koerner, *Who Controls American Education?* (Boston: Beacon Press, 1968).

25. Wirt and Kirst, *Political Web of American Schools*, pp. 85–88.

26. And the school board is often willing to legitimate the agreement to avoid further conflict. For a provocative view, see Norman D. Kerr, "The School Board as an Agency of Legitimation," *Sociology of Education* 38 (1964): 34–59.

27. The Department of Health, Education, and Welfare issues an annual report on Title I, and the state departments of education publish annual state reports. For special studies, see Wargo et al., "ESEA Title I"; and Ruby Martin and Phyllis McClure, *Title I of ESEA: Is It Helping Poor Children?* (Washington, D.C.: Washington Research Project and NAACP Legal Defense and Educational Fund, 1969).

28. Martin and McClure, *Title I of ESEA*, chap. 3.

29. Lawyers' Committee for Civil Rights Under Law, *Title I Comparability: A Preliminary Evaluation* (Washington, D.C., Septem-

ber 1972); U.S. Department of Health, Education and Welfare, "Comparability Task Force Analysis of Fiscal Year 1973 Comparability Reports and Corrective Action Plans for a Nationally Stratified Random Sample of Local Educational Agencies," November 6, 1972 (draft); Joel S. Berke, Stephen K. Bailey, Alan K. Campbell, and Seymour Sacks, *Federal Aid to Public Education: Who Benefits?* (Syracuse: Syracuse University Research Corporation, 1971).

30. Based upon calculations in M. Wargo et al., "ESEA Title I," table 6.2, p. 121. Exact breakdowns of personnel allocations are not available. Accordingly, they were estimated from the budgetary components presented in the Title I summaries. The budgetary categories are not necessarily descriptive of their functions. For example, the category "fixed charges" in the Title I allocations is almost exclusively devoted to employee retirement expenses, a personnel allotment.

31. This is another example of expenditures being allocated to functions that help teachers and administrators rather than students. The implications for educational opportunity are explored in Henry M. Levin, "Equal Educational Opportunity and the Distribution of Educational Expenditures," *Education and Urban Society* 5 (February 1973): 149–76.

32. See the documents cited in M. Wargo et al., "ESEA Title I," pp. 51–52.

33. Cited in Martin and McClure, *Title I of ESEA*, p. 69.

34. Ibid., p. 70.

35. Ibid., p. 73.

36. Ibid.

37. Ibid., pp. 75–79.

38. Michael Kirst has pointed out to me that in recent years there has been an increasing tendency for a portion of Title I to be allocated to teacher aides and other personnel hired from the community. This strategy reduces the concern of the community regarding the larger set of allocations and educational effects of the program by rewarding a small number of potentially vocal elements of the poor community with "paraprofessional" employment. This not only ameliorates criticism cheaply but also implicates the community in any educational failures of the programs. The total employment effect for poor communities is miniscule relative to the magnitudes of the school expenditures.

39. Harry Picariello, "Evaluation of Title I" (Washington, D.C., U.S. Office of Education, Office of Program Planning and Evaluation, 1969), p. 1. Mimeographed.

40. Ibid.

41. David G. Hawkridge, Albert B. Chalupsky, and A. Oscar H. Roberts, "A Study of Selected Exemplary Programs for the Education of Disadvantaged Children," Parts I and II, Final Report, Project No.

08-9013 for the U.S. Office of Education (Palo Alto: American Institutes for Research, 1968).

42. M. Wargo et al., "ESEA Title I."

43. Ibid., pp. 174–79.

44. Ibid., pp. 179–80.

45. See, for example, Benson et al., *Final Report*; and *Report of the New York State Commission.*

46. Averch et al., *How Effective Is Schooling?*

47. Such an assumption has no factual basis, but it follows from the "theory of the firm" of conventional neoclassical economics in combination with a liberal ideology. See Levin, "Concepts of Economic Efficiency," for a discussion of the maximization principle in education. See William Behn, "Social Reality and Education" (Occasional Paper in the Economics and Politics of Education, Stanford University, 1973), for a discussion of ideology and its crucial role in determining the acceptability of assumptions about the world.

48. An outstanding discussion of the conceptual approach to evaluating the "true" resources being allocated toward such educational objectives as academic achievement is found in Stephan Michelson, "The Association of Teacher Resources with Children's Characteristics," in *Do Teachers Make a Difference?* (Washington, D.C.: U.S. Office of Education, OE-58042, 1970), chap. 6.

49. See, for example, Henry M. Levin and Robert Singleton, "Equalizing Educational Opportunity and the Legislative Response to Serrano" (unpublished, 1972); and Henry M. Levin, ed., *Community Control of Schools* (Washington, D.C.: Brookings Institution, 1970).

50. In this sense the present power alignment is functional and corresponds to the larger economic, social, and political system of which it is a part. See Martin Carnoy, ed., *Schooling in a Corporate Society* (New York: David McKay, 1972), particularly Samuel Bowles, "Unequal Education and the Reproduction of the Social Division of Labor."

51. For a description of the experiment, see Center for the Study of Public Policy, *Education Vouchers: A Report on Financing Elementary Education by Grants to Parents* (Cambridge, Mass.: The Center, December 1970). The authorizing legislation as finally passed in 1973 provides for a district-level teacher organization veto over the participation of private schools in any voucher experiment.

52. Robert D. Hess and Michael W. Kirst, "Political Orientations and Behavior Patterns: Linkages Between Teachers and Children," *Education and Urban Society*, August 1971, pp. 453–77.

53. Doug Willis, "Teacher, Realtors, Insurance Firms Spend Big to Get Their Men Elected," Palo Alto *Times*, 21 October 1972, p. 1.

54. Surely the *Brown* decision did have an effect on the patterns

of school enrollment in the South, and this should not be ignored. See F. Wirt and M. Kirst, *Political Web of American Schools*, chap. 9.

55. As long as the present provision of unequal educational attainments by race and social class corresponds to the social control hierarchy, the educational system is truly functional. Since there is no contradiction between the educational subsystem and the larger social system, it is unlikely that any court mandate can produce a more equal effect with regard to educational outcomes that ultimately relate to the larger social outcomes. See H. Gintis, "Toward a Political Economy of Education."

8

Martin Carnoy

Is Compensatory Education Possible?

The social purpose of schooling can be defined in a number of
ways. Schooling can be viewed primarily as a place to train
workers for the labor market of the nation or community. In that
context, formal schools would teach the basic knowledge for
further specialized training. They would also instill the discipline
and the cooperative attitudes necessary for a trained labor force.
Social roles of children attending school would be associated with
the vocations for which the children were being trained. Early in
their school careers students would be grouped according to
ability and molded into social and economic roles that would fit
their abilities to society's "needs."

Although this is not exactly the theoretical basis for European
education, in practice it functions quite closely to this model. In
European state-capitalist countries such as the Soviet Union,
schooling is even more closely associated with future vocation
than it is in the West. This definition of the social purpose of
schooling essentially condemns students from low socioeconomic
backgrounds to low-ability tracks and low-status occupations.

In a more progressive view of schooling, the learning available to children and the training received in school is theoretically the same for all children. At the primary and secondary levels, all children receive a "general" education; this does not prepare them for a particular vocation, but is intended to give them the basic knowledge required of all good citizens. Students are not expected to absorb the material presented equally well, but the school does not define *what* material is presented to different students. All receive the same diploma; only the grades and recommendations accompanying the diploma differ. Once this general course is finished, it is in theory the option of the individual—on the basis of *his* criteria and needs—to shape his future occupational and social role. The U.S. system of public education is based on this theoretical model.

Nevertheless, in practice this model has also resulted in most students from low-income homes performing worse (and therefore taking less schooling) than students from higher-income families. It has also resulted in European-type "tracking" into vocational and academic branches of the same school. Even when the school system is centrally financed and does not—as in the United States—depend on the local tax base (Puerto Rico uses the U.S. model with central financing), low socioeconomic status (SES) students attend, on the average, schools with lower-quality resources per pupil than high SES students. A very small percentage of those who start out behind in the first grade catch up; on the contrary, even with dropouts biasing the comparison of test scores over time between low-SES and high-SES students, evidence seems to show a *growing* gap as more schooling is taken.[1]

Thus, if schooling is to correct for differential "education" opportunities in the family and environment, it should be *compensatory*. The ultimate objective of this recent compensatory philosophy of education in the United States is to equalize the performance of all *groups* of children going to school: groups of students entering with, on the average, different endowments in the first grade, would leave high school with, on the average, equal endowments. The function of the schools would be to allocate resources in a way that would fulfill this compensatory objective.

The equalizing nature of compensatory schooling hinges on several important assumptions:

1. The instruments used to measure equalization—for example, reading, verbal, or math test scores—reflect the hiring criteria of employers and the criteria for status set by society. In a society that practices racial, sex, or ethnic discrimination, however, reading-score equalization will not do much to equalize economic and social roles. Blacks or Mexican-Americans coming out of high school with scores equal to those of whites will not necessarily gain equal entrance to universities or equal pay on jobs.

2. Although social role perception, highly correlated with social origin, race, and sex, is reinforced by the school even after test scores are equalized, the choice of future roles among graduates is equal. The case of women's education (women's average test scores are equal to men's) is a good example of the inadequacy of this assumption. The perception of "desirable" vocations for lower- and higher-socioeconomic-class students may be very different at the end of high school despite equal test scores for the two groups. From this standpoint alone, the structure of the present schools is probably incapable of equalizing different social, ethnic, racial, or sex groups' life possibilities at the end of a given period of schooling. Schools tend to reflect and reinforce rather than counteract the prejudices and perceptions of the outside world.[2] As Gintis has pointed out, noncognitive knowledge learned in school may very well be more important in determining future economic performance than cognitive knowledge.[3]

3. The relationship between teachers and students in the school is such that improving the "quality" of the teacher will result in compensating low-performance pupils. Compensatory education models in the United States assume that this relation is capable of producing equal performance on the part of different groups of pupils. Nevertheless, teachers apparently use learning models that expect pupils to *behave* in certain ways while learning. Lower-SES children are expected to learn in approximately the

same way as higher-SES children, although the two have been exposed to different home and peer environments. Similarly, black, Mexican-American, Indian, and other ethnically different groups are expected to learn in the same way as white middle-class children do. Teachers from outside the cultures of these children may not even be aware of differential reward systems in the different cultures. The learning environment in the classroom leads the teachers to treat those children with whom they can communicate well much better (and reward them more often) than children with whom they are having difficulty. The hierarchical relationship in the school leaves the child no recourse but to take his rewards and punishment from the teacher. As this paper tries to show, this relationship between teachers and students is apparently such that large transfers of school resources to presently "disadvantaged" groups will not even equalize average reading scores of the "advantaged" and "disadvantaged."[4]

The purpose of this essay is to test only the last of these three points: does it appear possible within the structure of the present "progressive" U.S.-type educational schooling system to equalize achievement or reading scores between different social, ethnic, sex, and racial groups, given that these groups are currently performing at very different levels? To test this hypothesis, we will use a number of studies already made in the United States and Puerto Rico which show the relationship between student attributes, teacher "quality" (as measured by various teacher characteristics) and school output (as measured by student achievement or reading score).[5] Equalization of reading or verbal scores is neither a sufficient nor necessary condition for equalization of group opportunities after schooling. Other measures and other means may be much more relevant. Nevertheless, the reading or verbal criterion is widely held up as an effectiveness measure by educators themselves,[6] and it is therefore used here as our single criterion measure.

The studies used do not base their methodology on any theory of learning; rather, they assume that there are classes of variables that affect school outcomes. These classes of variables include the student's socioeconomic background (his family characteristics), his initial "endowment" when he enters school, the characteristics of the teachers he has in school, and the quantity of nonteacher resources available to him in school. The studies estimate the relation between components of these classes of variables and student achievement. They allow us to estimate the effect on achievement of incremental changes in school resources— especially the quality of teachers—holding constant the influence of other variables such as socioeconomic class of students, their age, and in one study, their performance in first grade. The studies further calculate the relationships of school variables, such as teacher characteristics, to student achievement for each *different* socioeconomic, ethnic, or racial group of students. Therefore, we are able to see whether the contribution of increasing the quality of teachers is different for one group than for another.

The results of the studies are strikingly similar. They generally show a positive relationship between so-called higher "quality" characteristics of teachers and exam score. They also show significantly different teacher input–school output relationships for different ethnic groups and, in Puerto Rico, for different class groups. Finally, they show that even if increasing teacher quality results in higher achievement, a large relative increase in teacher quality for those groups now getting low average achievement scores will at best bring them only part of the way toward equality with presently high scoring groups.

The Evidence

The following series of tables—numbers 8.1 through 8.5— present regression estimates of different studies for the relationship between home background of students, school inputs, and exam performance of students on verbal achievement or reading exams. The studies cover comparisons between Mexican-Americans and Anglos in California, Puerto Rican students from different sectors (urban/rural) and different socioeconomic classes, and blacks and whites in the northeast part of the United States. The results shown in these tables are regression coefficients; that is, the figure by each designated independent variable signifies the change in exam score resulting from a

Table 8.1

Third-Grade Reading Achievement Estimates, White Nonmanual, White Manual, and Mexican-American Manual Students, California Sample, 1969

Variable	Coefficients (t values in parentheses)		
	White Non-manual	White Manual	Mexican-American Manual
First grade test score	0.72 (3.0)	0.79 (18.8)	0.97 (9.7)
Sex female	—	2.81 (2.3)	2.84 (1.2)
Repeat	—	—6.38 (—2.8)	—8.92 (—2.0)
Father clerical	—5.1 (—1.9)	—	—
Teacher test score (3rd grade)	—	0.09 (2.4)	—
Percent of time spent on discipline	—	—0.07 (—2.1)	—
Teacher test score (2nd grade)	—	0.06 (1.6)	—
Years since most recent educational experience (3rd grade)	—0.79 (—1.2)	—0.57 (—1.5)	—
Years since most recent educational experience (2nd grade)	—0.66 (—1.8)	—0.68 (—2.9)	—
Years of experience with SES level (3rd grade)	0.10 (1.7)	—	—
Years of experience with SES level (2nd grade)	0.20 (*)	—	—
Skilled father	—	—	8.22 (2.7)
Semiskilled father	—	—	5.96 (2.0)

Source: Hanushek, "Production of Education, Teacher Quality, and Efficiency," pp. 91–94.
(*) No *t* value given in original equation.

Table 8.2

Estimated School Production Functions (Reduced Form), Sixth-Grade Male Students, Puerto Rico, 1967, Dependent Variable, Spanish Reading Score

Variable	Urban	Rural
Hours of school attended daily	1.038	2.755[a]
Parent conversation	13.280	2.105
Age	—5.630	0.447
Average social class in the school (4 = low, 0 = high)	—6.797[a]	0.428
Teacher academic preparation	0.888	0.888[a]
Percent teachers certified	1.056	—2.201
Teacher experience	0.328	0.370[a]
Percent teachers on permanent contract	—3.105	—2.437
Class size	—0.555[a]	—0.103
Percent teachers male	—5.859[a]	—0.281

Source: Carnoy, "Family Backgrounds, School Inputs and Students' Performance in School," table 5.

[a] 90 percent significance level. All other coefficients are not significant at a 90 percent significance level.

change in one unit of that independent variable, all other independent variables held constant.

On the basis of these figures, it can be argued that the contribution of school inputs, even when a child's home background is held constant, is significant and has an important effect on a child's performance in school. Now we are going to take these results one step further. We are going to ask how large these coefficients are in terms of the achievement-score difference between the low- and high-performance groups compared in each study. How much would increasing the average test score of teachers teaching black students, for example, contribute to eliminating the difference in exam scores between black and white students? Our numerical operations are, of course, nothing more than simple simulations. But the results of our simulations are remarkably consistent: in no case does a large increase in the

Table 8.3

School Production Functions (Reduced Form), Sixth-Grade
Urban Male Students, Puerto Rico, 1967,
Dependent Variable, Spanish Reading Score

Variable	Lowest Socio-economic Class, Urban	Highest Socio-economic Class, Urban
Hours of school attended daily	5.214[a]	—0.114
Parent conversation	21.000[a]	12.770[a]
Age	1.407	0.412
Average social class	—0.790	—9.101[a]
Teacher academic preparation	2.614[a]	—1.547
Percent teacher certified	28.130[a]	2.670
Teacher experience	—0.960[a]	1.063[a]
Percent teachers on permanent contract	—7.624[a]	—3.376
Class size	—1.297[a]	—0.108
Percent teachers male	—18.330[a]	3.713

Source: Carnoy, "Family Background, School Inputs and Students' Performance in School," tables 13 and 14.

[a]90 percent significance level. All other coefficients are not significant at a 90 percent significance level.

characteristics of school inputs allocated to the low-performance group result in equality of performance with the high-performance group. In each case, the increase in resources allocated to the low-performance group by our examples would leave that group with *more* (not equal resources per pupil than the high-performance group.

Table 8.6 (pp. 212–13) shows the results of these calculations. In each case the increase in the independent variable (usually taken as one standard deviation from the mean) is multiplied by the corresponding coefficient from the disadvantaged group regression to get the estimated increase in exam score. We assume that there is a constant marginal product of increases in quality; that is, we

Table 8.4

*Schooling Production Function Estimates (Reduced Form)
for White and Black Sixth-Graders in Eastmet, 1965,
Dependent Variable, Verbal Score*

Independent Variables	Regression Coefficients[a]	
	Whites	*Blacks*
Sex	0.846	0.277
Age: 12+	—6.806	—3.808
Family size	—0.613	—0.382
Possessions	1.344	1.159
Kindergarten	2.135	0.461
Mother *ID*	—0.532	—0.395
Father *ID*	—0.395	0.227
Father's education	0.385	0.322
Mother has job	—0.270	—0.002
Teacher test score	0.323	0.336
Teacher's undergraduate institution	7.718	—1.891
Teacher's experience	0.835	—0.237
Teacher's preference for another school	1.030	—0.540
Teacher turnover	—0.181	—0.133
Volumes per student	0.498	0.101
Constant	—8.030	12.497

Source: Michelson, "Association of Teacher Resourcefulness with Children's Characteristics," pp. 147–48.

[a] Michelson does not provide *t* values or errors of estimate of the regression coefficients since his purpose in the original article from which this table is drawn is to compare the signs and values of the coefficients for black and white students.

assume that the coefficient does not decline as the mean of the variable is increased.

The first case in table 8.6 estimates the increase in verbal achievement score (Stanford Achievement Test) of Anglo third-graders from homes where the father has a manual occupation if we "improve" four teacher characteristics by one standard deviation from the mean. This means increasing average test scores of

Table 8.5

Teacher Effect on Verbal Achievement,
Means and Standard Deviations

	Elasticity (t values)	Mean	Standard Deviations
White Model			
Teacher experience (years)	.020 (3.2)	11.9	4.6
Teacher test score	.117 (2.2)	24.8	1.4
Percent students with non-white teacher last year	—.024 (—7.1)	13.4	16.0
Black Model			
Teacher experience (years)	.045 (2.6)	11.3	4.0
Teacher test score	.178 (2.0)	24.0	1.8
Percent students with non-white teacher last year	—.026 (—1.7)	44.7	19.4

Source: Hanushek, "Production of Education, Teacher Quality, Efficiency," pp. 86, 97.

those teaching these low-SES Anglos from a mean of 67 points in the second and third grades to a mean of 85 points. Similarly, the number of years since the teachers' last educational experience would be reduced from more than two years to only a few months. The effect of each of these measures in reducing the exam-score difference between this group and Anglo third-graders from nonmanual-occupation homes is shown in Column 3. Since the coefficients used to estimate changes in exam score are themselves estimated with other variables held constant at their respective means, it is not altogether legitimate to *sum* the changes from the four increases, especially when the changes in the independent variables are large. There may be important interaction effects (either positive or negative) which could occur when the means of all these variables are changed simultaneously. Nevertheless, as a first approximation, the sum indicates that the mean score of the disadvantaged Anglo group would be increased from 55.7 to 61.0 points. The *mean* score of children from nonmanual-occupation homes is 64.8,[7] which is still significantly higher.

Hanushek's results are far less hopeful for compensating Mexican-American students. The results of table 8.1 show that the coefficients of teacher inputs are not significant for the Mexican-American achievement-score equation. This implies that increases in test score and other characteristics of those teaching Mexican-Americans do not have a significant effect on Mexican-American achievement test scores.[8]

The second and third examples deal with equalization of test scores between rural and urban Puerto Rican sixth-graders and between lowest- and highest-SES urban Puerto Rican sixth-graders.[9] The average academic preparation and experience of rural sixth-grade teachers is 3.5 years beyond high school and 8.3 years' experience. Urban sixth-grade teachers have training 4.4 years beyond high school and 15.1 years' experience. The difference in both academic preparation and experience of urban and rural teachers is approximately constant through the six years of primary school, at 1 year of preparation and 6–7 years of experience. The increase proposed here would take place with teachers who teach all six years of rural primary school and would result in nominally equal teacher inputs for urban and rural primary students. The average number of hours attended by urban and rural sixth-graders is already equal (5.6 hours), but we have increased rural hours by one-half hour daily. The result of all this is an increase of almost 5 points in the mean rural Spanish-reading score, from 43.0 to 47.9 points. The mean sixth-grade urban score is 49.8, which is significantly higher.

The situation between the highest and lowest socioeconomic classes of urban Puerto Rican students appears much more difficult to equalize. Average academic preparation (4.4 years beyond high school), experience (14 years), and percent of teachers certified (86 percent) are equal for those teaching lowest- and highest-SES urban sixth-graders. The average daily

Table 8.6

Examples of Estimated Exam-Score Increases of Low-Performance Students When Quality of Inputs for Such Students Is Increased

	Change in Independent Variable	Absolute Change in Test Score of Low-Performance Group	Percent of Difference Overcome Between Low- and High-Performance Groups
Third-Grade Children of Manual and Nonmanual Occupation Fathers			
Teacher (3rd) test score	+16.0	1.44	15.8
Teacher (2nd) test score	+19.0	1.14	12.5
Years since education experience (3rd)	−1.6	0.91	10.0
Years since education experience (2nd)	−2.6	1.77	19.4
Total		5.26	57.7
Urban and Rural Puerto Rican Sixth-Graders			
Teacher academic preparation	+1.0	0.89	13.1
Teacher experience	+7.0	2.59	38.0
Daily hours attended	+0.5	1.38	20.3
Total		4.86	71.4

hours attending school is also equal (5.5). Yet the Spanish reading score for the lowest SES group is 38.4 points and for the highest, 56.2. By increasing average teacher academic preparation by one year, reducing average teacher experience by three years, increasing the percent of teachers certified by 10 percent, and increasing the average daily hours attended by one-half hour,

Table 8.6—continued

	Change in Independent Variable	Absolute Change in Test Score of Low-Performance Group	Percent of Difference Overcome Between Low- and High-Performance Groups
Lowest and Highest Socioeconomic Class, Urban Puerto Rican Sixth-Graders			
Teacher academic preparation	+1.0	2.61	14.7
Teacher experience	—3.0	2.88	16.2
Percent teachers certified	+0.1	2.81	15.8
Daily hours attended	+0.5	2.60	14.6
Total		10.90	61.3
Black and White Eastmet Sixth-Graders			
Teacher test score	+4.8	1.62	14.2
Teacher experience	—3.1	0.73	6.5
Teacher turnover	—4.2	0.56	5.8
Volumes per student	+1.9	0.19	1.7
Total		3.10	28.2
Black and White Northeast Urban Sixth-Graders		*Percent Change*	
Teacher test score	+3.6	2.7	—
Teacher experience	+4.0	1.2	—
Percent students with nonwhite teacher	—22.3	1.3	—
Total		5.2	

Sources: Tables 8.1 through 8.5.

the average Spanish reading score of lowest SES students would be increased by 11 points, or about 60 percent of the difference between the two groups.

The last two cases compare urban black and white students in northeastern United States. The Levin and Michelson data taken from Michelson's study in the USOE volume (see table 8.4) indicate that raising the verbal score of those teaching black students by two standard deviations (4.8 points), lowering their average experience and turnover by one standard deviation (3.1 years and 4.2) and increasing the volumes per student (from 1.7 to 3.6) would only overcome about one-fourth of the difference between black and white achievement scores. The new mean teacher verbal score for black students would be 26.6 versus 24.7 for white students; teacher experience would be 6.1 years versus 15.1 for whites; and average teacher turnover would be 1.8 for black students and 6.9 for whites. The number of volumes per student would be 3.6 for blacks and 2.8 for whites. These relatively large changes in school inputs are estimated to increase average black verbal-achievement score from a mean of 23.6 to 26.7. This falls far short of the white mean of 35.1.

Hanushek made similar estimates for a different sample (see table 8.5) from the Coleman data. Again, using two standard deviations for the change in teacher verbal score and one standard deviation for the change in teacher experience and the percent of students with a nonwhite teacher, we estimate a total change in black verbal achievement as a result of these teacher changes of 5.2 percent (Hanushek's coefficients are elasticities rather than absolute values, so yield a percentage change in exam score). Taking the black student mean achievement as 25, the 5.2 percent translates into a 1.3 point rise in achievement score.

Conclusion

Many of the empirical studies presented here in support of our hypothesis were done primarily as a reaction to the Coleman Report of 1966. Coleman reported—erroneously—that once the socioeconomic background of children in school is accounted for, school inputs have negligible effect on students' achievement.[10] The studies discussed here show that it *is* possible to alter the allocation of resources in schools to increase the performance of those who are now receiving fewer schooling resources. But the data also make clear that equalizing resources spent on schooling for children of different socioeconomic, ethnic, or racial groups will not equalize academic performance among those groups. Even if substantially higher-quality teaching is made available to the low-scoring than to the high-scoring students, the change would result in only a partial reduction of exam-score difference between the two. In the case of ethnic and racial minorities in the United States, the reduction may well be negligible.

There is a fundamental belief in U.S. educational circles (and among the public at large) that lower-SES children cannot learn as quickly or as well as middle- or higher-SES children. The response to this belief on the part of those who wish to equalize the amount learned by all groups is a strategy of allocating much more resources to these "disadvantaged" slow learners so that they can catch up. The structure of schools would remain the same in this strategy, as well as the teacher-pupil relation and the student's social role perception. Schools would still have the goal of producing a certain type of citizen, but with a higher achievement or reading score than before. The difficulty, probably the impossibility, of achieving equality in this way is evident from the empirical studies presented here. The strategy, even in failure, would also turn out to be extremely costly relative to the benefits these lower-SES groups would gain in society as a result of higher scores.[11]

The alternative to this strategy is to reject the concept of a neutral school system implicit in the poor learners–good learners theory, and to assume instead that all groups of children can learn equally well but under different conditions. We may find that children's motivation is affected much more by the structure of the learning environment than by the number of years of teacher's academic preparation. The low probability of success of compensatory programs within the existing framework points to the need for new educational strategies for ethnic and racial minorities if equality is to be achieved. The solution may be to change schooling for all children and to create an educational process that does not preconceive social roles or even clearly define what or how a child must learn. This process would require new kinds of tests to measure results and a different kind of teacher to produce them. Education of this type could allow a child's own stereotypes of himself and others to be destroyed and be replaced by personal relationships. The alternative strategy, then, creates equality among groups of children, by believing that all children are equally *capable* of learning and building an educational structure that allows children to express themselves in various ways, all equally acceptable. This alternative would thus start from the premise that the structure of learning in the schools must be changed to produce something called "equality," rather than accepting the present hierarchical, role-reinforcing structure and attempting to overcome its deficiencies with massive infusions of traditional resources.

But is it possible to change the structure of formal public schooling, the relationship between teacher and student, without fundamental changes in hierarchies outside the school? Are not classroom relations modeled on economic and social relations in the society at large? If the schools are to produce workers and citizens to function in societal structures based on well-defined hierarchies and ethnic, racial, sex, and class discrimination, how can these same elements be eliminated from the educational system? Fundamental changes in schooling—as suggested here—will require fundamental changes in the basic structures of the society.

Notes

1. James Guthrie et al., "School and Inequality: A Study of the Relationship Between Social Status, School Services, and Post-School Opportunity in the State of Michigan" (Report prepared for the National Urban Coalition, Washington, D.C., September 1969).

2. See, for example, Edgar Z. Friedenberg, *Coming of Age in America* (New York: Random House, 1965).

3. Herbert Gintis, "Production Functions in the Economics of Education and the Characteristics of Worker Productivity" (Harvard University, Department of Economics, 1969). Mimeographed.

4. The period of school during which this equalization could be accomplished is taken here as six years. This choice is in part the result of data availability. However, from the standpoint of observed reality as well, almost all fundamental reading skills are part of the school curriculum only in primary school. Although remedial reading can be continued into high school, most subjects by the seventh year build heavily on reading ability.

5. See Martin Carnoy, "Family Background, School Inputs and Students' Performance in School: The Case of Puerto Rico" (Stanford University, 1971), mimeographed; Eric Hanushek, "The Production of Education, Teacher Quality, and Efficiency," in *Do Teachers Make a Difference?*, U.S. Office of Education (Washington, D.C.: Government Printing Office, 1970), OE-58042, pp. 79–99; Henry Levin, "A New Model of School Effectiveness," in idem, pp. 55–78; Stephen Michelson, "The Association of Teacher Resourceness with Children's Characteristics," in idem, pp. 120–68. Some of the studies also measure school output by other variables: math achievement, student attitudes, and the amount of school the student expects to take.

6. In performance contracting, school rank, etc., exam score is the single effectiveness measure used.

7. Hanushek, "Production of Education, Teacher Quality, and Efficiency," p. 93.

8. All of Hanushek's equations include a measure of initial endowment—the student's test score in the first grade. The coefficients of schools' input variables are therefore probably smaller than they would be if the first grade test score variable were not included. In the other studies discussed here, this "value added" aspect of schooling inputs is not directly accounted for, so the effect on students' achievement score of increases in teacher quality is probably *overestimated*; i.e., the coefficients of various teacher characteristics, not holding students' initial endowment constant, are upward biased.

9. See Carnoy, "Family Background, School Inputs and Students' Performance in School."

10. For a discussion of the errors in the Coleman Report, see Samuel Bowles and Henry Levin, "The Determinants of Scholastic Achievement: An Appraisal of Some Recent Findings," *Journal of Human Resources* 3, no. 1 (Winter 1968): 3–24.

11. For attempts to cost out increases in teacher quality, see Martin Carnoy, " A Systems Approach to Evaluating Education Illus-

trated with Puerto Rican Data" (Stanford University, 1971), mimeographed; and Henry Levin, "A Cost-Effectiveness Analysis of Teacher Selection," *Journal of Human Resources* 5, no. 1 (Winter 1970): 24–33.

9

William H. Behn
Martin Carnoy
Michael A. Carter
Joyce C. Crain
Henry M. Levin

School Is Bad; Work Is Worse

Introduction

One underlying tenet of American culture has been an enormous faith in the efficacy of its schools to create and sustain the "good society." Schools have been expected to provide universal attainment of literacy, an effectively functioning democracy, equalization of opportunity, and rapid economic growth. And, if some schooling has been considered good, more schooling has been thought to be even better.

But recent years have seen a sudden profusion of literature that has shattered this heroic image. Coleman et al. found that schools are neither as powerful nor as equalizing in producing cognitive achievement as we had tacitly believed.[1] Greer has questioned the legend that the enormous waves of immigrants of the late nineteenth century were successfully integrated into American society via the schools.[2] Illich has suggested that the effects of the schools are so pernicious in promoting an inequitable and economically wasteful society that "deschooling" should be the highest social priority.[3] And, most recently, Jencks has argued that there is little relationship between schooling attainments and economic outcomes.[4]

One of the latest entries to the debate on appropriate educational policy is the report of the Panel of Youth of the President's Science Advisory Committee, *Youth: Transition to Adulthood.* The committee was headed by distinguished sociologist James S. Coleman, and it saw its purpose as the examination of opportunities for youth to develop to adulthood, the transition represented by the age span 14–24. According to the committee, the aim of the report was "to stimulate the search for institutional inventions which will ensure that youth acquires the capabilities for fulfilling the demands and opportunities they will confront as adults, and thereby gain the self-esteem and self-fulfillment all persons need."[5]

The report focuses its criticism primarily on the schools by questioning the ability of extended schooling to prepare the young for the world of work and other adult roles:

> Schooling, as we know it, is not a complete environment giving all the necessary opportunities for becoming adult. School is a certain kind of environment: individualistic, oriented toward cognitive achievement, imposing dependency on and withholding authority and responsibility from those in the role of students.[6]

Further, it is asserted that the increased length of schooling has led to a sacrifice of other opportunities that are necessary for transforming a child into an adult:

> opportunities for responsible action, situations in which he came to have authority over matters that affected other persons, occasions in which he experienced the consequences of all his own actions, and was strengthened by facing them—in short, all that is implied by "becoming adult" in matters other than gaining cognitive skills.[7]

The study proceeds to set out a number of background aspects of youth including some historical aspects; rights of children and youth; demography and economic problems; biological, psychological, and cultural aspects; educational institutions, and youth culture. The treatments of these subjects are very uneven, and it is difficult to see their connection with the Issues and Recommendations that follow. Most of the issues address the limitations in youth development created by their segregation from adults and the workplace that results largely from an extended incarceration in schools. Obstacles to providing work opportunities for youth such as legal barriers—due to child-labor laws and compulsory-schooling codes—and economic hurdles such as minimum wage provisions are reviewed.

The final section of the report provides recommendations for changes or experiments that would increase the opportunities for youth to work, to undertake nontraditional types of training and experiences, and to have more contact with other age groups. Other recommendations address the need for greater research, for self-governance experiences for youth, and for more public service opportunities.

Since the principal thrust of the report addresses the relationship between education and work, it is this aspect of the study that we focus on. The most important recommendation of the report in this context is its emphasis on greater substitution of work experiences for schooling experiences. This change would be carried out by altering restrictive child-labor laws and by alternating work and schooling either within a daily schedule or by interspersing longer periods of work—several weeks or months—between periods of schooling. Increases in the demand for young people in work organizations would be provided by greater investment in public-service opportunities such as VISTA and the Neighborhood Youth Corps as well as by a dual minimum wage whereby employers could pay lower minimum wages to youth than to adults. Greater availability of training and schooling programs by private firms in conjunction with work would also be emphasized.

Before proceeding with an analysis of the report's assumptions and recommendations regarding the relations between schooling and work, it is important to note a puzzling aspect of the study. The overwhelming theme of the discussion surrounds the inadequacy of the present youth environments and particularly schooling for creating adults. If youth grow up to be less competent adults now than they did in the past, the report should substantiate this charge carefully. Yet one searches in vain throughout the report for an explicit and detailed analysis of this assumption. In what ways are young adults found to be lacking? What evidence supports this contention? Despite the crucial nature of the thesis as a basis for arguing that youth environments must be changed, it is neither addressed nor documented in any way whatsoever throughout the study.

Although it is argued that schooling is an incomplete environment because it neglects activities directed toward other persons —and presumably no other institutions are available to serve this role—it is never shown that youngsters grow up any more selfish or narcissistic today than they did in the past. Instead, the evidence of the deficiencies of schooling are documented by the following glib account:

> Signs of dissatisfaction abound, from parents and taxpayers who have an inarticulate sense that something is amiss, from school administrators and teachers who are experimenting with methods and objectives and forms that differ from those of the established system, and from youth themselves, many of whom are showing individual initiative in the search for extra-curricular experiences.[8]

Assumptions About School and Work Doubtless, no one would contest the assertion in the report that any single institutional environment, whether school, work, family, or community, is inadequate for socializing youth for adult roles. Therefore, the issue is not whether one should select schooling or work or any other single institution as an environment for youth, but rather, what combination of them is necessary for producing competent adults. In a sense this question can be answered only by knowing what kinds of competencies adults need and then exploring what kinds of socialization the various agencies provide.[9]

The report resolves this issue by defining it away with a sweeping generalization:

> Experience indicates that young persons need both activity directed toward self-development and useful activity directed toward the outside on which others depend. Neglect of the first results in an unskilled adult, impotent to deal with a complex world. Neglect of the second leads to frustration of the idealistic, creative, and constructive impulses of youth. For most persons these two activities, directed inward and outward, take the prosaic forms of school and work (though school does not always bring self-development and work does not always constitute productive and useful activity).[10]

Thus the issue is simplified for the reader in the following terms: only two major characteristics of youth development need be addressed, self-development and externally oriented development. The former is produced by the institution of schooling and the latter by the institution of work. Accordingly, we need not dwell on the role of family, community, the media, and other socialization influences since these do not enter the realm of socialization with which we are concerned. The report shows remarkable consistency in neither explicating further the basis for these assumptions nor documenting them in even the crudest fashion.

Further, the study informs us that: "Schools are the principal formal institutions of society intended to bring youth into adulthood. But the schools' structures are designed wholly for self-development, particularly the acquisition of cognitive skills and of knowledge."[11] That is, schools are viewed as having little or no socialization function with respect to other adult requirements, especially the competencies for being a "responsible" worker. Given these assumptions, it is not difficult to see why the report pursues the objective of getting students into the work force earlier in order to train them for their adult roles and to enable them to experience an outlet for their "idealistic, creative, and constructive impulses."

At this juncture it is useful to note several major differences between the views presented in the report and our analysis: First, while the report defines the socialization effects of schools and work in exceedingly narrow ways, we argue that the socialization literature does not support that conclusion. In contrast, virtually all agencies of socialization including family, school, community, media, and work contribute to the formation of the attitudes, values, skills, and knowledge required for work. We call this the "correspondence principal," since we assert that there is a direct relationship between the demands of work organizations and all agencies of socialization.

Second, the report ignores social-class differences in socialization experiences generally and in work experiences, school experiences, and occupational attainments particularly. The impression is given that all young adults share identical environments. In contrast we assert that a major role of the school is to reproduce the social relations of production; and that differential socialization of work traits takes place according to the social-class origins of youth in order to fill out the highly unequal work hierarchy inherent in capitalist production.

Third, the report makes no attempt to support its underlying thesis that young adults are inadequately socialized for their adult roles. We argue that they are well prepared for the adult roles that face them in society. Further, we assert that the problems of dissatisfaction with both school and work are more directly related to the alienating environments of both work organizations and schools than by inadequate socialization for meeting the demands of work.

Finally, we show how the recommendations that follow from our analysis differ from those of the report. In general, we argue for the transformation of adult roles, particularly work roles, and we contend that the socialization of youth for these new roles will follow closely.

Socialization for Work Roles

Any reading of the socialization literature tends to conflict with the extreme isolation of institutional roles reflected in the report.

To the contrary, all agencies of socialization overlap in their mission to transmit the culture. Surveys of literature on socialization of the young to occupational roles show links between family interactions, peer influences, schooling experiences, and occupational experiences on the one hand and work roles on the other.[12] Throughout this literature it is evident that many influences contribute to the formation of the attitudes, values, behaviors, and skills which are necessary to function in a given occupational role. The work of Inkeles on the formation of modern man indicates that among the six countries studied virtually all these influences contributed to the attitudes and behaviors which are necessary in modern industrial production as well as other facets of modern life.[13] In our view there is little support for the narrow stance that school and work perform narrow socialization roles and that other institutions are not important at all.

A second theme reflected in the socialization literature also differs from the presentation of the report. While the discussion of the report always refers to socialization requirements and adult competencies as generalizable to the entire male population, the socialization literature reports very important differences among both institutional influences and adult roles along social-class dimensions. That is, the set of socialization influences that affect an individual are largely predetermined by his socioeconomic origins. Families, communities, schools, and workplaces tend to inculcate different attitudes, values, cognitive skills, and behaviors according to their class orientation. The literature suggests that the institutional influences that affect the formation of children and youth tend to perpetuate these social-class differences.[14] By referring to some implicit common issue in the socialization of youth—although never specifying what it consists of—the issues of class are avoided. In our view these systematic differences in the socialization and preparation of youth are of as great importance as a national issue as is the overall question of youth environments.

Thus, the literature on socialization suggests that limiting the discussion of socialization to school and work and imputing narrow roles to each is not warranted, and that social-class differences in institutional influences and adult roles represent a significant obstacle to generalizing about the experiences of youth. But, more specifically, it can be shown that schools do indeed prepare the young for the realities of work in far more than a cognitive sense.

The view that schools are primarily a cognitive influence and that they represent the dominant instrument for cognitive socialization as reflected in the report is refuted by a number of empirical studies. Virtually all the statistical studies attempting to determine the causes of student achievement have concluded that most of the explainable variance in test scores is attributable to out-of-school influences rather than in-school ones.[15] While it is clear that children and young adults learn many skills and cognitive proficiencies in school, they also learn many of them out of school. Of course, the amount and nature of cognitive proficiencies and noncognitive socialization that takes place both in and out of the school seems crucially related to the social-class origins of the child.

Other studies attempt to determine what aspect of schooling is related to success in labor markets. That is, we know that educational attainments in terms of years of schooling on the one hand and earnings and occupational success on the other are closely related statistically. If the true effect of schooling on earnings and occupation were attributable to the cognitive effect of schooling, it would be expected that the statistical relationship between years of schooling and work success would be attenuated or eliminated once we controlled for the cognitive test scores of workers. That is, the cognitive theory of schooling's effect on such outcomes as earnings suggests that the reason that years of schooling have an important impact is because educational attainment is a surrogate for cognitive development.

Yet, when attempts have been made to explain the variance in earnings by both test scores and educational attainment of workers, the apparent statistical effect of years of schooling is only slightly diminished.[16] Different studies that have used test scores, years of schooling, and other variables to explain earnings suggest that the apparent effect of the amount of schooling on earnings is reduced by only 4 percent to a maximum of about one-third when test scores are introduced in the relations, and the increase in explained variance by using test scores is negligible.[17] Accordingly, it appears that the principal effect of education on labor-market success is through some other effect than the cognitive one.

We believe that a much clearer picture of the role of schooling in the socialization process emerges when one considers it in a context of correspondence. Following the model of Inkeles, every society creates specific demands for competency upon its adults, and it is the purpose of all institutions of socialization to fulfill these demands by socializing the population to attain these competencies.[18] Since work represents one of the most important adult roles, it is important to study the nature of work roles and their relations to the functions of schooling.

In contrast to the romantic descriptions of work used in the report—an outlet for idealistic, creative, and constructive impulses—evaluations of work in our society have found it to be alienating, dehumanizing, and violent to the spirit as well as to the body.[19] The recent study on *Work in America* sponsored by a special Task Force of the Department of Health, Education, and Welfare found the quality of working life to be one of the major issues of our time.[20] As we note later, greater questions should be raised about the competencies required for working life than about the environments that seem to be producing these competencies. What, then, are some of the requirements of work organizations, and how are they tied to school environments?

In his review of personality characteristics required for job performance in the bureaucratic and hierarchically organized enterprises that characterize our society, Gintis identifies four types of personality requisites: (1) proper level of subordination; (2) discipline; (3) supremacy of cognitive over affective modes of response; and (4) motivation according to external reward structures.[21] Each of these, in turn, can be shown to be linked to the agenda of schools.

For example, subordination and proper orientation to authority along hierarchical lines are necessary in virtually all modern work enterprises. "As the worker relinquishes control over his activities on the job, so the student is first forced to accept and later comes personally to terms with his loss of autonomy and initiative to a teacher who acts as a superior authority, dispensing rewards and penalties."[22] The discipline of the bureaucratic work structure with its requirements of highly regularized and conforming behavior to time schedules, regulations, and stifling conformity are reflected in the schools by Silberman's summary of the school environment: "how oppressive and petty are the rules by which they [the schools] are governed."[23]

Further, as Weber has noted, bureaucracies function best when social relationships are characterized by "rational matter-of-factness" rather than emotion. "Its specific nature which is welcomed by capitalism, develops the more perfectly the more the bureaucracy is 'dehumanized,' the more completely it succeeds in eliminating from official business, love, hatred, and all purely personal irrational and emotional elements which escape calculation."[24] Dreeben refers to the emphasis away from affect and toward "matter-of-factness in the accomplishment of tasks that governs the relationship between teachers and pupils."[25] Further, Gintis found that teacher ratings of students tended to be higher for personality traits related to the cognitive mode of expression and lower for those related to affective modes.[26]

Finally, since workers have little or no control over the attributes of the product or nature of their work, it is necessary to motivate them through rewards that are external to the work itself, such as money and prestige. Similar conditions exist in the school where the student has little control over his circumstances, and his activities are not determined primarily by his intrinsic interests and concerns. Rather, they are imposed upon him by a highly planned and routinized organization that manipulates his activities and the conditions under which he pursues those activities, and in order to obtain his conformance and cooperation with this reality there is a heavy dependence on external rewards such as grades, class ranks, and diplomas.[27]

In summary, the social relations of "production" in schooling serve to reproduce the social relations of work.[28] It takes little imagination to see the correspondence between grades for school performance and wages for work performance; to see the alienation and boredom of the assembly line mirror the stifling environment and boredom of the educational assembly line;[29] to see the competition among students for grades parallel the competition among workers for advancement; to see the teacher in the class- room impose his arbitrary values on his underlings just as does the boss on the job (neither legitimacy of authority resulting from a democratic election). These relations are reinforced by the findings of Gintis that higher grades are given to those students who exhibit traits that are functional in production (even when scholastic achievement is accounted for),[30] and by Brenner that teachers' evaluations of student conduct serve as better predictors of the students' later work success (as reflected in supervisors' work ratings) than do students' scholastic records.[31]

Social-Class Differentiation for Work Roles Without question, the schools are a major socializing influence in preparing youth for the realities of the workplace. What must be emphasized in this context is the fact that all individuals are not socialized for the same work positions. Since work organizations are character- ized by hierarchical roles with respect to such matters as in- dividual responsibility, authority, pay, and prestige, then the corresponding output of the schools must also contribute to the differentiation of workers for such roles. Accordingly, the schools serve to prepare workers to fill the work hierarchy by differ- entiating both the amounts of and types of schooling experiences that they receive. For example, low-level workers need only be inculcated with minimum cognitive attainments, the ability to follow orders, to show deference to authority, and so on. Middle- level workers need higher levels of cognitive attainments, and the abilities to give orders as well as follow them but with somewhat more independence than lower-level ones who are expected to conform completely to the work organization and its rules. Finally, individuals at the top of the occupational hierarchy must have the ability to show great independence in behavior, high cognitive skills, modes of self-presentation that denote authority, and so on.

The system of class socialization reflected in the schools and other institutions of our society tend to reproduce the social division of labor according to the class origins of youth.[32] On the average, a student whose father is working class will have less money spent on his education and will undertake fewer years of schooling than one whose father is in a higher-status occupation. Since educational attainments are a principal determinant of social and occupational mobility and attainment, the lower-class child finds that his relatively modest schooling limits him to lower-class jobs. This reality is a function of the many overlapping socialization influences that reinforce the class structure, but the schools represent a prime supporting ingredient.

Two aspects of schooling are especially noteworthy in this regard: the way that they are financed and the class-oriented nature of school environments. In general, elementary and secondary education are supported according to the wealth and income of state and local jurisdictions. That is, the present methods of financing education assure that a larger amount of support will be available for children in wealthy states and school districts than in poorer ones.[33] In turn, recent research has ascertained that the expenditure per student is directly related to the amount of education a student will obtain, even when social-class origins are held constant.[34]

At the level of higher education, too, financial arrangements tend to subsidize the rich more than the poor, even under the low-tuition policies of the public systems.[35] Children from lower-income families are less able to fund the nontuition and living expenses of higher education, and they are less likely to have fulfilled the academic requirements for gaining admission to colleges and universities. For example, they are less likely to have completed high school. Even when they do participate in the higher educational system, it is likely to be in the lower-cost community college segment. Studies of the higher educational systems of both Florida and California have found that the amount of public subsidy provided for students is a direct function of their family income.[36]

But systematic differences in expenditures in favor of the wealthy are only one of the ways in which the schools tend to reinforce the class structure. For example, school environments tend to differ according to the social-class origins of students so that students from lower-class families are inculcated with the traits requisite for being workers while children from more lofty class backgrounds are socializing to be managers and professionals. So-called ability tracking and testing represent one of the primary ways by which this is rationalized within schools,[37] but even more revealing is the class-related nature of education among schools.

The differential nature of schools according to the social origins of the child can be observed readily by anyone who lives within the proximity of a large city. One need only compare a high school in the inner city attended by children from low-income and minority backgrounds with one situated a few miles away in an affluent suburb. Although such a comparison focuses on the two poles of the social-class spectrum, the systematic influence of student social-class origin on school socialization can be generalized as a combination of these extremes for all stations in between.

The lower-class school and curricula are characterized by a high degree of external discipline. Rules abound and are rigidly enforced; written passes are required to leave classes during session, even to go to the restroom; and various types of corporal punishment, threats of suspension, and verbal abuse are used to maintain control. Decisions about each child's studies are made impersonally by counselors with little input from the student; and alternatives are few anyway in such schools. In such an environment the students learn to take orders and respond to authority. The institution provides them with few choices. They sense their lack of worth to the organization with the knowledge that they could drop out tomorrow, and someone would replace them. Only the school records would change. Of course, this socialization pattern corresponds with the needs of unskilled workers who need primarily to defer to authority; to respond passively to orders; to accept alienation from work and to become one of the faceless multitudes at the bottom of the work hierarchy.[38] Of course, since there will be many with these traits relative to job demand, employment will always be a transient and uncertain phenomenon.[39]

In contrast, the upper-middle-class students are attending schools where the rules are relatively few and less consistently enforced. It is well known among students that almost any rule can be violated under some circumstances, and plea-bargaining is common. Indeed, most conflicts between teachers and administrators on the one hand and students on the other are resolved through negotiation and discussion rather than through summary action on the part of adults. Students walk freely about the school at all times. Permission is not needed to leave class or to enter and leave the campus. Decisions about a youngster's program of studies are based upon discussions between counselor and pupil in order to select from among the large number of available course offerings. When certain learning experiences are not available in the curriculum, special programs of individual or small-group study can be arranged. Virtually all students are expected to study academic subjects in order to enter colleges and universities.

Such an environment tends to inculcate those traits that are functional in making decisions about the work organization itself and about the conditions that affect the workers at lower echelons. The experiences provided by the "flexible" nature of school rules and negotiation for special privileges represent preparation for those who will make the rules and engage in conflict resolution with other persons at high levels of decision making. The independence reflected in choosing among the large range of alternative educational experiences provides good training for selecting among alternative management strategies. The freedom to choose schooling hours and activities is also functional in preparing upper-middle-class students for the relative freedom that they will have in setting their work schedules in contrast with the wage-and-hour arrangements or fixed schedules of lower-level salaried workers. In a sense such youngsters are being socialized to be the "bosses," while the ones who are in the inner-city school are being prepared to be the workers or the unemployed. The former will learn to give the orders and the latter to follow them.

Nor is the process of differential socialization limited to elementary and secondary education alone. Higher educational institutions are also stratified in terms of the functions that they perform in differentiating the labor force for positions in the occupational hierarchy. The role of the community colleges is especially interesting in this regard. For example, Karabel has argued that such institutions serve primarily a "cooling out" function for working-class students who aspire toward bachelors' degrees, and the high dropout rates from these institutions as well as the applied types of course offerings tend to support this view.[40] A recent passionate defense of the community colleges against this interpretation argues that they are successful precisely *because* lower-class aspirants will meet the same conditions that they will face in the labor market (presumably in lower-status occupations):

> . . . the effort required of the community college student in order to maintain his status and progress within the institution is not unlike the effort that the same student will have to expend once he enters the workaday world. The sacrifices and commitment that he must make, the postponement of economic rewards, and hard work required are very much like those required of anyone who seeks to advance in a chosen career.[41]

Over time, it seems that community colleges have become the new prerequisite for integrating the working class into the class structure as the educational attainments of society have mushroomed.[42]

Finally, the socialization process needed to change an environment, rather than simply to adapt to a situation, does not occur in working-class schools, and it is less likely to develop in those higher educational institutions catering to a lower social-class clientele than in more elite institutions. The very group that is most likely to want to change its environment (those with the least rewarding jobs and political power and with the most frustrating existence) are least equipped by all the agents of socialization, including schools, to undertake that change.

Reappraising What Is Wrong

The major thesis of our discussion to this point has been that there is a direct relation—reflected in the correspondence principle—between the demands of work and the agencies of socialization that prepare people for work. We have emphasized that a worker needs special character traits in addition to cognitive skills to function productively in a hierarchically organized work environment. Not only do schools produce cognitive skills, they also develop those character traits which all workers need regardless of their position in the hierarchy. Moreover, schools differentially socialize children from different social-class backgrounds into the attitudes and behavior patterns appropriate to the position in the hierarchy which they are expected to fill. If our arguments about the correspondence of school and work social structures are valid, then the "problem" with youths and the young workers does not result from inadequate socialization, but is rooted in the alienating environments common to both workplace and school.

In our view the demands for competencies are created by adult society, and schools and other agents of socialization follow these demands. In short, we do not believe that schools can remake society. To the contrary, the schools serve society and tend to reproduce the dominant social, economic, and political values reflected by the prevailing institutions and ideologies. That is, educational reform is possible only when it does not conflict with the structure of its host society or polity.[43] Accordingly, given correspondence, what evidence do we have that anything is wrong? The report suggests that "signs of dissatisfaction abound" with schools, but specific details are scant. We agree that many youngsters are "turned off" to schools. They find them repressive, petty, and destructive of human values and feelings.

Since it is largely the demands of work organizations that have shaped school structures and environments,[44] it is the work process itself that is responsible for this alienation. What aspects of the work situation are responsible for making work (and schooling) alienating? Why don't the majority of jobs function as an outlet for "idealistic, creative and constructive impulses?" The answer lies at the heart of existing work organizations with their focus on wage contracts and pyramidal hierarchies rather than on human relationships. Through the system of wage contracts and hierarchical structure of production relationships, workers lose control of both the product and the process of their labor. They are separated and placed in structurally antagonistic relationships to one another in order to enhance the control function of the organization. It is alienation from work activity itself and from fellow workers that results in the degradation of work from a free, creative, cooperative activity to a coerced means of individual existence.

Under a system of wage contracts the worker sells his labor to the employer and in return receives a wage. It is then the job of the employer to extract labor from the worker. The use of force to extract labor would disrupt the production process and run counter to even the most superficial democratic precepts. Therefore, the employer seeks to obtain the "voluntary" cooperation of his labor force. There are many methods of doing this, but historically the dominant method chosen has been to design technology that routinizes as far as possible the tasks a worker must do. The worker need not think for himself, but need only follow prescribed routine. This procedure simplifies the task of supervision and increases the employers' control over the productive process. The history of technological development has reflected a tendency toward increasingly fragmented, routinized bureaucratized tasks.[45]

Employers rationalize the existence of hierarchical structures in production by arguing that increasing division of labor increases productivity and, therefore, wages. The workers labor neither for intrinsic satisfaction in their work activity nor to cooperatively create products and services which society needs, but merely to earn the wages that permit them to consume what they want as individuals. They don't experience productive activity as the unification of themselves with other workers in a network of mutual dependence and cooperation; but merely as a means to their individual consumption. The individualism, self-centeredness and competitiveness inherent in this situation are functional to and a structural characteristic of the hierarchical relationships among persons in the productive process.

Hierarchy is a natural outgrowth of the development of a technology which maximizes division of labor and minimizes thought and decision making by the direct producers of the product. Such a technology coupled with employers' desire to maintain control of the production process creates a "need" for foremen and supervisors, quality-control specialists, administrative personnel to coordinate production, engineers to collect data on and "improve the efficiency of" production, researchers and analysts to provide necessary data for the decisions made by the elite few at the top of the hierarchy, and so on. Leaving aside the question of the necessity of this proliferation of the hierarchy for the technical efficiency of production, it is clear that it serves to cement the control of those at or near the top of the hierarchy. The most direct effect of hierarchy is that it keeps those workers at the bottom of the hierarchy, whose pay is lowest and whose work is most boring and routinized, ignorant of the operation of the production process as a whole. This ignorance forces them to accept the fact that decisions about their productive activity must be made by those who are more knowledgeable and higher up.

Some workers might think that if they could gain some experience at higher job levels in the hierarchy they could perform as competently as those who currently hold those positions. This type of thinking is discouraged by the higher formal education requirements necessary for job entry above the lower levels. The explicit suggestion is that no amount of experience can substitute for a college degree in these types of jobs. With the absence of any chance for the worker to learn how well he can perform some higher function, he accepts the educational requirement as binding and doesn't seriously aspire to those positions. His major hope is that his children will receive a good education so they can attain the privileged positions in the hierarchy.

The worker is colonized through hierarchy into accepting the view that his "ignorance" inevitably relegates him to nonthinking and routinized jobs. Since work does not offer an outlet for gratification, he turns toward consumption activity for fulfillment, as well as toward such other forms of escapism as alcohol and drugs. Work represents only a means to earn the wages to consume; weekends, vacations, and retirement become the milestones of his existence. Personal "growth" is assessed not through the development of productive skills but through steadily escalating levels of consumption. New and faster cars replace older ones, and clothing styles and weed-free lawns become the basis for personal prestige. But his consumption can be augmented only by increasing his wages, and that means conforming with the demands of the employer and the work organization even when his sense of justice and fairness are violated.

While production workers cannot aspire to any of the choice jobs in the middle or near the top of the hierarchy, there are usually mini-hierarchies within which there is some possible movement. These mini-hierarchies or job ladders prevent workers from becoming completely frustrated and preserve the illusions of real mobility in this society.[46] At the same time they encourage stable work behavior, since promotion along the ladders depends on seniority which is attained by doing an "adequate" job and not causing any trouble. Moreover, since pay differentials between jobs at the top and bottom of these ladders can be on the order of three to one, workers who have moved off the bottom rungs acquire a vested interest in the preservation of the system. Thus, these mini-hierarchies legitimize the overall hierarchial structure of production.

A final stabilizing function of hierarchy is that the workers who have the most oppressive jobs seldom, if ever, come in direct contact with persons at or near the top of the hierarchy. Instead, the direct agent of their oppression is another worker—a foreman, or a quality-control supervisor. Workers in the lower- and lower-middle levels of the productive hierachy are placed in a directly antagonistic relationship. Their aggressions are channeled against one another. The ultimate cause of their oppression, the oligarchic elite of bosses who control production and reap the benefits of the extreme hierarchical fragmentation of production, is obscured.

In short, our thesis is that what is wrong with the socialization of youth is reflected in the adult roles we are preparing the young to undertake. Inequalities in adult status are reflected in similar inequalities in schools and other agencies of socialization. Alienation from both process and product of work are mirrored in the alienation from the schooling process. All these traits of schools that we wish to change are immutable as long as they are functional to the organization of work in our society. More generally, the real problems of youth socialization are precisely the fidelity of socializing institutions to the organization of adult life, particularly working life. The dilemma we face is that we are preparing youngsters only too well for relatively alienated and unfulfilling adult roles.

In contrast with the report, we believe that the transition of youth to adulthood cannot be understood without discussing the specific nature of adulthood. In the final section we argue that the democratization of the workplace is a necessary prerequisite to the democratization of the school. Rewarding relationships with coworkers and worker participation in decision making must exist before the schools will become more humane and participative themselves; and greater equality of work roles are a precondition of greater equality in educational outcomes.

What Is to Be Done?

If the problem is not directly in the socialization of youth as much as it is the nature of adult society, what is to be done to improve the environments that shape our children and young adults? In our view the agencies of socialization of youth replicate those of adult society, and they function well to prepare the young for the existing realities of adult life and to reproduce the class structure. Accordingly, any attempt to alter the socialization of the young must necessarily begin with the *transformation of adult roles* in society, particularly the roles presently assumed by low- to middle-income adults.

It is useful to integrate this view with one of the major themes of the report. "Adulthood cannot be accomplished merely by the acquisition of self-serving capabilities. These must be augmented by capabilities for mutually rewarding involvement with others."[47] The report goes on to list three characteristics of such "mutually rewarding involvement": (1) experience with persons differing in social class, subculture, and in age; (2) the experience of having others dependent on one's actions; and (3) interdependent activities directed toward collective goals. The report concludes that in order to achieve these capabilities, it is necessary to change certain youth-oriented institutions and to bring youth earlier into adult institutions—primarily the workplace.

But we have argued that the workplace is hierarchical and alienating. For most people, job experiences are not rewarding beyond pecuniary gain. Work is necessary in order to consume and consumption is the sphere of activity where people can express their "freedom" and "creativity" to the extent that they can afford to do so. Witness the campers, laden with motorcycles, snowmobiles, and motorboats on the nation's highways; the high-styled clothing of low- and middle-income blacks; and as the report itself points out, the massive consumption by youth.

The workplace is anything but free and creative for the average worker, and it is anything but a place where people have co-operative experiences with people from different social classes and subcultures. It is true that others may depend on a worker's actions, but often this dependence is an antagonistic one since many dependency relations are conditioned by the hierarchical context of the workplace; the foreman is dependent on the workers to follow the rules, and the workers are dependent on the foreman for favors and rewards, but such a relationship is not necessarily a cooperative one. Furthermore, as it now exists, the purpose of work is to maximize *individual* gain, even if it is at the expense of other workers. Thus skilled workers have traditionally been antagonistic to unskilled workers' needs, since the two groups have been set historically against each other in the struggle for wages. Racial antagonisms and sexual discrimination in the workplace represent similar types of conflicts among groups of workers.

The failure of existing work organizations to carry out these goals is not unlike the inadequacy of the schools in these domains. The obvious policy implication is that we must change the nature of work in order to make it more democratic, participative, co-operative, and interdependent in positive ways. Fortunately we are at a point in postindustrial society where this vision is truly a possibility. The very great alienation which has been so necessary for hierarchical production is now turning against the system, not in organized ways but in the more subtle forms of problems of quality control, wildcat strikes, and rising incidences of alcoholism, drug usage, employee absenteeism, and employee turnover.

These consequences have become so serious that the problem has been recognized at the national level by a Department of Health, Education, and Welfare Task Force.[48] This controversial report has suggested that if the nature of work does not change in such a way as to increase the participation of workers in decision making and to reduce worker alienation, major disruptions of normal production activities and reduced productivity can be foreseen.

In our view we should attempt to encourage and implement the changes that are being considered so that work environments become truly participative, cooperative, and humane and so that they provide an intrinsic satisfaction to workers. If we can transform the reality of adulthood, we believe that the socialization of youth will follow according to the correspondence principle. Parents, media, and the schools will begin to socialize youth for the new reality of sharing, cooperation, and a social consciousness. These will be the traits that will be functional under the new order.

It is through the democratization of the workplace that the primary institution of the adult world (the work situation) *could* be radically transformed. Workers in a democratized plant would, indeed, have a collective goal: the maximization of *their* well-being. This process might include both increases in production as well as a reorganization of the work process so that members of the work team experience a comradeship and sense of sharing. Gratification from involvement in the work process would replace alienation from it. No longer would the workplace be merely an oppressive environment for obtaining the money to satisfy a compulsive consumption pattern. And the social consciousness, sharing, and democratic participation for achieving the group-determined goals that would become a primary educational objective of the workplace would carry over to other institutions as well.

In many respects this transition would enable schools, families, and media to be more successful in their present quest to inculcate youth with civic responsibility—the duty to participate both politically and in the public service of their local communities.

The decline in hierarchy of production organizations and the increase in worker control of production would provide a major adult experience in democratic decision making and participation that would reinforce the efforts of and serve as role models for the media, schools, families, and other socialization influences. The dominance of humanism over property in such a society would pervade the youth environment.

Furthermore, industrial democracy would have an important effect on the distribution of *cognitive* knowledge: (1) Greater participation in the production process would tend to increase the training and education of all workers, but especially those drawn from the lower echelons who receive only limited training and work experiences at present. Under a democratized organization, the access to training and knowledge would be distributed more widely as a prerequisite to greater worker participation. In contrast, the present hierarchical structures tend to stratify access and exposure to knowledge, particularly that which is related to the management and financial aspects of production decisions. (2) Correspondingly, the schools would also have to prepare youth more equally for the world of work. They would have to find ways to develop much more general skills in working-class youth, including the abilities to handle an information rich environment, and to handle new situations, abilities that are presently limited largely to upper-class youth.

This is obviously an idealistic vision of a democratic industrial society. The transition to such a society is fraught with difficulties, but we do not believe that appropriate changes in the socialization of youth are possible without moving in this direction. More specifically, we do not believe that the young will be socialized to be creative, participative, and cooperative until the social relations of adults are characterized by those traits. The desirable portrait of youth that has been painted in the report cannot be achieved in a society which alienates worker from worker and worker from his product. Youth apparently understands this much better than the authors of the report; for the rise of the present youth culture is in part a reaction to a hierarchical, dehumanized adult world. We suggest that, rather than deemphasize the youth culture by an earlier incorporation of youth into this world, we should humanize and democratize the workplace *and* the institutions which prepare people for work.

Notes

1. James S. Coleman et al., *Equality of Educational Opportunity* (Washington, D.C.: U.S. Office of Education, 1966).

2. Colin Greer, *The Great School Legend* (New York: Basic Books, 1972).

3. Ivan Illich, *Deschooling Society* (New York: Harper & Row, 1971).

4. Christopher Jencks et al., *Inequality: A Reassessment of the Effects of Family and Schooling in America* (New York: Basic Books, 1972).

5. James S. Coleman et al., *Youth: Transition to Adulthood* (Chicago: University of Chicago Press, 1974), p. 7.

6. Ibid., p. viii.

7. Ibid., p. viii.

8. Ibid., p. 2.

9. Alek Inkeles, "The Socialization of Competence," *Harvard Educational Review* 36, no. 3 (Summer 1966): 265–83.

10. Coleman et al., *Youth*, p. 137.

11. Ibid., p. 146.

12. David Gold, "Socialization to Occupational Roles" (Menlo Park, Calif.: Portola Institute, February 1974); Marilyn Power Goldberg, "Sex Role Socialization and Work Roles: The Experience of Women" (Menlo Park, Calif.: Portola Institute, 1974).

13. Alex Inkeles, "Making Men Modern: On the Causes and Consequences of Individual Change in Six Developing Countries," *American Journal of Sociology* 75, no. 2 (September 1969): 208–25; Alex Inkeles and David H. Smith, *Becoming Modern* (Cambridge, Mass.: Harvard University Press, 1974).

14. Samuel Bowles, "Unequal Education and the Reproduction of the Social Division of Labor," in *Schooling in a Corporate Society*, ed. Martin Carnoy (New York: David McKay, 1972).

15. Coleman et al., *Equality of Educational Opportunity*; Harvey Averch, "How Effective Is Schooling: A Critical Review and Synthesis of Research Findings" (Santa Monica, Calif.: Rand Corporation, 1972).

16. Herbert Gintis, "Education, Technology and the Character-

istics of Worker Productivity," *American Economic Review* 61, no. 2 (May 1971): 266–79; Z. Griliches and W. Mason, "Education, Income, and Ability," *Journal of Political Economy* Supplement (May/ June 1972): S74–S103.

17. Gintis, "Education, Technology and Worker Productivity."

18. Inkeles, "Socialization of Competence."

19. Kenneth Lasson, *The Workers* (New York: Bantam Books, 1972); Studs Terkel, *Working* (New York: Pantheon Books, 1974).

20. U.S. Department of Health, Education, and Welfare, *Work in America* (Cambridge, Mass.: MIT Press, 1973).

21. Gintis, "Education, Technology and Worker Productivity."

22. Ibid., p. 274.

23. Charles Silberman, *Crisis in the Classroom* (New York: Random House, 1970), p. 11.

24. Max Weber, "On Bureaucracy," in *From Max Weber: Essays in Sociology*, trans. Hans Gerth and C. Wright Mills (New York: 1958).

25. Robert Dreeben, *On What Is Learned in School* (Reading, Mass.: Addison-Wesley, 1968), pp. 29–30.

26. Gintis, "Education, Technology and Worker Productivity," p. 276.

27. Dreeben, *On What Is Learned in School*, pp. 33–35.

28. Bowles, "Unequal Education"; Gintis, "Education, Technology and Worker Productivity"; Henry M. Levin, "Educational Reform and Social Change," *Journal of Applied Behavioral Science* 10, no. 3 (August 1974): 304–20.

29. Silberman, *Crisis in the Classroom*.

30. Gintis, "Education, Technology and Worker Productivity."

31. Marshall H. Brenner, "Use of High School Data to Predict Work Performance," *Journal of Applied Psychology* 52, no. 1 (January 1968): 29–30.

32. Bowles, "Unequal Education."

33. John E. Coons et al., *Private Wealth and Public Education* (Cambridge, Mass.: Harvard University Press, 1970).

34. George E. Johnson and Frank P. Stafford, "Social Returns to Quantity and Quality of Schooling," *Journal of Human Resources* 8, no. 2 (Spring 1973): 138–55.

35. W. Lee Hansen and Burton Weisbrod, *Benefits, Costs, and Finances of Higher Education* (Chicago: Markham, 1970).

36. Ibid.; Douglas M. Windham, *Education, Equality and Income Redistribution* (Lexington, Mass.: Lexington Books, 1970).

37. Samuel Bowles and Herbert Gintis, "IQ in the U.S. Class Structure," *Social Policy*, January/February 1973.

38. Marcus Raskin, *Being and Doing* (New York: Random House, 1971).

39. D. M. Gordon, *Theories of Poverty and Unemployment* (Lexington, Mass.: Lexington Books, 1972).

40. Jerome Karabel, "Community Colleges and Social Stratification," *Harvard Educational Review* 42, no. 4 (November 1972): 521–62.

41. David Bushnell and Mary Bach Kievet, "Community Colleges: What Is Our Job?" *Change*, April 1974, p. 52.

42. Samuel Bowles, "Contradiction in U.S. Higher Education," in *Political Economy: Radical Vs. Orthodox Approaches*, ed. James Weaver (Boston: Allyn & Bacon, 1972).

43. Levin, "Educational Reform and Social Change."

44. J. Spring, *Schooling and the Rise of the Corporate State* (Boston: Beacon, 1972).

45. Stephen Marglin, "What Do Bosses Do? The Origins and Functions of Hierachy in Capitalist Production" (Harvard Institute of Economic Research, Discussion Paper 222, November 1971).

46. P. B. Doeringer and M. J. Piore, *Internal Labor Markets and Manpower Analysis* (Lexington, Mass.: Lexington Books, 1971).

47. Coleman et al., *Youth*, p. 4.

48. HEW, *Work in America*.

10

Martin Carnoy

International Educational Reform: The Ideology of Efficiency

Part 1

> . . . today in this country we recognize that education has a variety of roles to play. Democratic institutions cannot exist without education, for democracy functions only when the people are informed and are aware, thirsting for knowledge and exchanging ideas. Education makes possible the economic democracy that raises social mobility, for it is education that insures that classes are not frozen and that an elite of whatever kind does not perpetuate itself. And in the underdeveloped economies education itself stimulates development by . . . demonstrating that tomorrow need not be the same as yesterday, that change can take place, that the outlook is hopeful.
>
> Dean Rusk, November 1961[1]

If books about education in underdeveloped countries were simply analyses by a few academics on a subject of passing interest, we could afford to discuss them on their technical merits alone. But the most important of these books are not written by academics. They are policy statements which influence both academic and nonacademic thought and, in turn, affect the thinking of investors and institutions offering assistance from developed countries toward the underdeveloped world. They therefore give important clues to the kinds of reforms which will be taking place in educational systems around the world.

Philip Coombs' *The World Education Crisis* (New York: Oxford University Press, 1968) is such a book. Although eight years old and many times favorably reviewed, it is worth returning to again, this time to examine the validity of its assumptions and how these affect the credibility of Coombs' analysis and recommendations.

The essence of Coombs' book is its definition of the world educational crisis, which Coombs suggests has several elements. First, he assumes that where social and economic aspirations are unfulfilled, a higher average education implies a greater propensity to demand radical change. Second, he assumes that in general the optimum path of social change for underdeveloped countries is in the historical footsteps of the developed countries, transforming economy, polity, and culture to conform with Western "modern" industrial standards.

According to Coombs, very rapid worldwide changes have occurred in all countries since 1945. These "revolutionary" changes have taken place in science and technology, economic and political affairs, and demographic and social structures. Educational systems have also changed rapidly, but not as rapidly as the surrounding environment. The changes have resulted in disparities between educational systems and their environments. Coombs singles out four particularly important causes of the disparities:

> The *sharp increase in popular aspirations* for education, which has laid seige to existing schools and universities; the *acute scarcity of resources*, which has constrained educational systems from responding more fully to new demands; the *inherent inertia of educational systems*, which has caused them to respond too sluggishly in adapting their in-

ternal affairs to new external necessities, even when resources have not been the main obstacle to adaptation; and
the *inertia of societies themselves*—the heavy weight of
traditional attitudes, religious customs, prestige and incentive patterns, and institutional structures, which has blocked
them from making optimum use of education and of educated manpower to foster national development. (p. 4)

If adjustment by both the society and educational system does
not occur, "the growing disparity between education and society
will inevitably crack the frame of the educational systems—and
in some cases the frame of their respective societies" (p. 4).

Coombs suggests that the educational crisis is worldwide, "more
subtle and less graphic than a 'food crisis' or a 'military crisis' but
no less weighted with dangerous possibilities" (p. 4). The nature
of the crisis is twofold. On the one hand, the enormous expansion
of education in the postwar period threatens world stability
because underdeveloped countries, and some developed countries
as well, have not changed their educational systems and economic
hiring policies rapidly enough to incorporate new graduates into
the labor force. On the other hand, most countries are far from
satisfying their future needs for skilled labor, so that school
systems still must be expanded.

To Coombs, primary consideration should be given to increased
output, so that everyone in the society eventually can prosper.
The impending crisis can be avoided through increasing the
growth rate, and all efforts should be toward that goal. Coombs
is not arguing that countries are in trouble because of unequal
distribution of education and consequent unequal distribution of
income. On the contrary, he tends to ignore the elimination of
social inequalities as an important objective for those in power.
This point of view is consistent with a belief in linear, evolutionary progress. Both internationally and within each developing
nation more equal access to resources can and should be achieved
through economic growth and by political persuasion and cooperation rather than radical structural change.

For Coombs, the principal problem of the educational system
is the inefficiency of its management and teaching techniques.

248 f MARTIN CARNOY

The schools are also inefficient because they teach curricula which
are not relevant to the needs of the country. Humanities majors
are being produced when engineers and scientists are needed.
Within this framework, he sees as crucial the relation between the
mass of uneducated people, the labor force, and the educational
system. He argues that society must provide many more resources
for schooling than in the past because of increasing population,
increased per pupil cost, and increasing level of schooling demanded by the average family for its children.

Coombs seems to believe that through a combination of technology, nonformal training, foreign aid, and national will, it is
possible to provide everyone with a level of schooling sufficient
to secure a decent job. At the same time, of course, internal
reform of the educational system is also necessary. The curriculum
has to be changed. People have to be trained for jobs that exist
or that will exist in the near future. The schools have to be run
more efficiently, with better teaching techniques, more feedback,
and more freedom for teachers and students. Other institutions
in the society also have to change. Bureaucracies have to be more
flexible. Throughout the economy, traditional man has to be converted to modern man. On a world scale, there has to be more
cooperation to transfer the knowledge and resources available
in the developed societies to the underdeveloped ones.

Equality for Coombs is a political issue. A government may
have to give greater income and educational equality to stay in
office, but at a cost of slower increases in national product. Therefore, equalization should be undertaken only as a necessity to
maintain political stability. In referring to the democratization
of school systems, for example, he argues that:

A selective [schooling] system for such a country [under-
developed] is no easier to manage from a political standpoint, but its adoption can be justified on practical grounds:
first the country is not in an economic position to afford a
more open system; second, by trying to adopt one, it may
slow its economic growth and thus postpone the day when
it can in fact afford one. (p. 33)

Coombs does not reject equality as a secondary goal of a society, but he certainly does not treat it as the possible basis for more efficient societal institutions or more rapid long-run economic development.

Coombs believes the greatest difficulty facing educational systems is the rising cost of schooling. But his analysis of why schooling is expensive is limited to statements about the structure and method of the current system of formal schooling. He also takes as given the social and economic structure which certifies teachers, rewards them, and causes them to relate to pupils in a particular way. Thus, the only solution to high costs of education —given the increasing social demand for formal schooling— is the introduction of capital intensive methods like technology to replace teachers (although there is unemployment even of skilled labor in many countries), borrowing funds from abroad, or extending the educational system to nonformal methods of training alongside formal schooling. This last solution would be applied to children and adults who cannot gain entrance to the formal system. In addition, Coombs would improve the management of both formal and nonformal education so that funds entering the system would be used more efficiently.

The Coombs analysis also concentrates on the efficiency of schooling without relating it to *multiple* goals. Like other planners, Coombs does little more than pay lip service to the significant issue of how a technician is supposed to measure the efficiency of a system when he avoids the issue of what the system is *supposed* to be producing, at least as defined by the ruling group. How can it be assumed that the system is inefficient if its outputs are not known?

Coombs' analysis also assumes that schools are primarily places to develop vocational (cognitive) skills. But in the real world that is not the only function of schools, and probably not the main one. Schools transmit culture and values and they channel children into social roles. This helps maintain the class structure and social order. Those who have the qualities most desired by the economy and society—verbal ability, awareness of time, and the internalized responsiveness to extrinsic rather than intrinsic rewards—perform best in school. The schools select people on the basis of qualities needed by capitalist economic structures, just as the feudal system relied on the family as a source of social position. Coombs' failure to analyze the role of the school system as an allocator of social roles is the most serious shortcoming of his book. He tells us that the objective of the schools is to produce graduates, and that schools are inefficient because large numbers of children drop out before graduation: "In any event, the objective of schools is certainly not to produce dropouts; it is to produce 'finishers,' and by this criterion their cost-effectiveness ratio must be judged very low."[2]

But if the objective of the schools is to produce finishers, why does the large majority of dropouts occur because there are either no classrooms available (for example, most rural primary schools in Latin America do not go beyond the third grade), or because of selective examinations? If we look at the structure of school systems and the way funds are allocated to schools, it seems evident that schools only expect a certain fraction of pupils to become finishers, and allocate funds, classroom space, and teachers accordingly. We therefore have to conclude that one of the objectives of schools *is* to produce dropouts.

Similarly, if the least powerful groups in a society are those who get the least benefits from the education system, does not this suggest that the system may be perfectly rational within that society? Why should significant changes in the distribution of schooling occur if social, economic, and political structures remain unchanged? Indeed, all the evidence we have shows that rapid increases in average education and in technology, and the other revolutionary changes to which Coombs refers, have not changed the distribution of income or social structure since 1945, even in the developed societies.[3] Only where radical and thorough overhauls of the entire society have occurred can we speak of significant changes in the efficiency of institutions for promoting employment and growth, and in the distribution of income, wealth, and education.

This brings us to a third characteristic of Coombs' analysis. He assumes that unemployment of the educated results from an ill fit between the output of the educational system and the needs of a modern economy. As in the case of education, Coombs approaches the issue of unemployment and of educated unemployment as a management problem: the economy and the schools must be aligned so there are more jobs available and more appropriate training in the schools to fill those jobs. This assumes that the economy in question is organized or can be organized to provide full employment without radical restructuring.

It seems much more persuasive to argue that any economy which is closely tied through trade and investment to the industrial countries is also going to have an employment structure and technology which is tied to the international system. This, in turn, will have a significant effect on the labor market and educational system. In such a system the maximization of employment, rather than profits, would require drastic alteration of its relationship with the industrial countries. What Coombs views as inefficiencies in labor markets and educational structures because they are not sufficiently modern, we argue are instead the result of imported capitalist forms, distorted to fit the condition of nonindustrialized economies. In large part, these forms only serve the needs of domestic elites and producers in the industrialized countries.

Many nonindustrial countries are now attempting to produce approximately the same set of consumption goods as industrial countries, using the same technology and organization of production. This pattern of production is promoted on the assumption that today's low-income economies can replicate, in temporally compressed form, the historical development process of already industrialized countries. But if a developing society is producing consumption goods appropriate for high income countries, only a small number of people in the economy will be active in producing or consuming these goods. Educational expenditures will be concentrated in urban areas to train only a few people, to function in the technologically advanced sector and to produce sophisticated consumer goods, especially consumer durables. Imported technology and organization of production thus make it more profitable and socially preferable to produce goods which higher income groups can consume. I would argue that the major source of the unemployment problem is not traditional elements in nonindustrial societies, but the most *modern* sectors—those tied most closely to metropolitan economies.

The problem of unemployment among the educated is an extension of this structural situation. If there is a constant rate of unemployment in an economy and the average level of schooling in the labor force rises, the average schooling level of the unemployed will tend to rise as well. This is particularly true since the young have a higher average level of schooling than older members of the labor force, and the young are more likely to be unemployed.

Coombs considers unemployment among the educated a serious matter on two grounds: first, it is a waste of resources, and, second, it may produce a threat to political stability and hence reduce the rate of economic growth. Indeed, Coombs is concerned with the role that schooling plays in the potential overthrow of social structures and political systems. In his book, the demands of the educated unemployed form only one of two threats to the system; the other is the unsatisfied demands of those who want more schooling. The validity of the proposition that these groups really do constitute a threat to the stability of capitalist societies relies on the premise that having education or wanting it is a liberating force and mobilizes people to action.

But his argument that these two groups will be catalysts of change is largely unsubstantiated. First, Coombs does not adequately support his contention that the *educated* unemployed are a greater threat to political stability than the *uneducated* unemployed. It is unclear that those with primary, secondary, or university education are in fact more radical than they would have been if they had not gone to school at all. People who attend school until a given level, when that level is limited to a lucky few, will tend to be employed in ways which meet their aspirations when they graduate. In most countries—at least in the last generation—this "lucky" group comes from higher socioeconomic backgrounds or more Westernized tribes.

The unemployment problem resides almost entirely among those from the lower classes, who, if they get to school at all, attend a level of schooling which has already expanded greatly relative to the demand for its graduates.[4] These are the very students, however, who not only come from less politically demanding families but also are socialized in school to expect less and to be less active politically.[5] Therefore, as schooling expands and children from the lower socioeconomic classes are schooled and then unemployed, the effect of schooling—which for all children may be negligible compared to the effect of family—may work in the opposite direction than Coombs predicts: potential discontents may actually be more effectively socialized into the system.

By political socialization, various institutions including the schools contribute to the maintenance of the political structure and culture. Ivan Illich[6] even argues that schools socialize children to accept *failure*, if that is to be their role in society. Higher aspirations upon completing some years of school are tempered by the stress in capitalist societies on individual accountability. Failure is the individual's fault. Certainly nothing that is learned in school, especially a school that reflects an institutionally rigid society, creates a propensity to promote radical institutional change. Coombs may want to argue that the existence of conservative schools, generally transmitting conservative values, conflicts with *other* forces which generate a radicalization of the population. But he has identified only one of those forces in the book: unemployment. If jobs are not available, people are sure to be upset. What he has not shown is that the unemployed with more education are willing to take more drastic action for change than those with less education.

According to Coombs, the second group—those who cannot get as much school as they want—are also a threat to political and social stability. In many cases, they are also educated and unemployed, and that is precisely why they want more schooling; they believe that by getting more schooling they will get employment. The very channeling of dissatisfaction into the demand for more schooling contradicts some of Coombs' fears. As long as people believe, as individuals, that the way out is to become better educated, the social and economic structure will never change. But Coombs assumes that education is such an important political issue among those who are not getting enough that they will be willing to overthrow the system to get it. There is little logic and little evidence to support that position. Unemployment, whether among the educated or uneducated, along with land tenure, racial and tribal conflicts, and imperialism have all been more important than access to schooling as causes of revolution in the past, and are much more likely causes of crises in the next generation.

It is difficult to pin Coombs down about what kind of economic organization he envisions. He could argue that each country has its free choice of an appropriate system, and that he is only concerned with efficient resource allocation within the system. If that is his position, then we feel that it is derived from an incorrect analysis of the way the international economy works. Even four years later, he makes it clear that he believes in an international system in which rich and poor capitalist nations can deal with each other as equals, without exploitation.

> In closing, we stress one further feature of strategy— namely, international cooperation. We agree that every nation must be the master of its own educational destiny, and that it must largely support its own education system, however poor the nation may be. But on the grounds laid out earlier, we assert that no nation—given the crisis conditions affecting all—can successfully "go it alone." International educational cooperation on a vastly extended scale must, therefore, be a cardinal feature of our educational strategy for rich and poor nations alike.[7]

Along with Schumpeter,[8] he implies that imperialism by trading and investment is an impossibility; that the spread of capitalist institutions are *antiimperialistic*. Not only do international relations in production lead to the highest possible rate of growth in all countries, but higher levels of ethical behavior are attained. The logical extension of Schumpeter's (and, to some extent, Coombs') analysis is that capitalism is a civilizing force coming from countries (in the United States and Europe) which reject domination as a means of settling disputes and distributing economic and political power.

However, another theory rejects this view of the world system and the notions of development which derive from it. This theory assumes that underdeveloped countries do not undergo the same phases of growth as the now highly industrialized countries. Instead, it is impossible for developing societies today to recapitulate the change which took place in the developing countries in another historical period. The problems of developing countries do not result from a *lack* or a *lag* of development; instead these problems result from a dependency which developing societies have on the highly developed countries.

> Dependence is a situation in which the economy of certain countries is conditioned by the development and expansion of another economy to which the former is subjected. The relation of interdependence between two or more economies, and between these and world trade, assumes the form of dependence when some countries (the dominant ones) can expand and be self-sustaining, while other countries (the dependent ones) can only expand as a reflection of dominant country expansion, which can, in turn, be a positive and/or negative effect on their immediate development. In any case, the basic situation of dependence leads to an overall situation for the dependent countries which places them behind and under the exploitation of the dominant countries.[9]

Dependency theorists argue that the only way to achieve development and a new national culture is through a national struggle for liberation from domination. The absence of struggle, or even of participation, by the colonized masses precludes the possibility of forming liberated cultural forms.

> We believe that the conscious and organized undertaking by a colonized people to reestablish the sovereignty of that nation constitutes the most complete and obvious cultural manifestation that exists. It is not alone the success of the struggle which afterward gives validity and vigor to culture; culture is not put into cold storage during the conflict. The struggle itself in its development and in its internal progression sends culture along different paths and traces out

entirely new ones for it. The struggle for freedom does not give back to national culture its former value and shapes; this struggle which aims at a fundamentally different set of relations between men cannot leave intact either the form or the content of the people's culture. After the conflict there is not only the disappearance of colonialism but also the disappearance of colonized man.[10]

There is a clear difference between the function of an educational system as seen by developmentalists and its function as seen by dependency theorists. Developmentalists view schooling as a liberating process, in which the child is transformed from a traditional individual to a modern one. This transition is supposed to enable the child to be creative as well as functional. Schooling is also supposed to enable the graduate to contribute to the economy, polity, and society. But according to the theory of dependency, the transformation that takes place in school cannot be liberating, since a person is simply changed from one role in a dependent system to a different role. While the new role may be more economically rewarding, it still leaves the individual in a conditional situation, one which is dominated by the culture, technology, and goods of the dominant, developed countries. The graduate cannot achieve his or her full potential, since the dependent society is limited in its ability to provide adequate work. Much of the labor force is not even able to enter the dynamic sector, which tends to be dominated by capital intensive technology. The inefficiencies of the school system as related to the social and economic structure are not inefficiencies at all, but derivatives of dependent status.

The large number of dropouts and illiterates in a particular society may, in fact, be accompanied by an *overdeveloped* school system, in which certain numbers of children go to school, but then are unable to find employment different from what they had before. This is not the result of irrelevant or low-quality schooling, as Coombs claims, but the result of a dependent economic system which is dominated by the international division of labor. An economic structure able to absorb all the educated is not possible under conditions of national dependency, and a system of schooling which complements all people's social utility also is not possible.

Where does all this leave us? I maintain that the most advanced management techniques—including Coombs' suggestions of systematic cost-effectiveness and cost-benefit analysis and program budgeting—will not solve the unemployment problem among the educated or reduce the pressure of the population for more schooling than the society can afford. These are primarily due to the nature of the capitalist world's social structure. Just as ability testing has been used to legitimize the class structure of industrialized capitalist societies by putting the onus on individuals for their failure to do well on such tests, so the efficiency criteria for school systems and labor markets are used to *legitimize the international class structure* by putting the onus on nonindustrialized peoples for failing to manage their own institutions efficiently or to mobilize adequate resources for economic growth.

If we accept dependency theory's analysis of underdevelopment, we understand that for the mass of people to emerge from their colonized passivity, their educational experience must be intimately related to a process of change which they themselves originate, consciously breaking the bonds of the social and educational structure which has oppressed them as long as they can remember. We understand that "cracking the frame of the educational systems"—and in some cases the frame of their respective societies—is a prerequisite to breaking the colonial relation and enabling all the members of underdeveloped societies to share in the growth process. If the educational system is suffering, we must find its root causes in the problems of society itself. These societal problems stem not only from relations internal to the nation, but extend to the relations among nations. If these relations are inequitable, the educational structures will also be inequitable; if relations are distorted, education will also be distorted. And ultimately if we believe these relationships should be changed we must deal with how they are to be changed.

This generation of educational planners, policy makers, teachers, and researchers has inherited a legacy. We still believe that although a statement such as Dean Rusk's quoted at the beginning of this essay may be naive and somewhat exaggerated, it is essentially correct. Now we are asked to question that belief. This is not an ethical choice, although some of us may want to see it as one. If we believe that world capitalism makes everyone prosper and that all countries, if they are wise and want their people to be happy, should continue to participate with the developed countries in the world capitalist venture, then we should continue to help that venture by supporting its theories and beliefs. If, however, we believe that world capitalism has created structures that *prevent* the mass of people in the world from achieving the fulfillment of their needs and aspirations, then we must contribute to radical changes in those structures.

Notes

1. Dean Rusk, "Economic Growth and Investment in Education," *Department of State Bulletin* 45 (13 November 1961): 821–22, quoted in James S. Coleman, ed., *Education and Political Development* (Princeton, N.J.: Princeton University Press, 1965), pp. 522–23.

2. Philip Coombs and Jacques Hallak, *Managing Educational Costs* (London: Oxford University Press, 1972), p. 95.

3. Robinson Hollister, "The Relationship Between Education and the Distribution of Income: Some Forays" (Unpublished paper, University of Wisconsin, 1970).

4. In Tunisia, the distribution of unemployed secondary school leavers shows the class effect very clearly. See Hans Thias, Martin Carnoy, and Richard Sack, "The Effects of Schooling, Socio-economic Background, Training, and Environmental Variables on Labor Force Characteristics of Middle Level Manpower in Tunisia" (Unpublished paper, World Bank, 1972).

5. See, for example, Richard Dawson and Kenneth Prewitt, *Political Socialization* (Boston: Little, Brown, 1969).

6. Ivan Illich, *Deschooling Society* (New York: Random House, 1971).

7. Coombs and Hallak, *Managing Educational Costs*, p. 172.

8. Joseph Schumpeter, *Imperialism and Social Classes* (New York: Augustus M. Kelley, 1951).

9. Theotonio Dos Santos, *Dependencia Economica y Cambio Revolucionario* (Caracas, Venezuela: Editorial Nueva Izquierda, 1970), p. 38.

10. Frantz Fanon, *Wretched of the Earth* (New York: Grove Press, 1963), p. 246. See also Albert Memmi, *The Colonizer and the Colonized* (Boston: Beacon Press, 1967).

Part 2

Learning to Be was an ambitious project: it attempted to summarize many of the profound issues in education which face planners, educators and all people interested in a better life for men and women everywhere. We cannot argue with the intentions and motivations of the International Commission on the Development of Education—*Learning to Be*'s authors; the Commission indicates deep concern for people and their welfare. Yet, there are great difficulties with the Commission's report, which threaten its value to the educational community. The recommendations and solutions to educational problems provided by the report mislead the reader and planner on the possibilities and manner of achieving those solutions. Furthermore, the report avoids some of the basic issues in economic and social development. In essence, *Learning to Be* tries, with some concepts of "universal truths," to transcend relationships of force and domination, and international, ideological, social, and inter-personal conflicts by ignoring that those relationships exist in the world. These universal truths are derived from an interpretation of educational history that is schizophrenic and from the Commission's pervasive reliance on science and technology to solve social problems.

The analysis by the authors contrasts education's historical past, which they characterize as fitting people into particular roles in a "traditionally" oriented or even industrializing society, and the historical present and future, which they believe is so qualitatively and quantitatively different that it cannot be treated with previous models. The Commission makes this leap with the following statement: ". . . for the first time in history, education is now engaged in preparing men for a type of society which does not yet exist." Taking this statement as truth, the Commission allows itself to treat the educational present as different from the educational past.

However, the statement is not correct. Formal education has often been used in the past by reformers to prepare people for visions of society in the process of change. Horace Mann and John Dewey are two examples of such reformers, but others would include missionaries in Africa and Asia, British and French colonial administrators, and philosophers in Latin America who saw in education the possibility of changing people to fit an organization of society which was largely a vision at the time they proposed their reforms. They did not always (or even usually) succeed. The Commission might ask itself why: the reformers who did succeed in having their ideas adopted had the support of powerful economic groups in their countries, and—in the case of the nonindustrialized economies—the support of even more powerful groups outside the country. But the report does not deal with the kind of support *its* proposed reforms would be likely to receive from various elements of the population and especially from the State apparatus itself. It fails to do this because to deal with the political-economic nature of school reform would have transferred the report from an idealist framework to a realistic one. Again, the rationalization for the framework was the historical schizophrenia of the report's analysis.

Four Historical Views

To understand this difficulty, let us consider four historical views of school development.

1. *Evolutionary Idealism.* In this view, schools in modern capitalist societies have as their mission to produce a liberated, integrated person. The failure of the schools to achieve this is a result of institutional bottlenecks, bureaucratic inefficiency and other societal imperfections. Nevertheless, evolutionary idealists believe—along with Joseph Schumpeter—that since modern capitalist society is essentially liberating and integrating, schools designed to fulfill the best form of capitalist organization of production are capable of producing the creative, socially committed, physically, intellectually, emotionally, and ethically integrated individual. Furthermore, evolutionary idealists

believe that these goals can be achieved by a continuous, evolutionary movement forward.

2. *The Pluralist View.* Here, the school is part of the struggle between the nether class and the elite. The nether classes have important power in the society; can effect change; and can use the school to achieve their purposes. The pluralist model admits a possible conflict in the aims of the nether class and the elite, but this conflict is not necessarily rooted in the economic and social structure of the society; rather, in purely political considerations which are highly variable over time.

3. *The Human Capital View.* The school's primary function is for the development of skills, and these skills are produced in response to society's economic needs. However, this approach cannot explain why skills are produced in a particular fashion; in particular, why are skills produced hierarchically as opposed to the way that the report suggests? One would ask an even more fundamental question: why is work organized hierarchically? The reason I raise that question in this context is because the report does not deal with this issue at all. If we are to reorganize schools so that they are not producing skills in hierarchical fashion, we must deal with the issue of the organization of work in society as a whole.

4. *The Structural Functionalist View.* It argues that schools are designed for fitting people into societal roles. The report understands this "correspondence principle" between schooling and societal roles, but does not deal with the fundamental issue of *why* certain roles for certain people emerge from the evolutionary process of school development.

Learning to Be at one time or another chooses to interpret the role of schooling from all these views. Yet, all of the views have conflicting elements and some of them conflict in fundamental interpretation. On balance, however, I would argue that, although the report gives much lip service to the structural functionalist concept of schooling, and although the report recognizes the class nature of schooling on page after page, its recommendations for the future imply the evolutionary, idealistic view of school development. The authors of the report choose ultimately to ignore an interpretation which puts schooling in the context of a class or conflict model of international society, and imply that development can progress as a *harmonious* process and that the role of the state is basically one of trying to benefit all of the people at the expense of no one. I profoundly disagree with this view of development and will now try to show how choosing that view —instead of a conflictual approach to development in schooling —results in completely different interpretation of fundamental issues raised in the report.

Once the report chooses harmonious development, it also chooses harmonious solutions. The underlying theme of the strategy sections is that science and technology will solve these problems. In order to show where this assumption leads the Commission, we can analyze three important issues dealt with in the report: the question of financing education, i.e. the *cost* of the programs the report proposes; the definition of equal opportunity and the relationship between equal opportunity and educational expansion; and finally the role of science and technology itself in education and society.

1. The report has recommended expanding education rapidly to provide all the young population with formal schooling and the adult population with continuing education. The cost of such a program would be enormous, and the Commission attempts to come to grips with this by suggesting several remedies for splitting up the burden of educational expenditures and introducing new technology into the educational system. I think the report shows itself to be incredibly naive, even to the point of using fallacious arguments, in its propositions.[1]

Although it is perhaps possible to reduce the cost per pupil in schooling somewhat in the long run by use of radio, programmed textbooks and so forth, in the short run the introduction of these new methods requires investment in teacher-training, technical assistance and other short-run expenditures which would increase cost per pupil for at least ten years. The Commission suggests that the burden of the additional expenditures required to expand education to both young people and adults should be borne by different ministries, business firms, etc. However, it is here that the Commission fails to convey the conflicts that occur under limited resources and expanding demands. It tries to minimize these conflicts, giving us the impression that in the harmonious model everybody will pull together to reach the universally desired goal. In practice what we find is that when there are limited resources for education (or, put another way, when those who control the resources are unwilling to spend them for education), those who have little power get very little of the educational resources and those who have a lot of power get almost all the limited resources. Thus, even if more resources for education are forthcoming, one could guess that these resources will be distributed in a way that may favor certain social classes over others. Instead of emphasizing this conflict, including all the tensions and crises that it foreshadows, the Commission gives us reassurance of remedies which in fact disguise the seriousness of the problem.

2. The report clearly separates equality and democracy in education from equality and democracy in the society, on the assumption that it is possible to democratize schooling separately from society, and that by democratizing education, it may be possible to democratize society. But the report ignores the relation between educational expansion and equality of social opportunity. It leaves us with the impression that by equalizing opportunity in education it would be possible to equalize opportunity in society. Ultimately, this objective is to be fulfilled by expanding education—making it available to all people on both an initial basis and a continuing basis—and by "shaking off the dogmas of conventional pedagogy," setting up "free and permanent dialogue . . . within the educational process," and "putting education into form of 'research, conquest, creative act.'"

Interestingly enough, the report defines equal opportunity for all not as nominal equality or even equal outcome at the end of the process, or even the equal chance to obtain economic and social resources in a society, or equal power in a polity. In the words of the report, "it means making certain that each individual receives a *suitable* education at a pace and through methods adapted to his particular person."

This very same definition of equality was used by U.S. educational reformers at the turn of the present century to rationalize a track system within the comprehensive high schools to rationalize a strictly vocational education for black people, to rationalize the aptitude testing that was used to discriminate against women, certain ethnic groups and certain races in American society.[2] Ultimately, these reforms were *class-based* reforms, because the society in which the word "suitable education" was defined was and is a class-based society. Because the Commission ignores the whole issue of class, discrimination and conflict, they can believe that individualized instruction will be used to compensate the poor relative to the rich. In practice, however, it is used to define inferior occupational and social roles for the poor and superior occupational and social roles for the middle class and the rich. The Commission believes that by opening up the school system and getting away from depersonalized and rigid examination systems it will be possible to create more social mobility. But all the evidence in a society like the United States (which is more "open" than most) seems to point to a reality that income distribution has not become more equal in the last twenty years, and that occupational mobility is very limited: education continues to prepare people for particular social roles and these social roles are based significantly on the family and social origins.

Even if we could equalize test scores by compensatory education, unless society itself is willing to equalize economic and social opportunity, equal test scores for different groups in a society do not guarantee that the people with equal test scores will have equal economic and social opportunity. The best example of this is the case of women. Women and men students at the end of high school have essentially equal test scores. Yet, women are socialized to accept different (and lower-paying) occupations than men. In the United States, the average income of white high school- and college-educated women is 40 percent that of which high school- and college-educated men, despite the fact that their scores on achievement tests are essentially equal at the end of high school. All these indications point to the fact that the opportunities for employment, the incomes of people and their occupational status in the society are a function of much more than their performance in school. The Commission does not deal with the fact that societies are class-structured, sex-structured and race-structured, and that these structures have a great deal to do with the organization of work in a society. The issue of equal opportunity is not going to be settled in the schools. Equal opportunity implies *equal* access to resources. But societies are not based on the harmonious model which the Commission would have us adopt.

3. This gets us to the third point that the Commission emphasizes: the important role of science and technology as an input into education and an output of education. In a society in which everybody does not have equal access to the decisions of the society, we must ask first whether technology can solve the problems which we ask it to solve, and secondly (and very relatedly), *who* will control the form and uses of the science and technology which the Commission so heartily expounds. Again, the report takes the view that science and technology are neutral, since in fact society can come to a harmonious agreement as to the best uses of science. But science can be easily used *against* people as well as for people, and this the Commission seems to ignore.

The question of *who* will begin the learning society and *who* will control the science and technology which is used to produce that learning society and which is then produced by a learned society is consciously avoided by the Commission. Rather, they seek to answer the question of *how* these things can be done, not ever connecting the who and the how. Yet to a large extent it is the *who* that determines the *how*: science can seek to benefit the masses of people and fulfill their rather simple needs, or it can be used to fulfill the needs of a dominant few, needs that are based on industrial country consumption patterns. Children can learn a science in school that makes them dependent on industrial concepts of technology, or they can learn a science that contains explicit social content as well as dealing with technical problems. All in all, the treatment of science and technology by the report is surprisingly mechanistic and doesn't leave the reader with the impression that the Commission gave very much thought to the relations between science and society.

Contradictory Recommendations

These three examples serve to indicate how contradictory are the recommendations of the report. As indicated above, these contradictions are rationalized by the evolutionary idealistic model which the Commission applies to the present state of the educational system and to their analysis of present-day societal change. It is very nice to think that the world is made up of people and nations who have common goals and are willing to achieve them in harmonious evolution. Nevertheless, it seems to me that it much more reasonable to assume that the reason that some nations are poor and others are rich can be found not in the fact that the rich nations are not willing to devote enough resources for foreign aid, but in the essential character of the economic *relations* between the rich and poor nations.

Similarly, it is much more reasonable to assume that, just as schooling in the past has been used to fit people into particular social roles based on their class background, it will *continue* to be so used in societies that are hierarchical and class-structured. The Commission hopes to create new kinds of societies through education. If that's the case, then the Commission should have spent much more time dealing with the nature of such new societies and how in fact the extension of formal and nonformal schooling will be able to achieve them.

Let us assume that, in contrast to the Commission's assumptions about the commitment of governments to everybody's liberation, a government represents particular class interests in a country, and that the distribution of schooling as well as its curricula depend on those dominating interests. Let us also assume that although some governments represent mass bases, many serve local and foreign owners of physical capital. What kind of education would be required to reach the Commission's education goals in cases where, for example, a bourgeoisie controls societal institutions? What kind of schooling should working-class and peasant children get in those countries where the middle class enforces its maintenance of institutions through military bureaucracies? Is the Commission suggesting that education in Brazil, Chile, Uruguay, Bolivia, South Vietnam, Taiwan, South Korea, Burma, South Africa, Angola, Mozambique and a host of other African, Asian, Latin American and even European countries like Greece and Spain has any possibility of developing creative, aware, self-fulfilling individuals?

It makes much more sense to speak of *defensive* education for most people of the world; an education that helps children and adults defend themselves against exploitation by dominant classes in their own societies and in the industrial societies. Such education would assume that the world is not a harmonious place, that industrial countries are primarily interested in the welfare of their foreign investors and domestic consumers, not in the well-being of the world's masses and that a dominant class of a country is not going to teach children or adults things that will destroy the control of institutions by the class in power.[3] Defensive education would have to be developed outside the normal school system or by highly conscious teachers within the schools. It would be oriented to the understanding of conflicts in and between societies and how to do better within such a conflict situation. *Learning to Be* would be based much less on science and technology and more on political consciousness and action. The solutions to development, both personal and societal, would not be promised by the triumph of scientific and technological know-how, as the Commission thinks they should be, but by the collective action of those who are now powerless and hungry.

Notes

1. See Michel Debeauvais, "Problems of Costs and Opportunities," *Prospects* 3, no. 3 (Autumn 1973): 307–16.

2. See Joel H. Spring, *Education and the Rise of the Corporate State* (Boston: Beacon Press, 1972).

3. For a more detailed exploration of defensive education, see Martin Carnoy, *Education as Cultural Imperialism* (New York: David McKay, 1974).

11

Martin Carnoy

The Role of Education in a Strategy for Social Change

In these chapters we have discussed the limits of "reformist" educational reforms in achieving social change within a society in which fundamental political power relations and economic structures remain unchanged. Indeed, we argue, even if these reforms are well-meaning, their results will be much more conditioned by the needs of groups in power than the intentions of reformers themselves.

We suggest that the "problem" of education is generally not a problem that resides in the educational system; but that if an educational system is "inhuman" or "unjust," it is largely because the economic and social structure it is preparing children for is inhuman and unjust. In order to change the educational system, the type of education it offers, the human relations it fosters, and the types of attitudes and capabilities it helps produce, we suggest that we must change the way goods are produced and the kinds of goods produced by the economy, with all that this implies for the relations among producers and the full democratization of society. On the other hand, we argue that societal

269

structure not only affects the nature of education, but also that the institution of formal schooling, once solidly entrenched and crucial to the continuation and operation of the economic and social system, may influence the course of economic and social development. On the basis of this premise, we try to develop a strategy for working within the educational system to help create social change.

What Is the Economic Problem?

If we define the economic problem only in terms of increasing overall output, we can reduce the issue to two variables: the amount of savings/investment that can be generated from different sources and the output-capital ratio (productivity of capital). Of course, the economic problem is much more complex. Not only are we concerned with *how much* the society produces, but *what* it produces, *how* it produces, *who* gets to *produce* the output, and *who* gets to *consume* the output. We are concerned with human rights and physical and mental health. Thus it is important to analyze development much more broadly than the limited view provided by increases in material product.

In the United States, goods are produced with a capitalist organization of production; a major thrust of our thesis is that while it is possible to increase material output rapidly under capitalism, much of the economic problem defined in broader terms arises from the *way* capitalism produces this increased output. We can generalize several main features of this economic system which help us understand the roots of the problem:

1. Capitalist development is based on the private ownership of property, including the means of production, and the right of the individual to the protection of that property against infringement by other individuals. In theory, anybody in the capitalist economy can own capital and use it for production; but in practice, the distribution of capital for production is highly concentrated. A relatively small number of individuals in a capitalist economy make decisions about what kinds of things should be produced and how they should be produced. Furthermore, since owners of capital are primarily interested in maximization of

returns to that capital, they are likely to use all means at their disposal, including, if possible, the state apparatus, both to increase returns to their capital and to ensure that they maintain control over the means of production.

2. Under these conditions, it is not surprising that technology developed by capitalists is oriented to lowering labor costs, both through controlling worker organizations and through eliminating as much as possible of the skilled-worker component of any production process.[1] If we consider that technology was developed by capitalists at least in part to solve labor problems in production which had little to do with *overall* wage levels—the elimination of the skilled-work component and the control of management over labor—the existence of high levels of unemployment, for example, is *not* the result of the misallocation of resources or of using inappropriate technology in terms of capitalists' and managers' class interests, since this technology has been proved effective in helping solve these two principal production problems. Work is therefore organized in capitalist countries primarily by owners and managers of capital to maximize the return to capital, not to make work more humanized or to employ fully all those who want to work.

3. We further observe that many important economic sectors are characterized by *monopoly* production—a few large firms producing a high percentage of output and employing a high percentage of labor in those sectors—while some "traditional" sectors are characterized by highly competitive conditions—many small firms competing in the market for their goods. Thus, one set of capitalists is rapidly expanding production of goods produced under monopoly capitalist conditions in domestic markets while also trying to establish monopoly positions for their goods abroad.

Both sectors, however, while differing in type of capitalist organization in production (monopoly corporate versus competitive),[2] produce goods to maximize profits and distribute goods to those who can pay the highest prices, not those who *need* the goods. Furthermore, in each sector, goods are produced *in a way* which maximizes profits: if this means holding wages down, so be it; if this means increasing unemployment, so be it; if this means increasing control over the work process by the capitalists/managers, so be it; if this means impairing the health and safety of the workers, so be it.

As a result, we observe even in industrialized capitalist countries the phenomenon of continuing unemployment as the economy expands. We also observe largely unchanged inequality of income distribution since 1945 in the United States despite rapid economic growth.

Education for Development

We have gone into this description of the characteristics of capitalist development because it is essential to understand that development in order to comprehend the nature of educational systems and educational change in the United States. What kind of educational system would we expect the state to provide in this kind of "development" situation? Would we expect all individuals to receive an education that helps them participate in the economic growth process and in decision making for production? Or would we expect that children would be educated by the institution of formal schooling to fit into *capitalist* labor needs which include some highly paid workers as well as large numbers of unemployed and to believe in an ideology that justifies the inequity of the capitalist system of production? How would the educational system distribute education in a society where the fruits of production and access to jobs is inequitably distributed?

As we discussed, the explicit and implicit purpose of mass schooling as it was instituted in the United States in the nineteenth century was to make people useful in the new capitalist hierarchy, not to help to develop societal relationships which carried them beyond that social structure to others. So schooling was not organized to help people reach stages beyond this class-controlled hierarchy, but tried to fit people to the needs of that hierarchy whether it benefited them or not. We define this as the *colonizing* aspect of schooling. Transformation from traditional to capitalist hierarchies occurs, at least in certain sectors, but the *tools of change* are not taught in the schools. Schooling is a colonial institution whose employees, through their role in the system, end up trying (though not always successfully—see below) to make children fit certain molds, to shape them to perform predetermined roles and tasks based on their social class. Neither children nor adults (including teachers) are brought to understand their relationship to institutions (including the school) and how they can change those institutions to suit their needs. The structure and content of learning are set by a state bureaucracy representing certain class interests, and these interests are served by the schools. The introduction of school itself constitutes a type of change, but once that introduction is carried out, people are brought to a certain level of social consciousness and no farther.

The state in a capitalist economy is crucial to our understanding of the role of the schools in the "development" process. The state acts to "guide" development along a certain path;[3] it therefore presents an ideology of development through the school system and other institutions that reflects the dominance of certain groups in the society who manage to control the state apparatus over certain periods of time. In the United States, state governments that supported the type of capitalist development described pushed an ideology conditioned not by the needs of the local bourgeoisie. Thus, the school system reflects this conditioned approach to development, not only in preparing children to fit into various pieces of a class-based hierarchy that has been structured to produce goods under this conditioned development process, but in attempting to nurture in children cultural forms which are also conditioned by the intermediary role of the state.

The state's provision of formal schooling is therefore organized in large part (or entirely) to supply the needs of the group (or groups) that dominate the state apparatus. In the case of capitalist countries where a domestic "modern" bourgeoisie controls state power, we observe that state is used as a support mechanism for the labor needs and ideological position of that bourgeoisie in its interpretation of the optimum way to development.

It is not unusual, under these conditions, that rural schooling and schooling for colored minorities has low priority for urban capitalists and technocrat/managers who dominate industrialized "modern" economies. Yet the same capitalists and managers are concerned about producing a large reserve army of skilled and semiskilled workers in urban areas who put downward pressure on skilled workers' wages, making industrial expansion and capital accumulation (profits) more rapid. They may also be concerned with socializing children from marginal populations to accept the fate in store for them at the bottom of the urban class structure. The modernizing state may therefore expand mass urban primary and even secondary schooling both to produce a large reserve of schooled labor and to help legitimize the inequalities in the development process.[4]

We observe, then, that the U.S. educational system is characterized by an enormous disparity between minority and middle-class educational systems, even at the primary level. Minority schools are ill equipped, and the curriculum for such schools is a white middle-class curriculum, developed by the state apparatus and textbook publishers catering to a capitalist ideology and a white middle-class style which has emerged from the ideology. The quality and quantity of public schooling also varies greatly between the different social classes among whites. Those children from working-class families who reach secondary school are usually channeled into vocational training (now junior college), rather than the preparation necessary to qualify for an academic university education. Finally, when the university level expands in response to corporate and state bureaucratic needs, there are large salary differentials between those occupations followed by children of lower-income families who attend a university, and those occupations such as medicine and engineering which require full-time study (making it difficult to work while attending university) and are taken primarily by youths from higher-income families.

The entire school system, therefore, is highly class stratified, with the majority of the state's resources for education going to support those kinds of education that prepare children to work in the monopoly sectors and for the managerial and technical levels of training required by that sector. On the other hand, those children who are not likely to be working in that sector receive a very small share of the state's resources for education. In addition, the curriculum at different levels of schooling is designed to prepare people for corporate work. If children do not get managerial or technical jobs, much of the schooling they have taken does not prepare them for the tasks they will perform in menial or even skilled work. Yet, schooling does play an important function in socializing these children to believe that their failure is not the failure of the *system*, but their own failure in not succeeding in school and thus not being able to get the kinds of jobs that are highly rewarded. This is the principal "legitimizing" function of public schooling. Nevertheless, even as the school system expands rapidly and the average level of schooling increases, the number of managerial and professional jobs available does not expand as rapidly; we find that succeeding in school still does not buy jobs for the mass of people in the high-paying sectors.

But is it possible to devise a strategy within the present U.S. educational system that will contribute to nonreformist reforms— to structural changes in U.S. economy and society? The answer to this question depends on (1) whether changes in the educational system have a significant effect on the way people relate to one another in the economy and society, on political power, and on political participation; and (2) whether it is possible, given the organization and function of the formal school system, to produce significant nonreformist reforms in the schools.

We are somewhat skeptical that either of these premises is true. At least, there is little evidence that anticorporate capitalist schooling changes can be initiated on a large scale in the face of corporate economic/political conditions. Similarly, there is serious question whether, even if changes in the schools could take place, the school environment would overcome the powerful socialization of the workplace and the sociopolitical conditions impinging on students during schooling and in postschool life.

Nevertheless, the school system *is* a major employer in the United States, and, as we point out below, is an important component in the overall socialization and preparation of children for the labor force. Under these circumstances, it is useful, at minimum, to discuss alternative strategies for those in the school system who see themselves trying to change their own place of work in a nonreformist way.

In order to develop such strategies, we think it is fundamental to analyze the place of schooling in capitalist societies and to define the type of society one is aiming for in changing the schools. In the preceding chapters, we indicate our belief that schools in the United States are class stratified and that individuals do not receive an education which either maximizes their learning capability or helps them to comprehend fully the economic and social forces around them. This is not, we argue, an accident, nor a result of "inefficiencies" in the school system. Rather, the schools were historically designed to function in a way which left the mass of people learning less than their intellectual capacity permitted and in jobs which required even less knowledge than learned in school. All this because the economy was and is organized to maximize learning and knowledge utilization for the few rather than the many.

The type of society *we* desire is one that is primarily oriented toward *human* welfare rather than the output of goods or the maximization of returns to capital. This means that everyone who wants to work should be guaranteed a job at a livable wage under working conditions developed and controlled democratically by those who do the work. In other words, the kinds of changes we strive for in the schools would promote attitudes and values that contribute to the dismantling of corporate capitalism and to the creation of a humanistic democratic socialism governed primarily from the local level and pervading all aspects of economic and social life.

Eduational strategies which point toward this kind of society have to deal with the *mechanism of control* in the corporate capitalist educational system and the possible *contradictions* produced by such education. We explore these two concepts now.

The Mechanism of Control

The state, in our model, serves as a principal mechanism through which the mass of people is *controlled* during the capitalist development process both through the schools, media, and through the state's repressive apparatus. We consider that the schools serve as part of that control mechanism, and within the school system, two principal elements are used for control. The first of these is the teacher corps. Teachers generally come from urban working-class or lower-middle-class backgrounds and aspire to a higher-middle-class position in the social structure. We think it is useful to view teachers employed by the state as managers or supervisors of the production of knowledge and social behavior in children. Since they generally identify with the values of the domestic bourgeoisie and middle-class professionals, they follow the lead of the state in pushing those values and adherence to the capitalist mode of production. Thus, we observe that teachers seem to act as a middle-management or supervisory group primarily interested in its own position in the hierarchy (teachers' unions are a manifestation of this) that gets rewarded for the ability with which it produces children who are suited to fit into different parts of the economic and social structure.

Second, besides using this middle-management group to control the behavior and values of children in different kinds of schools and in different levels of schooling, the state distributes access to knowledge through the schools in different amounts to different social classes. Access to knowledge—technical knowledge—probably forms a very important part of people's attitude toward political participation, particularly in an industrialized society. We would argue that if a person is comfortable with "modern" technology and has a certain depth of understanding of it, it is much more difficult to convince that person that he should not participate in decisions about what goods are to be produced and how they are to be produced. The schools function to distribute this knowledge differentially, first, by giving very different amounts of knowledge to children at different levels of schooling. Therefore, children who attend only primary school will gain very little understanding of the phenomena occurring around them, while children who attend high schools and universities will have much more understanding of those phenomena. Second, at each level of schooling, *different* schools study a phenomenon in different ways. Schools that cater to higher-income students have much more equipment available; bring children in contact with a wide variety of experience with technology; and even, in some cases, teach children to explore technological alternatives, or to question the technology used to produce certain kinds of goods. Children from lower-income families in general do not get this kind of experience and therefore later in life probably have a great deal of difficulty understanding the changes occurring around them and tend to be mystified by them. The curriculum and the teachers are important instruments of social control of students within the school system and function to reproduce the class structure through an ostensibly meritocratic system.

Contradictions in the Educational Process

Although the dominant domestic bourgeoisie in capitalist countries attempts to use the educational system to reproduce this class's control over the means of production and the surplus, and although it is generally successful in convincing people to accept this inequitable system of "development," it can also fail to convince children and their families that the reality described in the schools is indeed the reality they face. Formal schooling in a state-controlled system can create aspirations which are not met, which *may* lead people to question the economic system;[5] formal schooling can teach skills such as reading which may give students access to literature not in the curriculum; and the schools can introduce students to adults—their teachers—who may be against the established system, and these teachers may introduce ideas to students whose families have taught them things different from the things being taught in school. Thus, just as the factory helped capitalists increase control over workers in the work process, it also brought workers together in the same place in close proximity and created the conditions for working-class organizing. The schools also attempt to subordinate people's values and behavior to a particular development process —in the case of capitalist development, an inequitable one in which a few people will participate fully, and the vast majority may attend the school but will not participate in the growth of the national product. At the same time, however, the schools bring children together in school, introduce them to one another as people, their ideas, and occasionally give them a teacher/manager who is not completely convinced that he or she should present to the pupils a reality that does and will not exist for them.

Furthermore, the use of schooling as a selector for different strata in the capitalist work structure creates a demand for ever more schooling among young people, which eventually produces a labor force with more schooling than "necessary" to carry out production tasks. Since capitalists and managers are constantly pushing for more schooling in order to increase the degree of socialization and the cognitive knowledge of their work force, the state feels compelled to increase the amount of schooling available for the general population. However, this ever-increasing average level of schooling tends to create frustration in the labor force once it reaches the job market and finds that increased schooling has prepared it for jobs which their fathers may have done a generation ago with much less training. Only a small percentage of graduates are able to find work that makes the additional schooling seem worthwhile.[6]

As Gintis has pointed out: on the one hand, the school system becomes essential to producing socialized and cognitively prepared labor for the production of goods, so if it does not function properly, it may create problems for the system; on the other hand, while the school system actively tries to socialize and prepare this labor efficiently, the bringing together of large numbers of young people in the schools and the possibility of teachers sympathetic to the young may create the conditions under which students will act to disrupt the schools or use them as a place to organize in order to create a politically sensitized output of the schools which is not useful for the capitalist production process.[7] As we have added, the schools may also create aspirations that cannot be met by the economic system. In this case, one of the most important products of the school, a labor force that accepts its position in the system as equitable and just, fails to materialize from the schools; to the contrary, under these conditions, the output of the schools may be a frustrated and alienated labor force which again creates increasing problems for capitalist production.

It is difficult to say to what degree these contradictions develop in the schools, but we do know that in high-income countries, the school has become a significant element in supplying socialized labor for capitalist production and for the reproduction of the capitalist system. This makes it an essential institution for the continued development of capitalism, and in a sense, it is an integral part of the capitalist production process. At the same time, there is evidence that bringing together masses of young people in the schools can create unintended values among the young which makes them less useful in the capitalist production hierarchy.[8]

A Strategy

We have argued that the persistence of poverty, unemployment, and differential access to schooling is not the result of *inefficiencies* in capitalist development, but the direct *product* of that development. According to our analysis, therefore, in order to have a society in which human needs and development are put before the accumulation of capital and the production of goods as ends in themselves, it is a necessary condition to dismantle the capitalist system of production. Once that occurs or *as* it occurs, capitalism must be replaced with a humanistic social and economic system that emphasizes the production and distribution of goods for the satisfaction of human needs, putting those needs *before* the accumulation of capital.

We have also argued that the educational system in capitalist society *is* inefficient in not being able to legitimize the inequalities of capitalism completely: some students are not convinced that the values developed by schools for them are consistent with their own or others' needs; some are not socialized to accept their role in the capitalist hierarchy or to accept capitalism itself. Furthermore, the school system produces some labor which aspires to much more than it can receive from the production system. Teachers in the schools—the schools' middle-line managers—cannot be completely controlled in what they tell students or how they affect their attitudes and perceptions. Thus, the schools *are* inefficient in that they are not completely isomorphic to capitalist production and cannot completely legitimize the inequalities of that production system. These inefficiencies are contradictory to continued capitalist growth, and they can be exploited in order to both make further capitalist control difficult and to raise consciousness of the need to dismantle the existing production system. Organizing within the educational structure to achieve these ends may well play a small role compared to similar efforts aimed directly at workers in production. It is difficult to argue on theoretical grounds that the revolution will be made within the educational institutions of capitalist society, even though the 1960s did convince many temporarily that students were the vanguard of the revolution (among them, Herbert Marcuse).[9] Nevertheless, those institutions employ large numbers of people and, as we have argued, these people are essential in capitalist countries to the production of socialized labor and to the reproduction of the system. Organizing in the education sector may also help build the kind of society which emanates from the struggle against capitalism in the low-income countries.

But what are we to organize *for* in the schools? What is the overall strategy for dismantling the capitalist system which this organization will serve? According to Andre Gorz,[10] the revolt against society in most high-income countries has lost its natural base of misery and lack of necessities; thus, the internal contradictions of capitalism may not be great enough in these countries to persuade workers or peasants to engage in armed struggle against the state apparatus and to take it over. Once taking over the state, revolutionary groups would destroy the capitalist system of production and create a new form of producing and distributing goods. Within the strategy of armed struggle, revolutionaries organize in the schools to prepare students to participate in the armed confrontation itself or to support the confrontation once it occurs. Universities, in particular, are an important source of revolutionary soldiers to participate *directly* against the repressive force of the state. Furthermore, as the repressive forces of the state become more powerful and sophisticated, a strategy of armed struggle becomes more difficult. It is an all-or-nothing strategy which may succeed because it accepts the fundamental premise that capitalists or the state will not go down without a fight and the strategy confronts that fight head-on. But it may also fail because it exposes anticapitalist forces to the armed might of the state.

Under most conditions, other strategies for dismantling capitalism must be developed. Gorz has argued that "socialism as a necessity has never struck the masses with the compelling force of a flash of lightning. There has never been direct transition from primitive revolt to the conscious will to change society. Those content with their condition have never spontaneously led even the most organized workers to attack those structures of society which made their lives unbearable."[11] Gorz goes on to suggest an "encroachment strategy" in which people organize in the production sector to "encroach" on capitalist prerogatives in the capitalist system. This strategy exploits existing contradictions but, more important, creates *new* contradictions in the system.

> The only way to unite and mobilize a differentiated working class at present is to attack the class power of the employers and of the State; and the only way to attack the class power of the employers and the State is to wrest from each employer (and from the State) a vital piece of his power of decision and control.
>
> Concretely, the goal of this attack should not be to achieve modifications and accommodations of the workers' condition within the framework of a given management policy and a given stage in the technological development of the industry; for such a victory, besides being nongeneralizable beyond the individual company, could rapidly be taken away from the workers, as rapidly as improvements in techniques and in the organization of production permit. On the contrary, the working class movement must demand permanent power to determine, by contract, all aspects of the work situation and the wage scale, so that all modifications in the productive process must be negotiated with the workers, and so that the workers can materially influence the management of the enterprise and orient it in a given direction.[12]

The strategy, then, is to establish in the workplace—and we suggest, in other institutions as well—an antagonistic pole of power of challenge to management decisions. This antimanagement organization, once it achieves its power, will be able to anticipate management decisions and to influence them before they are made; "it will place workers [students and possibly even teachers] in an offensive, not a defensive position; it will elevate their level of consciousness and competence; it will deepen their knowledge of the production process [and the production of knowledge]; it will force them to specify their goals, scaled according to a strategic and programmatic vision, goals which they intend to oppose the capitalist plan on the company [or the school], industry, or regional levels, and on the level even of the national economy; it will give rise to partial and local demands . . . within the framework of an overall and coherent perspective of response ("alternative") to monopoly capitalism, a perspective which will reciprocally influence and clarify the local demands; in this way it will stimulate a continually resurging struggle with more and more advanced goals, at a higher and higher level."[13]

An "encroachment" strategy for the schools would have to deal with the complex set of production forces in the school: students are at once workers and the raw material being transformed; teachers are at once workers and the supervisors of the production process; parents, to the degree to which they identify with their children's transformation, are at once consumers of their children's education and its comanagers, and most parents are also workers elsewhere in the production process. In capitalist development, the student workers/raw material are forced to be the antagonists of their managers/knowledge intermediaries, the teachers, with parents usually caught between, on the one hand siding with the students' (their children's) grievances, on the other, siding with the teacher-managerial view of how students should behave and what they should learn.

Furthermore, any strategy has to deal with teachers' organizations (unions) as they exist in the United States: these are usually unions which, as described by Gorz, limit their action to achieving "modifications and accommodations of the workers' condition within the framework of a given management policy."[14] The given management policy in this case is largely concerned with the teachers' relationship to students and to the distribution of knowledge among the students. The state management defines these relationships through the method of presenting the curriculum, the organization of the classroom, the use of tests, and pass/fail policies. Teachers' unions, as we know, have defined their role as bargaining for increases in teacher salaries, higher nonwage benefits, and improved promotion policies and job security. None of these issues affects the conditions of teaching in the schools, which are determined from above.

Since teachers' unions are already extensive in the United States, it seems reasonable that any encroachment strategy should start by organizing within those unions to change the limited nature of union bargaining, expanding it to include control over all aspects of the school-work situation.

It is important to stress that any organizing among teachers, students (at the secondary and perhaps primary level), and parents of students is fraught with difficulties and has a great likelihood of failure. As we argue, the school system is viewed by most teachers not only as their employer, but also as their escape from other, less desirable kinds of work. Many also probably view the classroom as a manager might view a department of a plant, with a certain sense of propriety. Furthermore, teachers' organizations are usually extremely conservative and primarily concerned with the wages per hour worked of their members. Parents and students are likewise often mesmerized by the imperative of succeeding in the schools as the only way out of the even worse economic situation facing the nonschooled. Exploiting the contradictions of schooling by organizing in the schools is a tough row to hoe. The proposed strategy is therefore suggested as the *most fruitful* strategy for organizing in the educational system for radical social change, even though organizing for that kind of change through education may not be as productive as, say, organizing in other parts of the productive structure, like the factories, or among municipal employees, etc.

Moreover, it must be recognized from the start that even if teachers could begin gaining control over classroom conditions and school administrative decisions, the antagonistic relation between teachers and students that is inherent to capitalist schools may produce a situation where teacher control over the classroom makes for even less control over learning (work) conditions by students, who are the teachers' coworkers in the school. Thus, while teachers' unions may be the logical place to start to encroach on management decisions over the nature of the educational process, there has to be a simultaneous effort to ensure that *all* workers in the school participate in this increased control over what is to be learned and how it is to be learned.[15]

There are a number of alternative ways to do this. First, unlike other types of workers whose training is carried out in a variety of institutions and forms, a large percentage of teachers are trained and certified in teachers' colleges and the education schools of state universities. Student-teacher organizations oriented toward raising the consciousness of teachers-to-be with regard to the present role of the teacher corps as manager-intermediaries and with regard to the role of schools in the capitalist production process would probably help alter the nature of teacher-union demands in the bargaining process and would shape the nature of schooling process to favor student rights.[16]

Second, pupils themselves should organize for control over the management of the education process, encroaching on the right of the state education board to set educational standards, who can pass and who fails, what the students must learn, and how they must learn it. Characteristically, such student organizations in universities and even in secondary schools have attempted to shut down the schools because they serve the capitalist system. But we would argue that—under the encroachment strategy— shutting down the schools is generally a misdirected action. In the encroachment strategy, the struggle for control is based on the *continued operation* of the plant. The school in this case would continue to graduate students, but students with a different kind of knowledge; it would continue to employ teachers, but teachers who play a different role in the education process— participants instead of managers.

In a sense, it may be easier to achieve the continued operation of the school under student-teacher control than to achieve the continued operation of a plant under worker control: if capitalists can no longer derive profit from the plant, they will attempt to close it (if necessary, with the help of the state). While the federal government could cut off teachers' salaries in a school that produces the "wrong" kind of good, the municipal government or the families of the students attending the school could threaten to continue to pay those salaries, since the school produces services which the community may value highly. The workers in the schools (students and teachers) can also attempt to produce other goods besides knowledge which are valued by people both inside and out of the community. Schools in both China and Cuba produce material goods a part of each day in order to finance the cost of teacher salaries and the food and clothing of the students attending.[17]

The short-term objective of the encroachment strategy, then, would be to win increasing control over what goes on in the classroom and what constitutes the educational curriculum. However, it is crucial that this control be won by teachers at the expense of central management, not students, and that control be won by students *together* with teachers. This requires reducing the antagonism between teachers and students which is inherent to the production of knowledge in capitalist societies, and implies a strategy of not only raising consciousness of teachers as worker-managers to demand permanent power over all aspects of work, as Gorz suggests, but also to raise teacher and student consciousness as coworkers to demand *joint* control over the learning process.

Although this should probably be the main thrust of an encroachment strategy, we also have to consider the students' families in the strategy, particularly in the case of young children, but also as a community element in supporting such changes in the educational system. One aspect of the strategy for parents is the movement for community control of the schools. The pitfalls of community control were nowhere more obvious than in New York and Michigan in the 1960s. Students' families, mostly blacks, demanded control of the schools in the face of not only central state administrative opposition, but the opposition of white teachers, many of whom stood to lose their jobs if the local community took over. The parents saw the teachers as the principal villains in the children's failure to do well in school.

Finally, when schools were taken over, teachers fired, etc., parents found that the state legislatures had no intention of giving them control over the state funds allocated to their schools. Also, the parents did not wish to change the nature of the education their children were receiving, nor did they want to change the student-teacher relationship. They were fighting for increasing pupil test scores in those schools so that their children might better succeed in the capitalist economic system.[18] Even so, as Levin has argued elsewhere,[19] the community-control movement may produce some of the effects which Gorz predicts for his encroachment strategy, inasmuch as parents' awareness of the role of schooling in capitalist societies may be raised to the point where they take further and more radical action.

Our emphasis on the control of classroom structure and student-teacher-parent relations in the education process is intentional: it is the worker-participants who will have to alter the nature of the production of knowledge and encroach on capitalism's use of that knowledge of labor prepared with that knowledge for the purpose of capitalist production. But it is also worth discussing the kinds of changes in curriculum that would also encroach on the role of education as a legitimizer of capitalist inequalities and as an *allocator* of knowledge. For example, if even teachers would organize to demand control over the workplace, what kind of change in curriculum could they demand in order to affect the kind of labor produced by the schools? The most obvious answer is that students would no longer be taught that private property is inviolate, that capitalism is the best and only way to produce things, and that the social structure emanates from the distribution of ability. In other words, the curriculum would no longer legitimize the capitalist system. It is difficult to imagine such a demand being met and the schools kept open by the state; but it is not difficult to imagine that those teachers who wished to teach such opinions would be protected by the union, and that the union contract specify that teachers could not be dismissed for what they taught as long as the students met the average competency levels on reading, math, and science examinations.

We also suggested that the distribution of access to technology and information about technology should be radically altered in any curricular change designed to disrupt capitalist control over the distribution of knowledge. Our argument is based on the use of knowledge about technology in the advanced capitalist state to legitimize managerial control over production, to facilitate managerial control over the work process and the increased division of labor,[20] and to make more difficult worker encroachment on control over the work situation. By increasing access to technological/scientific understanding at lower levels of schooling, teachers and students would ensure that workers-to-be would not be mystified either by management-inspired technological innovation at the plant level or state policies at the regional and national level designed to increase monopoly corporate power over economic and social development.[21]

We have not really discussed what schooling should be like in a "new" noncapitalistic society. However, the encroachment strategy we have outlined for education implies that the development of new forms of schooling would emanate from a situation where students and teachers control the classroom and the curriculum. This very process of joint decision making should radically alter the hierarchical relation between teachers and students, and should produce a joint learning-teaching process. Since many of the goods produced in the society would not change, and the development of technology, the use of tools, the allocation of resources, and communication among people would still require mathematical and reading skills, the curriculum in the new schools would include mathematics, reading, social studies, and science. The content of social studies would be different, and the way reading and math is taught may be somewhat different as well.

But the schools would be producing knowledge and labor for a different production process, a process that would require different *social skills* and much more sophisticated understanding among workers of production processes and interpersonal relations. Achieving these new institutions will require an enormous effort and long struggle for those involved, and the product of that struggle is hard to predict, since it will so profoundly condition those who participate in it.

Notes

1. Harry Braverman, *Labor and Monopoly Capital* (New York: Monthly Review Press, 1974).

2. Without going into detail on these differences, we can mention that monopoly corporations face much more stable markets than competitive firms, and therefore may attempt to stabilize their labor force and their markets through a host of control mechanisms and management hierarchy which competitive firms cannot afford (David Gordon, Richard Edwards, and Michael Reich, "Labor Market Segmentation in American Capitalism" [Harvard University, Center for Educational Policy Research, 1973]. Mimeographed).

3. William Appleman Williams, *The Contours of American History* (Cleveland: World, 1961).

4. Martin Carnoy, *Education as Cultural Imperialism* (New York: David McKay, 1974).

5. On the other hand, the schools generally serve, if successful, to socialize children and their families to place the blame for failure both in the school and in the labor market on their own personal inadequacies.

6. See James O'Toole et al., *Work in America* (Cambridge, Mass.: MIT Press, 1973); Braverman, *Labor and Monopoly Capital.*

7. Herbert Gintis, "The New Working Class and Revolutionary Youth," *Schooling in a Corporate Society*, ed. Martin Carnoy (2nd ed.; New York: David McKay, 1975).

8. For a proposed response to this problem, see James Coleman et al., *Youth, the Transition to Adulthood* (Chicago: University of Chicago Press, 1973); for a response to Coleman, see William Behn, Martin Carnoy, Michael Carter, Joyce Crain, and Henry Levin, "School Is Bad; Work Is Worse," chapter 9 in this volume.

9. See Herbert Marcuse, *One-Dimensional Man* (Boston: Beacon Press, 1964).

10. Andre Gorz, *Strategy for Labor* (Boston: Beacon Press, 1968).

11. Ibid., p. 3.

12. Ibid., p. 43.

13. Ibid., p. 53.

14. Ibid., p. 43.

15. It is also crucial to organize around particular issues that can rally both students and teachers. In most U.S. cities, the conditions in high schools are bad for everyone, and these conditions of work (learning) should serve as a central focus for restructuring the school situation.

16. The Work Research Institute in Oslo, Norway, is currently

working with student teachers to change the curriculum and organization of learning in vocational courses and even primary schools.

17. Martin Carnoy and Jorge Werthein, "Cuba: Economic
Change and Educational Reform, 1955–1974" (Stanford: Center for
Economic Studies, 1975).

18. Unfortunately for this effort, increased reading ability, for
example, does not increase blacks' economic success per se, even
though it may increase the probability of entering college, which in
turn has some effect on blacks' incomes. See Martin Carnoy, "The
Social Benefits of Better Performance in School," in *Analytical Models
in Educational Planning and Administration*, ed. Hector Correa (New
York: David McKay, 1975).

19. Henry Levin, "The Case for Community Control of Schools,"
in *Schooling in a Corporate Society*, ed. Martin Carnoy (2nd ed.; New
York: David McKay, 1975).

20. Braverman, *Labor and Monopoly Capital*.

21. Good examples of this in the high-income countries are the
"public" utilities' attempt to develop nuclear power as an alternative
source of energy and the expenditure of billions of dollars on the space
program in the name of vague scientific advances. In low-income
countries, the introduction of satellites for educational television is an
example of vast expenditures on technology whose main purpose is
probably the more efficient control of the educational process but
whose value to the public is presented in glowing terms. See Martin
Carnoy and Henry Levin, "Evaluation of Educational Media: Some
Issues" (Stanford University, 1975). Mimeographed.